Missions to Mexico

Missions to Mexico

A tale of British diplomacy in the 1820s

HENRY McKENZIE JOHNSTON

British Academic Press
London · New York

Published in 1992 by
British Academic Press
45 Bloomsbury Square
London WC1A 2HY

An imprint of I.B. Tauris & Co Ltd

175 Fifth Avenue
New York
NY 10010

In the United States of America
and Canada distributed by
St Martin's Press
175 Fifth Avenue
New York
NY 10010

A CIP record for this book is available from the British Library

Library of Congress catalog card number: available
A full CIP record is available from the Library of Congress

ISBN 1-85043-553-5

Photoset in North Wales by
Derek Doyle & Associates, Mold, Clwyd.
Printed and bound in Great Britain by
WBC Ltd., Bridgend, Mid Glamorgan.

CONTENTS

LIST OF ILLUSTRATIONS

(plates section between pages 144 and 145)

Maps

FOREWORD

by Viscount Montgomery of Alamein

Henry McKenzie Johnston served his country well as a diplomat, and has now done further service by writing this fascinating insight into the world of diplomacy in the early part of the last century. There are many different views of diplomats and diplomacy, and most informed people have strong views about the British Foreign Office – past, present and future. I stand four square in support of an institution that has done well for Britain and frequently diverted politicians from making wrong decisions – that is decisions which might be politically expedient in the short term, but not necessarily in the long-term national interest.

In the period covered by this book, the head of an overseas Mission was in a most independent position. The advent of instant communications changed the role but, since all international relations depend on human interaction, the accredited representative, whomsoever he or she may be, is still of vital importance. Nowhere is this more so than in Mexico.

It is a matter of pride and satisfaction that Britain was so influential at a crucial time after independence. Amongst other factors Britain was obviously striving to establish a sound mercantile position. This still holds good today when, with mutual advantage to be gained from increased trade, Britain needs to be very active in an increasingly competitive market. Although Mexico is, and always had been, heavily committed to the United States of America, there is a distinct need for a spread of interest, admirably provided by the European Community, into which Britain might serve as a useful bridgehead.

I have been visiting Mexico very regularly for more than thirty years – on business, for industrial exhibitions, on government trade missions, as a back bench politician, and as a tourist. I have grown to love the country and its people, observed the changes, and been impressed with the dynamic political awareness in a constantly changing scene. Every visit has illuminated a new facet of a beautiful, rich and diverse country, and this book will further increase the general knowledge.

Montgomery of Alamein
London
February 1992

PREFACE

Few who have the opportunity to live for a while in Mexico fail to come away without a lasting interest in the land, its people and its history. My wife and I were no exceptions after serving for nearly three years in our embassy there in the 1960s. Much has been written, and is still being written, about this country and its history; but very little has been published specifically on British-Mexican relations following the declaration of independence from Spain in 1821. My attempt much later to find out for myself how my predecessors as the first British diplomats in Mexico set about establishing diplomatic relations with this former Spanish colony has been for me a fascinating piece of research, during which I began to feel that possibly others might like to share my discoveries with me. By accident, therefore, rather than by design, I have been led to write this book.

In my view (and this is shared, among others, by some of my Mexican friends), insufficient attention has been paid to the key role British diplomats played in the development of the first Mexican republic. Although the influence of the United States, both politically and economically, on its southern neighbour has been pervasive in all sorts of ways, and the importance of Britain to Mexico's economic development has waned sharply since the end of the nineteenth century, at the start of that nation's independence Britain's attitude towards her was crucial. Central to this, of course, were the policies adopted by George Canning; but the friendship which developed between a young British diplomat, Henry George Ward, and the man who became Mexico's first president, Guadalupe Victoria, had an important effect. The parts played by Lionel Hervey and James Morier (not to mention the strange intervention of Dr Patrick Mackie) have their significance; but it is to Ward that should go much of the credit for the development of friendly relations between the two countries and the successful conclusion in 1826 of the first treaty between them. Not only did he fight off the efforts by the United States minister in Mexico to prevent this; he even had to counter the occasional irritation and impatience shown by Canning himself towards people he thought were insufficiently grateful for Britain's interest in their future.

In the days of sail it took months for the likes of Ward to exchange correspondence with the Foreign Office over 6000 miles away across the ocean. In such circumstances it was a challenging task, requiring the use of initiative and the assumption of great responsibility, to set up diplomatic contacts with a country so little known in Britain as Mexico then was. This tale is an attempt to give some idea, with the benefit of both private letters and official correspondence, of the characters of the main players, of the problems they had to overcome, and of the background of intrigue and personality clashes against which their task had to be performed.

Naturally I owe great debts of gratitude for help received from many people. First among these is Professor Luis Márquez, who with enthusiasm over several years acted as my researcher in Mexico, helping me to clear up points which arose from my study of material available in Britain; and it was thanks to him, and the permission he secured for me to examine documents in the archives of the Mexican Foreign Ministry, that I was able to complete my personal researches there in a mere ten-day visit (during which I enjoyed generous hospitality in the home of Licenciado Raul Ortiz y Ortiz and his mother). I also received valuable help in Mexico from Señora Graciela de Cantú and Mrs Virginia Young, and I am grateful to Señora Concha Noriega for allowing me to examine papers of Lúcas Alamán in her possession. Both the British Mexican Society and the Rayne Foundation in London gave me grants towards the cost of my visit to Mexico. Mr George Mays, a friend of many years, obtained much relevant information for me from the Texas State Archives in Austin, where he lives.

I am grateful for the help of many people in Britain for their readiness to respond to requests for background information or to allow me to consult documents in their possession and to quote from them. These include the Hon. Mrs Alice Cunnack and Mr Bernard Bevan, descendants of the Morier family; Miss Philippa Richards and the Rev. Arthur Mead, descendants of the Ward family, and Mr Geoffrey Bishop (the latter in New Zealand) married to a Ward descendant; Mr John Browne-Swinburne descended from the family of Emily, wife of Henry George Ward; the great-granddaughter of Arthur Goodall Wavell, the Hon. Mrs Pamela Humphrys; and the Earl of Harewood, Lambeth Palace Library, the Warden and Fellows of All Souls College, Oxford, the Cumberland County Record Office, Dr M.J. Orbell (the Archivist of Baring Brothers & Co. Ltd) and Dyfed

County Libraries Officer. I am also grateful to the Countess Waldegrave, the National Maritime Museum and the Hydrographic Office of the Ministry of Defence for so readily answering my questions, and to numerous bodies and people from whom I vainly tried to discover the family background of, and check on the alleged medical qualifications of, Dr Patrick Mackie.

Finally, but no less importantly, I acknowledge with gratitude the trouble taken by Professor Michael Costeloe of Bristol University to give me advice and look over my manuscript as it grew; but he must be absolved from blame for any shortcomings in the final version.

Quotations from original documents are as written, except that the punctuation and most spelling has been modernized, and the use of capital letters for nouns so prevalent in those days suppressed. Translations from the Spanish are as made contemporaneously where available; otherwise they are the author's.

Henry McKenzie Johnston
January, 1992

OUTLINE CHRONOLOGY

Background	
1521	Hernán Cortés defeats Aztec king Cuauhtémoc and founds Spanish Empire in America
1796	King Charles IV of Spain joins France in war against Britain
1806	Abortive attempt by British to capture Buenos Aires
1807	Napoleon Bonaparte attacks Portugal through Spain: start of Peninsular War
1808	French occupy most of Spain and Napoleon's brother, Joseph Bonaparte, put on throne: King Ferdinand VII in exile in France. 'Junta' formed in unoccupied Spain loyal to Ferdinand
	Revolt against viceroy in Mexico: subsides on appointment of new viceroy
1810	Representatives of Spanish colonies in America summoned to join 'free' parliament in Cádiz
September	Start of revolt in Mexico against Spanish colonial government led by Hidalgo
1811	
July	Hidalgo captured and executed: leadership of revolt assumed by Morelos
1812	Promulgation of 'liberal' constitution in Spain by 'free' parliament
1814	King Ferdinand VII restored to Spanish throne and abrogates 1812 constitution
1816	Revolt in Mexico suppressed apart from isolated guerilla activity
1820	Military revolt against Ferdinand in Spain revives revolt in Mexico. Iturbide ordered by viceroy to suppress it but joins revolutionaries
1821	
February	'Plan de Iguala', setting out future constitution for

	independent Mexico, agreed between Iturbide and revolutionaries
August	Spanish representative, O'Donojú, accepts Mexican independence and signs Treaty of Córdoba with Iturbide
September	Iturbide enters Mexico City in triumph
1822	
May	Iturbide made emperor of independent Mexico
December	Santa Anna inaugurates revolt against Iturbide.
1823	
March	Iturbide deposed and goes into exile
April	French troops enter Spain to restore Ferdinand, a prisoner of the rebel government, to the throne
October	Ferdinand back on throne and revokes Treaty of Córdoba, refusing to recognize independence of any of the Spanish colonies in America.

British dealings with Mexico

1822	
August	Canning becomes Foreign Secretary
December	Canning sends Dr Mackie on secret mission to contact Iturbide
1823	
February	Dr Mackie finds revolt in progress against Iturbide and withdraws to Havana
July	Dr Mackie returns to Mexico and has discussions with Victoria
October	Canning sends the Hervey mission to Mexico
1824	
January	Hervey sends his second commissioner, Ward, back to London with recommendation for immediate recognition of Mexican independence
December	Hervey recalled and replaced by Morier
1825	
January	Canning announces intention of negotiating treaties with Mexico and other former Spanish colonies, thus extending *de facto* recognition. Ward returns to Mexico with draft treaty
May	Mexican ratification of treaty agreed with Morier and Ward. Morier returns to England with text. Ward

	becomes Chargé d'affaires
November	Mexicans expel last Spanish troops from off-shore fort of San Juan de Ulloa
December	Morier returns to Mexico with amendments to treaty required by Canning
1826	
January	Breakdown of negotiations in Mexico for revised treaty
March	Morier returns to England
July	Mexicans sign treaty with the USA (never ratified) and send Camacho to England to continue negotiations for treaty with Britain
December	Treaty with Britain finally agreed in London
1827	
March	Mexicans ratify treaty signed in London
April	Canning becomes prime minister
May	Ward returns to England on recall
July	British and Mexican ratifications of treaty exchanged in London
August	Canning dies

PROLOGUE

In the early evening of Monday 12 January 1942 damp snow and the gloom of a blacked out railway station was the chilly introduction to London for the newly appointed Mexican Envoy Extraordinary and Minister Plenipotentiary to the Court of St James, Alfonso Rosenzweig Díaz. There was no formal reception, not even a car to meet him, only a charming lady speaking impeccable Spanish from the Ministry of Information. A lesser man in his position might have taken offence, but not this one. However, as he peered into the penumbra and saw the hurrying homebound office workers, each with a gas mask, and the groups of kitbag-burdened soldiers, he could not help feeling a frisson of forlorn loneliness. Why had he agreed to leave the sunny safety of Mexico for exposure to air raids in a country which seemed to be on the brink of being brought to its knees by Hitler? But he knew the answer before he had even formulated the question. This was the nation which, nearly 120 years earlier, had defied France, Russia, Prussia and Austria to support his country's newly won independence from Spain, the only European great power to extend the hand of friendship at that critical time. Now this nation, once again alone, was facing a threat to *her* independence. He was glad that President Ávila Camacho had chosen Britain's darkest hour, in 1940, as the appropriate time to repay that debt by proposing the resumption of the diplomatic relations which had been so needlessly broken in 1938. It had been in that year that President Lázaro Cárdenas had expropriated the foreign oil companies in Mexico and, taking offence at the tone of an official British communication, had withdrawn his minister from London. It had not been the first such break since the 1820s. In 1867 President Benito Juárez had decided that he could not have dealings with a country which had recognized the 'Emperor' Maximilian imposed on them by the French in 1864; and that break had lasted until President Porfirio Díaz had agreed to mend it in 1884. Then there had been another short quarrel in 1925. But all that was in the past. Rosenzweig was sure that now, once and for all, there would be an end to such bickering between two great peoples who should be able to respect each other in genuine friendship. Despite the inauspicious personal circumstances in which he found himself he was proud to be playing his part in this significant development. (And he did not know then that a few months later Mexico would decide to join the allies and declare war on Germany.)

The first practical step, back in 1822, on the four-year-long journey to the conclusion of the first treaty between the two countries was also taken in chilly darkness. At 7.15 on the morning of Tuesday 24 December of that year the deck watch of the 28-gun class 6 frigate, HMS *Ranger*, toiled in the low lying mist of Gillingham Reach on the River Medway to raise the single anchor to which they had lain overnight. It was the slack of the tide before the ebb which would help them down Queen's Channel against the freshening breeze to clear the shoals of Margate Sands and round Foreness Point and North Foreland so that they could then settle into a good reach heading west-south-west. It was a routine which Captain Peter Fisher RN and his ship's company of some 175 men knew well; but they were unaware then of the part they were playing in history. All Fisher had been able to tell his men was that they were to make best possible speed to Plymouth where they would pick up a civilian passenger, head south-west and open sealed orders when 50 leagues beyond Scilly. It was a good passage to Plymouth, which was reached at 11.30 on the morning of Boxing Day. Fisher went ashore immediately and found that his passenger, Dr Patrick Mackie, had arrived from London a few hours earlier. They wasted no time. High water was expected about 4.0 p.m. and they were aboard by then with anchor a-weigh by 4.30 and plenty of ebb tide in hand. The wind was still favourable, moderate from the south-east. Fisher's orders, which he was able to open soon after noon on the 28th,[1] instructed him to sail direct to Vera Cruz in Mexico. His passenger was on a secret mission to establish the first direct contact between the British government and the new rulers of that former Spanish colony. Fisher was to land Mackie and wait up to about three weeks to bring him back to England.

Mackie's mission had come about in a curious way (and developed even more curiously). A Mexican revolt against their Spanish colonial rulers had begun in 1810. After many set-backs, victory had come in 1821, 300 years almost to the day since Hernán Cortés had first brought Mexico under Spanish dominion by his victory over the Aztec king Cuauhtémoc. The final success had been the result of a deal between the revolutionary guerrilla chief, Vicente Guerrero, and Augustín Iturbide, then a colonel in the Spanish colonial army who decided to change sides. By skilful political manoeuvering Iturbide, after declaring independence from Spain, had succeeded in having himself crowned emperor in July 1822. Shortly after this, Mackie, a self-styled physician (no trace can be found of his ever having qualified as such) who had been living in Mexico for several years, had decided to return to Britain, determined to persuade the government of King George IV to recognize Mexican independence from Spain and establish diplomatic relations with Iturbide.

Nothing is known of Mackie's origins or background. There is some circumstantial evidence pointing to Glasgow as his native city. He was unmarried and probably then in his late forties or early fifties. Small of stature, he must have combined a cocky determination with a persuasive manner, for against all the odds he persuaded the Foreign Secretary, George Canning (who had succeeded Castlereagh on the latter's suicide in August 1822) to go along with his ideas, at least up to a point. On reaching London in September he had written a memorandum about conditions in Mexico which an influential friend had put in the hands of Joseph Planta, the Permanent Under Secretary at the Foreign Office, who had read it with interest.[2] Although a substantial amount of second hand information about events in Mexico was reaching the Foreign Office (notably from Henry Kilbee, a member of the mixed British-Spanish commission in Havana for the regulation of the slave trade) this was the first to be provided by someone now actually in London who apparently had first hand knowledge; and it had been presented at a time when Britain's policy towards the revolted Spanish colonies was beginning to change. It was true that there had been two letters from a Mr John Hall resident there.[3] In August 1821 he had reported that he was

> commanded by [Iturbide] to express to your Lordship [Castlereagh] … his great desire to enter into arrangements with Great Britain founded on the most liberal principles and having in view the reciprocal interests of both nations …

Hall had added that he was convinced 'that this country has arrived at that point at which they have not only gained their liberty but are also capable of maintaining it'.[4] A few months later he had written again to say that

> Iturbide has opened himself to me on various occasions, and I am confident that Great Britain might at the present moment make an alliance here which in the event of any future rupture with the United States would make us perfectly independent of that Republic.[5]

But these had reached the Foreign Office in January and March 1822, at a time when it was not considered to be in Britain's interest to take any overt action which might be seen by Spain and other European powers as supporting such revolted colonies. She was not unsympathetic to their aspirations, a genuine desire to assist the spread of democratic freedoms mixing pragmatically with a wish to gain commercial advantage; but developments in Europe meant that she had to appear to be at least neutral. France was threatening to invade Spain in support of King Ferdinand against whom a revolt had broken out in 1820. The 'Holy Alliance' of Russia, Prussia and Austria was eager to support France, and if it did it might lead to military intervention on Spain's behalf to recover her South American possessions, something Britain was determined to prevent. For the present nothing could get in the way of diplomatic efforts to remove this danger.

By the time Mackie's memorandum was presented, however, Canning had come to the conclusion that Britain's commercial interests could be damaged if the revolted colonies felt that she was not interested in their fate and they turned instead to the United States for help. So he had decided to call Mackie in for interview. Mackie's aim had been to persuade Canning to send him back to Mexico as his messenger with some promise of help. In his memorandum he had described Iturbide as 'shrewd, cautious and reserved, though by no means morose … a sincere admirer of the English nation … a kind and warm friend, but I should also think a bitter enemy … the son of a settler from Old Spain'. Of the Mexicans in general he had written:

> The natives are particularly well disposed towards the English .... They well know the sterling worth of our national character, and will consequently the more highly appreciate any overtures of friendly intercourse between the two Governments: indeed steps to that effect should immediately be taken as the advantages resulting from it to this country in a commercial view will be incalculable .... Great Britain has little to dread from any

> partiality in favour of the Americans, as none really exists. On the contrary, the Americans from their meddling character are generally looked upon by the Mexicans with a jealous eye.

Canning had not at first responded with any enthusiasm to Mackie, whom he later referred to somewhat derisorily as 'our little Doctor'.[6] Mackie had followed up this interview with another memorandum and two letters. He claimed to have known Iturbide for seven years and to have twice treated him as his doctor. He had suggested that communication should be opened with the emperor personally 'in a secret manner, as coming through the medium of a confidential acquaintance of his, without the publicity of the usual credentials'. He had put himself forward for this task with a total lack of modesty:

> Aware of the many accidental qualities that must unite in the person so selected to insure any chance of success, such as perfect knowledge of the language, the character, and disposition of the people ... few if any I imagine could be found here competent to undertake it .... I am willing to forego, for a few months, the plan of retirement I had proposed to myself, amongst my relatives and friends ...[7]

Getting no reply he had tried again, writing

> that an anxious desire to be instrumental in rendering your Administration glorious in the annals of our history, induces me, however unimportant a part I bear in society, to repeat the offer of proceeding immediately to Mexico, and at my own expense, under the impression of my having the means of effecting for you the most essential services with the actual Government of that country .... I am most anxious and eager to avail myself of the credit and influence I enjoy with the Emperor, the principal Officers of State, and the Congress, to counteract designs [of the Americans] so injurious to the interests of Great Britain ...[8]

And he requested passage in a ship of the Royal Navy.

By now it was the end of November. What finally induced Canning to take up Mackie's offer is not known, but three weeks later he had drafted instructions to him and arranged for *Ranger* to take him to Mexico, £82 being paid later to Fisher by the Foreign Office to cover the cost of 'entertaining' Mackie for 75 days.[9] But in no way did Canning intend to use Mackie as a negotiator. His purpose was simply to gather information by means which would not compromise His Majesty's Government. In Mackie he seemed to have someone who would be trusted by the man now leading one of the key countries in Spanish America. Through him he might be able to discover whether this new Mexico was really a stable political entity, and whether its rulers were prepared 'to receive and to treat with proper attention and courtesy commercial agents sent out [from England] to reside at the capital and at several ports where trade is carried on and to afford to British subjects generally all the civil rights and the unmolested exercise of their religious worship.[10] He also wanted Mackie to discover whether the Mexicans wished British help in persuading Spain to accept their independence. Such information was an essential preliminary to deciding whether it would be in Britain's commercial and political interest formally to recognize the separation from Spain. Mackie was most emphatically not being sent out as an agent of His Majesty's Government with a political brief. He was intended to be no more than a messenger to show that Britain was not taking sides in the quarrel between Spain and her colonies, but did hope, pragmatic as always, for friendly trading relations with the latter.

Ranger reached Vera Cruz on Saturday 22 February 1823. The safe anchorage was right under the walls of San Juan de Ulloa, the strongly built castle on an islet only a few hundred yards off shore from which the Mexicans had not yet succeeded in expelling the last of the Spanish troops. Ships would secure to the massive iron rings set in the walls in order to avoid dragging their anchors in the fierce northerly winds, the 'nortes', which could sweep down the coast with little warning and blow for days at a time. The governor of the castle, who, in the absence of a Mexican navy, controlled all traffic in and out of the port, permitted trade with the mainland, but charged his own duties on goods in addition to what the Mexicans levied. Some foreign merchants lived in the castle rather than on shore, for greater security. But as Britain was observing a strict neutrality between Mexico and Spain, her naval vessels had taken to avoiding the risk of compromising that by using this anchorage. They exchanged complimentary salutes with the garrison as they came and went, and used the services of local pilots; but they then anchored in the lee of Sacrificios Island, a couple of miles further along the coast and about a mile off shore near Point Mocambo. This island, a sandy spit no more than half a mile long and a quarter wide, had 'only one wretched Indian family living upon it' and was 'strewed with the bones of British subjects who have perished in this unhealthy climate, and whose remains are not allowed to be buried in consecrated ground'.[11] From there Mackie was landed at Vera Cruz by ship's boat early next morning.

William Bullock, one time proprietor of the London Museum in Piccadilly, who landed there from a merchant ship a week later, noted that the mole was 'partially paved with pigs of iron, each bearing the broad arrow of the king of England', which he was told had been the ballast of one of HM frigates discarded to make room for the silver specie being shipped back to England for merchants. 'Thus' he wrote, 'the first step an Englishman takes … is upon what was once English property. May this be an auspicious omen of the future good understanding and commercial intercourse between the two countries.'[12] It was not a good omen for Mackie, however. When he landed he discovered that the military governor of Vera Cruz, Antonio López de Santa Anna, had instituted a revolt against Iturbide. Mackie's instructions did not specifically say he was to deal with Iturbide and no one else; but, despite Santa Anna's assurance 'that it was by no means his wish, nor that of his party to depose the Emperor, notwithstanding their public declaration to the contrary', he decided that it might be unwise to try to go to the capital while Iturbide's position was in doubt. 'The communication with Mexico [City] having been for some time back interrupted' he reported later to Canning, 'I did not consider myself authorised to ask for a passport, being well aware that under existing circumstances any anxiety on my part to proceed to the Capital would naturally excite in the mind of General Santa Anna that I had matters of importance to communicate to the Emperor.'[13] He decided to reembark in *Ranger* and go to Havana (still in Spanish hands) from where he would seek further instructions from Canning.

1

BACKGROUND

It is advisable, before beginning to read the tale that now follows, to have some understanding of the historical background to the independence movement among Spanish colonies in America, of the course of Mexico's own struggle for independence in particular and of the various political factors which shaped Britain's policies towards these developments. For the last, the classic work is C.K. Webster's two-volume *Britain and the Independence of Latin America* published in 1938 (Oxford University Press), particularly the introduction. For the rest, there is a large selection of published works from which to choose.* In this chapter an attempt is made to distil the essence of all these three background elements. Many readers will already know it: they can go straight on to chapter 2. Others, if they wish, may skip it, for every effort has been made in relating the tale which follows to make it comprehensible on its own. Nevertheless, here and there are references to matters explained in this introductory chapter which are therefore left with little or no explanation later on. The reader must now choose whether to be armed with these explanations in advance, or find later that it may be necessary to refer back to this chapter.

After Hernán Cortés in 1521 defeated the Aztec king Cuauhtémoc at what is now Mexico City, the Spaniards rapidly extended their conquests over the remainder of what we now know as Latin America – except for Brazil, conquered by the Portuguese. By the middle of the sixteenth century this Spanish continental empire extended from what is now the south-west of the United States to the Magellan Straits. Although not all was so soon fully colonized and under close Spanish administration, from then until the end of the first decade of the nineteenth century control of this vast continent by Spain, exercized through viceroys and captains-general, was absolute. There were

* Some of which are listed in the recommendations for background reading at the end of this book.

occasional revolts – against social injustices, corruption and the misuse of power rather than against colonial status as such – but all were suppressed. Then suddenly, in a matter of a dozen years, it was all over. By 1821 all the various constituent parts of this empire had declared their independence from the mother country. Britain, however, although the first European power to do so, delayed some years before formally recognizing the new governments.

The fabric of Spanish colonial rule had in fact begun to weaken about the middle of the eighteenth century. The empire was by then divided into four viceroyalties: New Spain which was the present Mexico plus Central America (excluding Panama) and including much of the present southern USA; New Granada which was the present Panama, Colombia, Ecuador and Venezuela; Peru, which included most of present Chile; and La Plata, based on Buenos Aires and including the present Argentina, Uruguay, Paraguay and Bolivia. In this empire the Catholic Church, although controlled from Madrid, had a privileged position, great influence and much wealth. The populations were divided into four broad classes: the Spaniards from Spain (known in Mexico as the *gachupines*) who kept all the top positions of government to themselves and, with the Church, owned most of the land; their locally born descendants, or *creoles*, who, with rare exceptions, could not aspire to any of the positions of power, although many of them became rich landowners; the *mestizos*, the offspring of mixed Spanish or creole and Indian marriages, who occupied generally the lowest social echelons above the Indians; and the native Indians who had virtually all embraced the Catholic faith, at least superficially, but had almost no rights and lived for the most part in abject poverty as forced labourers.

Important changes in the way the empire was run began to be made from 1762, the year in which Britain captured Havana from Spain. Prior to this the administration of the colonies was very much in the hands of the viceroys and their appointed subordinates, and over the years many of the wealthier creoles had been able to share in the profits to be made from the opportunities for syphoning off taxes due to the Crown and from contraband trade. All trade was in theory a Crown monopoly. Hardly any was allowed between the colonies themselves and all with the rest of the world had to go through only two Spanish ports. This had an inhibiting effect on the economies of the colonies, but not on those individuals powerful enough to reap personal advantages. With the capture of Havana, however, King

Charles III of Spain realized that he had to take the defence of his colonies seriously. Although the Treaty of Paris of 1763 led to the return to him of Havana, he instituted new measures to increase the income he received from the colonies in order to pay for better defence. Tax collection was improved, control over colonial administration was tightened and, for the first time, colonial armies were formed. Not only did this upset some of the ways the creoles were making money, it meant an influx of gachupines (to use the Mexican word for convenience), both military and bureaucratic, which resulted in an increase of discrimination against the creoles. Charles also reduced the privileges and influence of the Church, even expelling the Jesuits entirely in 1767 and confiscating their estates. It was not surprising that many in the colonies began to feel less loyal, to say the least, a tendency reinforced as it became easier to get access to the writings of the Enlightenment emerging from France. Moreover, the gachupine proportion of the population began to fall dramatically as the birth rates among the creoles and mestizos rose. The effect of all this was gradual, however. The gachupines retained their grip on society, while the wealthier and more influential creoles found it possible to go on making money as the control over trade by Madrid was relaxed. There was certainly not enough dry revolutionary tinder around to present a serious risk to Spain simply from the spread of liberal ideas and the examples of the American War of Independence against Britain and the French Revolution.

It was in fact political developments in Europe that eventually stimulated revolution. Charles III was succeeded in 1788 by his son, Charles IV, who joined in war against France intended to revenge the execution of King Louis XVI and prevent the spread of this dangerous revolutionary spirit. But he made unilateral peace with France and in alliance with her turned upon Britain in 1796. This led to the blockade of Cádiz by the British fleet during the last three years of the eighteenth century, which had a serious effect on trade with the colonies in America. Spain decided to bow to the unilateral actions taken by Cuba and Venezuela to start direct trading with neutral countries, which of course included the United States. And in 1805 Britain won undisputed supremacy of the seas with the defeat of the French and Spanish fleets at Trafalgar. In desperation, to raise more money, the Spanish Crown forced sales of property both at home and in the colonies against paper money, thus seriously disrupting the colonial economies and the personal finances of both gachupines and the wealthier creoles. Charles IV became personally unpopular in Spain, especially when he allowed Napoleon to bring in his armies in order to attack Portugal in 1807, thus starting the Peninsular War. In 1808 Napoleon forced Charles to abdicate in favour of his son, Ferdinand, and then forced Ferdinand's abdication so that he could place his own brother, Joseph, on the throne of Spain, while Ferdinand became a 'guest' in France.

For the majority of Spaniards this was too much, with the French occupying a large part of their country. A 'junta' was formed in the unoccupied part, loyal to Ferdinand and determined to continue the war against France. It summoned representatives of the viceroys and captains-general in the American colonies to join them and in 1810, while besieged in Cádiz, it converted itself into a regency and created a *cortes* (parliament) which included elected deputies from the colonies. This cortes confirmed Ferdinand as the legitimate monarch, but also introduced liberal measures such as civil equality, abolition of privilege, freedom of the press, all intended to be applicable equally in the colonies. The principle of constitutional monarchy and the sovereignty of the people was the aim, but at first it simply led to the breakdown of the 'social contract' between monarch and people, leaving something of a political vacuum; and in the colonies the new liberal measures were applied with considerable reluctance by some of the viceroys, particularly in Mexico. Thus did the climate become favourable for the flowering of the dormant seed of revolution and self assertion against the metropolitan power.

The first serious overt manifestation in fact appeared in Buenos Aires. In 1806 British forces made an unauthorized and incompetent attempt to take possession of the city. The gachupines ousted their equally incompetent viceroy in order to defeat this external enemy. No declaration of independence from Spain followed this; but effectively power had passed from Madrid to the colonials. Then, following the events of 1810 in Spain, the creoles in their turn ousted the gachupines and in due course declared for independence. By the end of that year active revolt against viceroys elsewhere was in train. There had been a similar gachupine revolt against the viceroy in Mexico in 1808, when news of Ferdinand's abdication was received, but this was inspired mainly by fears that he would not defend their positions against pressure from creoles for more liberal government. It was not a bid for independence from Spain, and another viceroy soon took over. As elsewhere, however, it was not long before the gachupines in Mexico too found themselves in trouble. But there was one important difference in Mexico.

In South America the revolts against the gachupines were instigated with political motives by the wealthier creoles, and support from mestizos and Indians was at first only partial and reluctant. In Mexico, although the revolt was planned by creoles and may have been intended as a political move, it quickly developed into a spontaneous rising by the poor against oppression. Indeed, in the earlier stages the better off creoles saw it as a danger to themselves. It began dramatically on 16 September 1810 when, in the small hours, Father Miguel Hidalgo y Costilla, a scholarly and idealistic priest in the small parish of Dolores, some 170 miles to the north-west of the capital, took premature action on realizing that the plotting had been discovered by the authorities. He summoned his flock with the tolling of the church bell, and, so tradition has it, called upon them to 'recover the lands stolen three hundred years ago from your forefathers by the hated Spaniards'. Whatever his exact words, the effect was electric. Within a few days he had a motley, ill-armed and ill-disciplined force rallying to the religious banner of the Virgin of Guadalupe, who was particularly venerated by the poor, and gathering strength as it surged through the countryside. More by the exercise of terror than through the skilled use of arms, they got as far as the gates of the capital before unaccountably turning back. The royalists, who included most of the better off creoles, recovered their nerve and defeated this 'army' in January 1811, Hidalgo himself being captured and later executed, after trial by the Inquisition, on 3 July.

Hidalgo's place was taken by another parish priest, José María Morelos y Pavón, a mestizo without Hidalgo's scholarship or intellectual abilities, but with the organizing flair to create a much more effective fighting force, and the political sense to forge alliances across class frontiers. The movement then became more respectable, taking on a clear political goal of complete independence from Spain, and formulating a programme of social reforms. It promised to maintain the Catholic Church's status and not to interfere with property. Even so, however, Morelos gained the support of only a minority of the better off creoles and professional classes. Militarily he had early successes, but the viceroy, helped by reinforcements from Spain, turned the scales and he was captured in November 1815 and executed.

Meanwhile, in Spain there had been more constitutional

developments. In 1812 the 'free' cortes in Cádiz had promulgated a new and relatively liberal constitution. This still retained a hereditary monarchy, but it provided for much of the former powers of the Crown to be exercised by parliament. (It also abolished the Inquisition.) In practice this still did not bring to the colonies the equality with the metropolis they were looking for, but in Mexico at least it assured the loyalty of those not actively involved in the revolt. Then in 1814, with the defeat of Napoleon, Ferdinand was restored to his throne and immediately abrogated the 1812 constitution. The viceroy in Mexico stepped up the military campaign, using extra taxation and forced loans to pay for locally recruited militia, at the same time taking action against those with liberal sympathies who had been unwise enough to show their hand. By 1816 the revolutionary forces had been scattered and they steadily lost such support from the population at large as they had managed to gain under the leadership of Morelos. A new viceroy, Juan Ruiz de Apodaca, built upon this by offering amnesties, which were widely accepted, and by 1819 armed resistance to his authority had virtually ceased. He reported to Madrid that all was under control and no further military reinforcements were needed.

Beneath the surface, however, there was still much smouldering liberalism, and this received encouragement when a military revolt in Spain in 1820 forced Ferdinand to restore the 1812 constitution. News of this, accompanied by Apodaca's decision to apply its liberal provisions in Mexico, produced a new wave of support for the independence movement, and Vicente Guerrero, the only revolutionary leader then still active in harassing the authorities, began gathering support. In the autumn of 1820 Apodaca put Colonel Agustín de Iturbide in command of a force to seek out and destroy Guerrero's band. Iturbide, however, decided to change sides. In November he met Guerrero to discuss joint action to bring about independence from Spain. It took some time for Iturbide to overcome Guerrero's suspicion, but on 24 February 1821 they agreed and announced their proposals for the basis of a future constitution. This did not, like the earlier American Declaration of Independence from Britain, denounce the 'mother' country. On the contrary, as a deliberate bait for the more conservative elements in the population, this *Plan de Iguala* (so called after the place on the road to Acapulco where it was agreed) gave credit to Spain for her achievements in and magnanimity towards Mexico. Another bait was the provision that Mexico, although independent, would be a constitutional monarchy, the crown to be offered to Ferdinand or some other appropriate European royalty. It was made quite clear, however, that after 300 years as a Spanish possession it was time for independence.

Iturbide's political skill in getting this *Plan* adopted led to its almost universal acceptance, even by the Spanish community, and the other great revolutionary leader who had refused the amnesty and gone into hiding, Guadalupe Victoria, now emerged to join again in action against the Spanish forces. By this time the Spanish Council of State (which, following the 1820 military revolt, was in control of policy) had decided to abolish the post of viceroy and had despatched Juan de O'Donojú as Captain-General of New Spain with instructions to enforce the constitution and persuade the Mexicans that their grievances could be resolved peaceably. He landed at Vera Cruz on 30 July 1821 (by coincidence just as an earthquake shook a large area of central Mexico). Discovering the state of affairs he arranged to meet the insurgent leaders in Córdoba, then a mere village, on 23 August. Realizing then that his task was hopeless, on 24 August he signed the Treaty of Córdoba, based closely on the *Plan de Iguala*, recognizing Mexican independence. Iturbide entered Mexico City in triumph on 27 September 1821.

O'Donojú, pending a decision from Spain whether to approve this treaty, became a member of the junta then formed to govern the country. Possibly he hoped in this way to defuse revolt and eventually bring about the restoration of Spanish rule; but it is improbable, as Mackie reported, that he had actually been authorized to act as he did with this end in view.[1] As a staunch constitutionalist his aim would have been to do what he could to see constitutional rule develop in Mexico, and as a Spaniard he would have wanted to do what he could to ensure that relations with Spain would be amicable, and that commercially the mother country would suffer minimum harm from the loss of direct rule. But he died on 8 October after a short illness, believed to have been pleurisy. Rumours that Iturbide had him done away with have generally been accepted as mischievous. It is certainly possible, however, that had he not fallen fatally ill so soon he might have been able to convince Spain of the advantages of recognizing Mexican independence and, perhaps, agreeing to some kind of dominion status. As it was, however, Spain repudiated the Treaty of Córdoba and until 1836 maintained a state of war with the 'revolted' colony.

Iturbide himself was not bent on severing all connections with

Spain. But he had ambition to wear his own crown, not merely to be the representative of a higher authority, and he was skilful in achieving his aim. He had introduced a significant modification to the *Plan de Iguala* when drawing up the Treaty of Córdoba. There was now provision in the constitution for the selection of a Mexican as emperor should no suitable European monarch be available; and his opportunity came when a republican movement began to stir up opposition to his presidency of the provisional government. He managed to ensure that his soldiers staged an impressive demonstration in his favour, and, with a show of reluctance, on 19 May 1822 he allowed himself to be chosen as constitutional emperor. His coronation took place on Sunday 21 July.

Iturbide's triumph, however, was short-lived. He was unable to stem the continuing decline in his country's economy, suffering as it was from years of civil war. Moreover, he made the mistake of trying to suppress opposition by force and arbitrary arrest, even suspending the Congress, as well as appropriating to himself large sums of money with which to run a court on lines of which Louis XIV might have been proud. A substantial anti-monarchist movement grew up under the leadership of Antonio López de Santa Anna, Iturbide's military governor at Vera Cruz. On 1 December 1822 Santa Anna proclaimed a republic in that city and quickly gained the support of three more generals, Vicente Guerrero (with whom Iturbide had made his original pact at Iguala), Nicolás Bravo and Guadalupe Victoria. Iturbide appointed José Antonio Echáverri, Captain General of Vera Cruz, to put down the revolt. Echáverri, however, decided to join Santa Anna, and this new band of insurgents began to advance on Mexico City, gathering support all the way.

Iturbide did not wait for an attack on the city before offering his abdication on 8 March 1823. This was not accepted, so he repeated it ten days later. This too was refused, because the insurgents did not want to imply that they recognized his right to the crown by accepting his voluntary relinquishment of it. They compelled him to submit to dismissal. But he was treated with dignity and allowed to leave Mexico with his family and a large retinue, and a generous pension of $25,000 a year (about £5,000). The new rulers even paid 15,000 pesos to Captain Quelch of the armed British merchant ship *Rawlins* to give him passage to Leghorn; and persuaded the British navy to provide HMS *Tamar* as escort for the first part of the passage, through waters much troubled by piracy.

It was with this republican regime that Britain eventually established diplomatic relations; but this came about slowly because of the need to avoid upsetting the delicate balance of power in Europe. Since the middle of the eighteenth century Britain had kept in mind the possibility of helping revolutionaries in Spain's American colonies to achieve independence, more from a desire to secure valuable trading advantages than from idealism (although the latter was not entirely absent); but in practice nothing was done. The attack on Buenos Aires was an unauthorized and bungled attempt to take advantage of unrest for British gain. A military expedition was proposed in 1808 in support of Francisco de Miranda, who was planning revolt in Venezuela, but this had to be diverted to the task of freeing Portugal from Napoleon. Britain was now at war with France and in alliance with Spain, and from then on her objective was to persuade Spain to come to an accommodation with her American colonies and to open up free trade with them. In 1814 Spain went so far as to admit Britain to equality with other countries in respect of trade with her colonies, in return for which Britain had to promise neutrality in the independence struggle. (British military and naval help given to the independence movement in South America – none was given to Mexico – was unauthorized by the government.) In 1812 Castlereagh, then Foreign Secretary, had tried active mediation. He was particularly keen on getting Spain's agreement to mediation first between her and Mexico because of the perceived importance of stopping an insurrection which was interfering with the supply of bullion on which both Spain's and Britain's ability to finance the war against France so much depended. So keen was he that he was even prepared to offer a British guarantee as backing for any agreement reached by Spain with her colonies.

Castlereagh urged the Spaniards to recognize that unless they put the colonies on an equal footing with the metropolis their eventual separation was inevitable; and he even told them that the British had derived positive commercial advantage from the independence of her former colonies in North America.[2] But, as he wrote to the British ambassador in Madrid,[3] treaties with Spain required 'Britain, as a fundamental duty, to preserve by all means in her power the integrity of the Spanish monarchy' and she would have to 'counteract … by every suitable means' any attempt by the colonies to 'throw off their allegiance' to the Spanish Crown. Castlereagh, however, considered that this duty stopped short of going to war, refusing to agree to a Spanish condition for accepting mediation that in the event of its failure Britain would support a Spanish attempt to recover her colonies by force. In 1817 Castlereagh ensured that the European powers were left in no doubt as to Britain's position (and, incidentally, surely at the same time ensuring that the struggle for independence would succeed) by circulating to them copies of a Foreign Office memorandum setting it out. In addition to making it clear that Britain would not countenance any use of such force, it emphasized that she was not 'aiming at any exclusive commercial preference for the subjects of Great Britain in the ports of Spanish America' although some degree of preference for Spain herself would seem reasonable in the event of reconciliation.[4]

This British policy became even more important after the 1820 revolt in Spain. After the defeat of Napoleon, the political developments in Europe had fallen effectively into the hands of the quadruple alliance of Britain, Austria, Prussia and Russia which was intended to defend the territorial provisions of the Treaty of Vienna and prevent any attempt at restoring the Napoleonic dynasty. To do this, they had had to be prepared to go to war again. With the restoration of the Bourbon monarchy in France the danger from that quarter was seen as slight and the military occupation by the allies had in fact been brought to an end in 1818. The monarchies of Austria, Prussia and Russia had then attempted to broaden the purpose of the alliance to become a moral or 'holy' defence against any attempt by radicals to upset constitutions based on the divine right of kings and emperors to decide how their countries should be governed. Although King George IV would personally have liked to be a co-signatory with his fellow monarchs of this 'Holy Alliance', as a constitutional monarch he could not have done so without ministerial approval, and of course this was something that Parliament would never have sanctioned. The British government, however, although with some reluctance, had continued to participate in the Congress system of high level meetings of the alliance from time to time to deal with European problems. And after 1818 the French had also taken part.

Tsar Alexander saw the 1820 revolt in Spain as a threat to all established monarchy and called on the allies to join in restoring Ferdinand's full 'legitimacy'. Castlereagh took a firm stand against this. He acknowledged the danger to the stability of all existing governments, but made it clear that Britain was not going to be party to interference in the internal affairs of sovereign states. Armed intervention in Spain was averted – at least for the present; but almost immediately a new problem arose with a revolt in the Kingdom of Naples. In this case, there was justification of a sort, arising from Austria's treaty with Naples of 1815, for that country's armed intervention in 1821. Nevertheless, Castlereagh objected strongly to the line taken by Austria, Prussia and Russia at the Congress held in Troppau at the end of 1820 when they called upon England (and France) to join in 'delivering Europe from the scourge of revolution [and] diverting or checking … the evils resulting from the violation of all the principles of order and morality', and he confirmed his policy of non-interference in the internal affairs of other countries. This was particularly welcome in the Spanish colonies and raised hopes of early British recognition of their independence. This, however, could still not be overtly given at that time without possibly serious consequences for the balance of power in Europe.

The situation became even more difficult two years later when King Louis XVIII of France, concerned at the civil war then in progress in Spain, in which the 'liberal' government was maintaining the upper hand against the 'conservative' supporters of Ferdinand, moved a large army to the frontier. At the Congress of Verona in the autumn of 1822 he declared that he was not prepared to stand by while his brother Bourbon king in Spain was deposed or, worse, murdered. His plenipotentiary at the Congress invited the allies to say whether they would join France in breaking diplomatic relations with the government in Spain if necessary, and to make clear what moral and other support they would lend if war broke out between the two countries. Even though Canning (who was now Foreign Secretary after Castlereagh's suicide) was reasonably sure that at least Austria and Prussia would not rush to offer military help, he saw that it was vital to do nothing in relation to Spanish America which would bring all four European powers into an alliance in support of Ferdinand. At Verona, the Russians offered to send an army to back up France. All three promised to break diplomatic relations with Spain if necessary, and Austria and Prussia offered armed aid provided 'the extent, quality and direction of this aid' was agreed between all the powers concerned. Canning was prepared to break up the quadruple alliance rather than see it approving armed intervention in Spain on behalf of Ferdinand, and instructed the British plenipotentiary, Wellington, to make clear that Britain would not be a party to this.

While this at least made it unlikely that the other three allies would be prepared to engage in open military intervention on the side of

Ferdinand, France was in fact more interested in having a free hand in Spain and Canning's task now was to try to prevent this, and with it the risk of renewed war with Britain's old enemy. He determined to do what he could to mediate, and for this he had to convince the Spanish government that he was not about to take action in America which they would regard as hostile. On 10 December 1822 he had announced that a naval squadron had been despatched to the West Indies with instructions to protect British shipping by force against pirates, including if necessary attacking their bases in Cuba, still a Spanish possession. On 7 January 1823 he suspended these orders and offered to negotiate a commercial convention with Spain. This offer only reached Spain, however, after Austria, Prussia and Russia, in accordance with their promise to France, had announced the withdrawal of their ambassadors. The Spanish government's reaction to this had been to tell France that they refused to make any concessions over Ferdinand. However, as soon as Canning's offer was received, they immediately asked him to use his good offices with France; but by then France too had withdrawn her ambassador. And almost immediately after this, King Louis, in his speech from the throne at the opening of Parliament, threw down the gauntlet. He announced that 100,000 Frenchmen were ready to march to the help of a brother Bourbon, and he called upon Spaniards to 'let Ferdinand be free to give to his people the institutions they cannot hold but from him'. This return to the cry of 'legitimacy' was too much for Canning. His policy was based on the principle that 'England should hold the balance, not only between contending nations, but between conflicting principles: that, in order to prevent things from going to extremities, she should keep a distinct middle ground, staying the plague both ways.'[5] In the face of this danger of the anti-liberal influence prevailing, the preservation of equilibrium demanded British support for the liberal cause. He led public opinion in Britain in wholehearted condemnation of such reactionary ideas. He told France that he could recommend Spain to modify her constitution, but not on such a principle 'which strikes at the root of the British constitution'. King George's speech from the throne was drafted deliberately to omit any mention of British neutrality in the quarrel between France and Spain,[6] and in a public speech on 11 February Canning said that if a state of hostilities were unavoidable, England 'was fully prepared to meet the emergency'.

In fact, Canning did not believe that Britain would be justified in going to war unless France were to help Spain to recover her American colonies or attack Portugal. Nevertheless, he provided what comfort he could to the government of Spain, and continued to try to make France believe that war was a possibility, while at the same time appealing to moderates in both countries. His bluff was called in March 1823 when it became obvious that the Spanish government was not prepared to make any modifications to the constitution to give Ferdinand greater powers and that France was about to invade. He then made clear that Britain would remain neutral, but only if France pledged not to establish a permanent military occupation of Spain, not to appropriate any Spanish colonies and not to violate the territorial integrity of Portugal. He considered that the colonies had by now effectively separated themselves from the mother country, and let it be clearly understood that he might be prepared, depending on circumstances, to extend formal recognition to them. (He had already begun, secretly through Dr Mackie, to make contact with those in power in Mexico.) He stated publicly that Britain had no intention of trying to gain territorial advantage in any of these colonies, and called upon France to do likewise. On 6 April French troops entered Spain. Canning explained the reasons for his policy of neutrality in the House of Commons on 14 April and got approval by a large majority.[7] But it was obvious that he hoped that liberalism in Spain would win the day. In this he was disappointed. By the end of September the French had rescued Ferdinand, who had been imprisoned by the liberals, and he was back on the throne able, with French backing, to get his own way.

Canning's policy, by assuring France of British neutrality, at least ensured that she refused offers of armed help from Austria, Prussia and Russia. But he had in reality suffered a diplomatic defeat, so he determined to take steps to prevent another in relation to America. On 3 October 1823, before news of the rescue of Ferdinand in Cádiz had reached London (but after he had already decided to send official missions of enquiry openly to both Mexico and Colombia), he summoned the French ambassador, Polignac. They held discussions over several days, at the end of which Canning drew up a memorandum which he got Polignac to sign as representing what they had agreed. This 'Polignac Memorandum', as it became known, was not made public until March 1824; but its contents were made known immediately to the governments of the USA and the European powers. In brief, Polignac had agreed that it was hopeless to attempt to bring back Spanish America under Spain; had disclaimed French intentions to obtain exclusive advantages in those countries; had agreed that Spain was entitled to preferential commercial privileges there, but that any privileges extended to others should be available to all equally; and had abjured the use of force against the colonies. Canning for his part had declared that recognition of the independence of the former colonies was not dependent upon the actions of Spain, but on time and circumstances, and that Britain was not prepared to discuss their future with other European powers. In a part of the memorandum which was not revealed to others, Canning had suggested that a European congress could hardly discuss Spanish America without bringing in the USA, a proposal in which Polignac, speaking personally, saw no insuperable difficulty.

Canning's suggestion that the USA might be invited to participate in any congress to discuss Spanish America was really intended to discourage such a congress from assembling at all, for he had good reason to suppose that the USA, if invited, would refuse to take part. He had already tried, unsuccessfully, through the American Minister in London, Richard Rush, to suggest a joint British-American declaration on Spanish America as a way of forestalling a European congress. Rush had been receptive, but had insisted that Canning should first recognize the fact of the independence of the colonies, as the Americans had done in 1822. (They appointed a consul general to Mexico in March of that year; but a full diplomatic minister was not appointed until May 1825, although a Mexican minister had been formally accepted in Washington in December 1822.) This Canning was not prepared to do, partly because he would never have got it through the cabinet at that time, partly because he was still hoping to influence and help the Spanish constitutional party. However, his suggestions did play a part in the formation of the Monroe Doctrine, announced to the world at the end of December 1823, which effectively put an end, at least for the time being, to any European ideas of meddling in Spanish America. The essential part of this famous declaration was that which made quite clear that the USA could not in any way approve of the political systems of Europe and 'would consider any attempt on their part to extend their system to any portion of this hemisphere as dangerous to our peace and safety … The American Continents, by the free and independent condition which they have assumed and maintained, are henceforth not to be considered as subjects for future colonisation by any European Powers'. With the existing colonies or dependencies of any European power the USA would not interfere, but any European intervention would be, as the American Secretary of State, Adams, put it 'the manifestation of an unfriendly disposition to the United States' which would not be regarded 'with indifference'.

Canning always believed that his policy would have prevented the French invasion of Spain, and had it done so the course of subsequent events would have been different. Part of the reason why it did not was the clear indication given by some of his cabinet colleagues and the king himself that they were not behind him. The king was delighted with the French support of 'legitimate monarchy' and let this be known in the courts of Europe. Several ministers made it clear to the French Chargé d'affaires in London that if the French invaded Spain quickly Britain would remain neutral. But even Canning himself, while genuinely opposed to the type of despotic monarchy represented by Russia, Austria and Prussia, and to attempts by those countries to suppress by force popular efforts to create more democratic constitutions, continued to hope that he could persuade Spain to accept the independence of her colonies, and that the colonies, in such circumstances, would choose to be constitutional monarchies. This, he felt, would ensure the proper equilibrium between despotism and rampant republic liberalism. (In a letter at the end of 1823 he expressed the view that 'monarchy … would cure the evils of universal democracy and prevent the drawing of the line of demarcation which I most dread – America versus Europe'.[8]) It was therefore European politics, the attitude of King George IV and some of his ministers, and Canning's own leanings that combined to delay formal British recognition of the independence of these new nations. But British sea power ensured that neither Spain herself nor any other country could in practice take military action to recover dominion over them, and in the end it was the need to ensure that Britain had full access to the lucrative trade with and opportunities for investment in Spanish America that brought about that recognition. The idealism of those who hated European absolutism and the self-interest of those whose livelihood depended upon trade across the Atlantic combined to give these new republics the status they sought.

2

SECRET DIPLOMACY MISFIRES – 1823

Mackie, after discovering that Iturbide's position was in the balance, left Sacrificios on 2 March 1823 and reached Havana on the 17th. From there he wrote to the Foreign Office asking for further instructions.[1] While waiting for these he learned, in early May, that only four weeks after he had left Vera Cruz Iturbide had been deposed and had been allowed to leave the country for Italy, with all his family and a generous pension. He wrote again to the Foreign Office.[2] By 30 June, having heard nothing from London, and deciding that his existing instructions from Canning would be valid for making contact with whomsoever was now at the head of affairs instead of Iturbide, he left for Mexico in an armed Spanish schooner, informing the Foreign Office of this in a third letter.[3] (In fact the Foreign Office never replied at all to him.) Reaching Vera Cruz on 14 July he there learned that there was now a supreme executive of three men running the country, Nicolás Bravo, Pedro Celestino Negrete and Guadalupe Victoria. Although all three were nominally equal, it was clear that Victoria (who later became President) was the real power and regarded himself as head of the Executive.

Victoria had become a national hero during the long years of struggle against the Spanish Crown. He had been born José Manuel Ramón Adausto Fernández y Félix on 26 September 1786 into a middle class creole (locally born Spanish) family of modest means. He had been orphaned while quite young and, with his four brothers, cared for by an uncle, a priest in their small village. At the age of 19 he had set off for Durango with only a few pesos in his pocket and there had managed to get instruction in philosophy and do well enough to move to the capital two years later to study law, which he had completed in 1811. He had then joined the revolution which had begun the previous year, quickly gaining a reputation for bravery and military skill. In 1814, after a particular military success on the day of the Virgin of Guadalupe (much venerated by the poor and who had become the patron saint of the revolution) he had adopted the name Guadalupe Victoria (by which he was always thereafter known) and been promoted colonel in charge of the important insurgent operations in the province of Vera Cruz. His reputation had continued to grow and he had become a general in 1817. He had then met a series of set-backs as the Spaniards began to gain the upper hand. Many of his co-revolutionaries had accepted the pardon offered by the viceroy, but Victoria had resolutely refused this, continuing the struggle with an ever dwindling band of guerrillas until eventually forced into hiding in the mountains. Here he had disappeared for some 30 months during which he had endured extreme privation entirely on his own. When Iturbide had changed sides and revived the revolt in 1820, Victoria had been found and had immediately joined him. Later he had opposed Iturbide's harsh and demagogic policies and had been arrested. He had escaped and again gone underground before joining Santa Anna's revolt. Now once more he was the popular hero, one man who had consistently held out for independence from Spain and democratic liberty.[4]

Mackie found that Victoria was at Jalapa, some 60 miles inland, charged with organizing defence against any attempt by the Spaniards to attack from their remaining base at Ulloa, and with preparations for dislodging them entirely from Mexican soil. The Spanish government, however, had taken an unexpected initiative. Mackie was told that two Spanish commissioners 'had lately arrived from Spain' and had gone to Jalapa, where they were 'holding daily conferences' with Victoria. Greatly alarmed by this news, he immediately set off on horseback for that place, reaching it on the 16th. He 'waited on the General from whom [he] endeavoured with the necessary caution to ascertain the object of the Spanish Commissioners'. These had in fact made their first approach to Mexico in May 1822, while Iturbide was still in power, hoping to strike a deal with this troublesome colony in which, by the offer of some degree of self-government, it would remain part of the Spanish empire. This approach had been rejected, but in January 1823 Iturbide had responded to a second approach with a cautious readiness to hold discussions. When he was deposed shortly after this, the commissioners had waited patiently in Ulloa and had then, in April, approached Victoria, who was authorized by the supreme Executive to open discussions with them in Jalapa. By the time Mackie arrived there, Victoria had indeed reached agreement with the commissioners on the text of a draft treaty which he had sent to the capital, and he was awaiting further instructions.[5]

Mackie gained the impression that this agreement allowed Spain a trade monopoly 'to the exclusion of all other nations' and he decided that he must somehow prevent 'a step so pregnant with evil to the interests' of Great Britain from being ratified. He therefore presented himself to Victoria as having negotiating powers on behalf of the British government and set about trying to persuade him that if he wanted the friendship of Britain and her recognition of Mexican independence he could not possibly grant Spain commercial privileges from which Britain would be excluded. This was an astonishing initiative. Canning had specifically made clear to him that his mission was entirely informal and that he was to 'be particularly careful not to convey the notion of your being charged with any political mission or invested with any political character whatever', although he was to 'state on all occasions with the utmost confidence your persuasion of the friendly disposition of this Government, of its determination to maintain, so long as Spain and her late Colonies are at variance, a perfect and scrupulous neutrality between the contending parties, and of its desire to see the contest brought to a conclusion on terms consistent with the interests and happiness of both'. Not only, therefore, was Mackie deliberately ignoring that specific instruction, he was actually misrepresenting Canning's policy, which was to encourage Spain to recognize Mexican independence even if this meant she would obtain special advantages.

Victoria, however, wanted British recognition above everything. On receiving the conditional approval of congress for the agreement he had reached with the Spanish commissioners he therefore decided to say nothing to them. To Mackie he gave the impression that he had been persuaded by him to annul the agreement with them. Mackie, fearing that if he now went to the capital to discuss the situation there the Spaniards might get at Victoria again (and in any case wanting to keep his activities out of the public eye), had no difficulty in persuading Victoria to get authority to negotiate with him in Jalapa. He even went so far as to write himself to the Foreign Ministry to explain that he had been 'sent by the British Government to show to the Supreme Executive of Mexico its ardent desire to establish friendly and commercial relations in a spirit of freedom and resting on the dignity and interests of both countries', that he had been instructed, when given this 'delicate commission', to deal directly with Victoria, the only one of the governing executive of whom Canning had heard 'because of the fame of his name throughout Europe' and 'in order not to compromise, by my going to the capital, the absolute secrecy which is the essence of the proposed negotiations and in the interest of the whole position of my nation'. He said he would exhibit his powers if the Supreme Executive would authorize the proceedings; and he asked for a speedy response as the frigate *Phaeton* was waiting at Vera Cruz to take him back to England.[6] (This was the same ship that had carried the 7th Earl of Elgin and his wife on his embassy to Constantinople in 1799.)

Perhaps Victoria, susceptible to flattery, simply ignored what should have been an obvious inconsistency in this explanation. But he did understand enough about Britain's need at the time to avoid conflict with Spain to appreciate that Canning could not possibly have been prepared at that stage to make a more formal and open move. And he was prepared to believe, because he wanted to, that this was nevertheless a serious approach behind the backs of the other European governments which should not be rejected. He was at pains to make clear to his colleagues on the executive that he expected them not to miss this opportunity of forming an alliance with Britain. In forwarding Mackie's letter he invited them 'not to lose a moment' in giving him full authority to negotiate 'in order that as soon as possible this envoy can return to the bosom of that nation from which we expect all kinds of help which otherwise may be delayed or even denied; and which, if negotiated in good time, may be the basis of Mexican prosperity and greatness which, in my opinion, needs only to seek such respectable protection under which to grow rapidly to its full maturity'. As the 'nature of this negotiation requires prompt and delicate treatment', he did not doubt but that the executive 'would resolve as wisdom dictates, avoiding all proceedings which could prejudice them or bring them to public notice' so that 'the violent machinations of the jealous enemies and rivals of liberty and national independence which exist in the country's press' would not hurt 'the English, so circumspect in all their actions'. He assured the executive that he would 'not lose sight of the dignity and respect due to my country, proposing always as the unalterable basis the solemn recognition of its independence, of its territorial integrity, equality of rights in external trade and the speedy granting of all the help it needs.[7]

Some historians have considered that Victoria was indecisive and too much swayed by the opinions of cleverer politicians. There may be some truth in this, for there were many around him whose intellectual abilities were greater than his. But he was nobody's fool, and it would be fairer to say that his main endeavour – in which he was largely successful during the next few vital years in the early life of this new republic – was to balance the different political influences so that none came out clearly on top, with the risk that that would have had of reopening civil strife. He was himself an honest man, with a determination to do his best for his country and a fairly clear idea of how to do it. And he was sufficiently respected and trusted to be able to get his own way in a body in which he was nominally, at that time, only one among three equals. Fortunately he had then the full support of the man who had been appointed to take charge of foreign affairs, Lucas Alamán. Alamán knew Europe and was a man of outstanding abilities, later playing a crucial part in negotiations with Britain. He had been born in Guanajuato in 1792 of a wealthy Spanish aristocratic family with large mining interests. During most of the years of revolt against the Spaniards he was in Europe, studying mining among other things, and he visited London in 1815. He did not return to Mexico until February 1820 and soon after this he was chosen to be one of the Mexican deputies in the Cortes (parliament) in Madrid. He left Spain in 1822 to return once again to Mexico, travelling via Paris and London in an effort to raise capital for the mines in Mexico and form his own mining company. He was therefore unusually well qualified among leading Mexicans, in the difficult time of adjustment after the fall of Iturbide, to play an important part in developing relations with Europe. It has been said that Victoria did not like him, possibly feeling a sense of intellectual inferiority; but he shared most of Victoria's political ideas (even if they did not always see eye to eye on how best to implement them), and this was a vital factor over the next few years. To him Victoria also wrote, privately, begging him, with 'the knowledge you possess of the different characters of all the nations with which we must treat', to support his proposal of negotiating with Mackie and his arguments for absolute secrecy in the negotiations 'in which the English seriousness and circumspection seem to be so interested'.[8]

These two letters from Victoria had the effect he wanted and his Full Powers were signed on the 27th, within 24 hours of receipt of his request. They were accompanied by formal instructions (no doubt drafted by Alamán) for the carrying out of the task being entrusted to one 'to whom the country owes so much in the achievement of its independence'. He was required to secure 'absolute recognition of the independence of the Mexican territory … including the Castle of San Juan de Ulloa, the method of repossession of which Your Excellency should agree with the English envoy'. The importance was emphasized of acceptance by England of Mexico's right to have whatever form of constitution and government it thought best, and an assurance, in the light of feared French intentions, that no European power would be allowed to interfere in Mexican internal affairs or with her independence. He was to assure Mackie that Mexico would 'open her ports to the ships of the nations which recognised her independence and keep them closed to those which did not … [and] … as it seems that the English Commissioner is opening the door to providing the help which our circumstances require, Your Excellency should ask for a loan of £150,000 per month for one year, doing your best to ensure that this would begin from the date of the treaty, as well as armaments for 50,000 infantry and 12,000 cavalry'. Further loans would be sought once the treaty became public: Mexico's needs were such that it was essential that England should give massive aid, and an agent would therefore be appointed in England to pursue this. The negotiations with the Spanish commissioners were to continue as might seem appropriate in the light of those with Mackie, and further instructions would be sent as necessary. For the present, however, Victoria was not to reactivate them, giving no reason for not doing so; and he was certainly not to reveal to them the contact with England.[9] (Nor did he reveal to Mackie that the Spaniards were in fact being kept in the wings in this way.)

Mackie was by now committed to a difficult course of action. At the first formal meeting on 31 July it was agreed that 'an exact copy of the credentials [of both parties] be transcribed in a book prepared for that purpose to be placed in the archives' and that an agreed record of all the proceedings would be prepared in both Spanish and English. Mackie had no 'powers' to exhibit. His only credentials were Canning's written instructions, which contained the specific disclaimer of his having any political status. To get round this, Mackie simply covered that passage with a piece of plain paper; and this was noted in the Spanish language record where it reproduced the remainder of Canning's instructions in English. Mackie, however, simply noted in his English version of the record of the meeting that a copy of his instructions had been taken into the Spanish record. Both versions recorded that Victoria had acknowledged Mackie as 'fully authorised to present proposals on the favourable development of which depends the opening of the doors to relations …'

What, one wonders, did Victoria make of this? Did he merely think it only natural that there might have been something in Canning's instructions which his agent would consider confidential? Or had he himself discovered the truth from Mackie and, wishing to conceal it from his colleagues in the capital, suggested this subterfuge? There had been a lot of discussion between them before the first formal meeting and it might have become evident from these that Mackie did not have authority to agree anything. Or possibly the truth only emerged during their further unrecorded talks about this first formal meeting. What does seem likely is that Victoria did at some stage discover the limitations on Mackie's powers but was so keen to have some kind of understanding with Britain, and if possible avoid one with the Spaniards, that he was prepared to join in an arrangement which would avoid the possibility of his colleagues calling off the discussions with Mackie.[10]

Whatever may have been Victoria's understanding of Mackie's position, he certainly managed to get enough into the agreed records to persuade his colleagues that Britain was serious in wanting close relations, even though he could not in the end carry out in all detail the instructions they had sent him. He formally recorded the hope that despite Britain's determination to remain neutral in the dispute with Spain she would 'prevent any invasion that may be attempted' and would 'afford every assistance that may be required by the Mexican nation for its defence'. He also placed on record two specific questions, with Mackie's answers to them. First he wanted to know 'Will Great Britain declare war against any country trying to invade Mexico?' To this Mackie replied, with admirable caution, that the only answer was what was contained in his written instructions and in statements that Canning had made in the House of Commons. In other words, Mexico could not count on this.[11] Secondly, Victoria wanted to know whether Britain would supply everything needed for Mexico's defence. Here Mackie was less cautious, suggesting 'that the Mexican nation may rely on receiving every class of supplies from Great Britain under such conditions and indemnization as may be determined by both governments'. This was stretching the concept of strict neutrality. And he also wrote into the record his 'certainty that the Mexican government will not on any account form any treaties of commerce, or grant any privileges to Spain, or any other nation whatsoever, until the two governments may as soon as possible agree on what may be the most conducive for their mutual advantage' and that any such concessions would be 'opposed to the interests of both nations'. This went a long way beyond what Canning intended.

Although Victoria did not formally put to Mackie detailed demands for armaments and loans, as he had been instructed to do, in their informal discussions he was frank about Mexico's needs. He constantly 'reverted to the unpleasant situation in which as the Head [*sic*] of the Supreme Executive Power he found himself placed with respect to the possession of the Castle of San Juan de Ulloa by the Old Spaniards', explaining that he dared not take military action to cut off the castle's supplies from Havana as this 'would be the prelude to a general massacre of the Old Spaniards in all parts of the Kingdom, so great is the animosity excited in the minds of the creoles against them'. He asked Mackie, however, whether he could not arrange for 'a King's ship to be stationed in the port of Vera Cruz to put a stop' to the governor's practice of demanding taxes on goods being imported into Mexico. Mackie told Canning that although this suggestion 'met my view and decided approbation', he had 'hesitated to adopt so vigorous a measure from the apprehension of exceeding the powers with which I was entrusted', leading Victoria 'to request me in the most earnest manner to represent to you the expedience of adopting the most prompt and effectual means of checking the evil complained of'. (Quite how Mackie could have adopted 'so vigorous a measure' if he had felt it would not exceed his powers is unclear: one can hardly suppose that the naval commander-in-chief at Jamaica would have taken orders from him.) Victoria also hoped that Britain would help him get rid of the Spaniards in Cuba, and told Mackie that he was in favour of a Mexican union with that island. Mackie had the good sense (or so at least he told Canning) to tell Victoria that he 'considered an union with the island of Cuba would from its locality inevitably be the means of embroiling the Mexican nation with the powers of Europe at a future period, from which they would be exempt by remaining altogether a separate State, as it was evident that the island of Cuba required the protection of a formidable maritime Power, without which it would be impossible to preserve its independence'. Victoria also spoke bitterly about the attitude of the United States, showing 'his contemptible opinion of them as a nation, and representing them as an ambitious people always ready to encroach on their neighbours without a spark of good faith'.

After the third formal meeting, Victoria sent the records to the capital for approval. In doing so he did not, in so many words, point out that Mackie had not turned out to have all the powers he had at first suggested; he merely said that it was easy to see 'that it would not be possible to take another step forward in the circumstances without compromising the position of the Mexican nation or that of the envoy whose credentials only permit him to present proposals which show the readiness of a government to open the relations from which surely we should expect every support once it is certain of ours'. But he excused this by expressing the view that the British government could not have proceeded in any other way, given their relations with other European countries, and that, considering how little they could know of conditions in Mexico, they could not have expressed more good will. 'How' he wrote 'could they have ventured to authorise a Minister to conclude a definite treaty without assuring themselves of the good will and stability of our government?' Mackie had confessed to his earlier attempt to make contact with Iturbide, and Victoria, revealing this, urged the executive, despite the uncertainty of the situation, to show a positive response to his mission.[12] Mackie, too, wrote to Alamán, to express his satisfaction that he had been able

> to fulfil the object of the delicate commission entrusted to me … having displayed to [Victoria] … the lively desire which my nation has for the prosperity and welfare of this privileged land; and being able now to assure Your Excellency with the greatest frankness that as soon as the British government is informed by me of the sincere and friendly disposition of the Supreme Executive of Mexico, of which it was completely ignorant at the time of my departure, it will unfold its grandiose and beneficent regard and all its influence and power in order that this nation, which justly may call itself the pattern of all the Americas, may fulfil its burning desires.[13]

It is unlikely that Alamán put great faith in such bombast, even though Mackie (quite improperly) had stated, on the record, at his first meeting with Victoria, 'that on his return to England a public Minister will, without any delay, be sent out fully empowered to conclude a definitive treaty competent to fulfil the intention of both governments, and may respect inviolably and religiously the basis of absolute independence, the integrity of the Mexican territory …' He must have known that if Mackie were really someone whose views would influence the British government to that extent he would have carried something more directly relevant in the way of credentials than the request he included in this letter from the brother of the Duke of Wellington (William Wellesley-Pole, 1st Baron Maryborough), to buy 'the twelve paintings, kept in the Convent of Carmel in Puebla, by the Spanish painter Murillo representing the history of the Virgin' which Lord Maryborough wanted to present as a gift to the king.[14] There would surely have been at least some personal letter from Canning to Iturbide, however carefully worded. But Alamán shared Victoria's eagerness to get Britain committed to recognition of Mexico and was prepared to use Mackie's approach as a means of extracting something from her if at all possible. He made sure that the Executive approved generally of Victoria's proceedings. Their only reservation was over Mackie's suggestion that Mexico should refrain from giving privileges to Spain, or any other country, before a treaty could be concluded with Britain. The response to this was that 'if England recognises our independence it would be possible to forbid access [to Mexico] by ships of nations which have not done the same, and this would provide a form of privilege in her favour which could in no way offend others and which would show them the advantages to be gained by granting recognition'.[15]

So Mackie was able to return to England well satisfied with what he persuaded himself had been the exercise of wise initiative in an unexpected situation. He was the bearer of a personal letter to Canning from Victoria expressing his

> particular inclinations towards Great Britain, from my full persuasion that its position invites us to form a perfect amity, and that its interests are allied to ours, as well as from its good faith, which is the soul of all the relations of England .... It therefore only remains for me to entreat Your Excellency to bestow on this concern your great influence. I can desire nothing further, as it will be the surest means of rendering my country happy and raising it to the rank which belongs to it ...'[16]

He also carried a formal letter from Alamán informing Canning that they were appointing an agent 'at the British court' to pursue the question of establishing relations.[17] Moreover, he believed that he had not only extracted a promise of facilities for British merchants, but had persuaded the Mexicans to reduce import duties on British goods from 27 per cent to 15 per cent, with the prospect of special rates for cotton goods at 2–4 per cent lower than those charged to other countries. No wonder he expressed himself so enthusiastically in his formal report to Canning:

> From my long and personal knowledge of the Mexican character I am induced to attach the greatest confidence to the General's declarations made to me in the name of the Mexican people, and I could readily perceive in the sentiments … a most decided prediliction for Great Britain, as being the only nation with which Mexico should be most desirous of forming the closest connections .... From Great Britain they confidently expect the realisation of their hopes, and I beg leave to add my feeble voice to join them in their desire of the accomplishment of them. And from the confidence inspired by your speeches in Parliament they look up to you as the saviour of their country and the author of their rank as an independent nation.[18]

It was as well that Mackie did not know that, as soon as he had left, Victoria reopened discussions with the Spanish commissioners. But his luck held. The draft treaty earlier agreed by Victoria with these commissioners had been only provisional, subject to formal Spanish recognition of Mexican independence. In the renewed discussions, the commissioners showed no inclination to grant this, and in any case they began to get the impression that even if the treaty were signed it would not be accepted by all the provincial governments. But before any further progress could be made, their efforts were unexpectedly sabotaged by the Spanish governor of the castle when he attempted to take possession of Sacrificios Island. The Mexicans immediately suspended the negotiations, and shortly after this, when the castle started to bombard Vera Cruz, thus turning the dormant war between the two countries into open hostilities, the commissioners were asked to leave. That particular attempt by Spain to heal the breach with Mexico had ended, and Victoria was left holding onto his belief that he would soon be receiving the formal mission from England promised by Mackie.

In fact, although Mackie left Mexico at the end of August 1823, he did not reach London until 20 November,[19] and when Canning later discovered that he had represented himself as having negotiating powers, he was furious and arranged to inform Victoria that all Mackie's proceedings were to be disregarded. Fortunately, however, Canning had by then already decided, without waiting for Mackie to report, to send an official mission, and when this arrived in Mexico it was assumed to be the direct outcome of Mackie's recommendation. Although, therefore, Mackie cannot claim any official part in the process of establishing formal British-Mexican relations, by chance his disregard of his instructions contributed positively to creating the atmosphere in which these could develop. But during the four years that followed, Victoria's patience was tried severely.

3

SECRECY IS ABANDONED – 1823

Why Mackie should have acted as he did is a question that cannot be answered with any confidence. He may have genuinely felt he was defending important British interests and, by going beyond his instructions, performing a service for his country which would earn him the grateful thanks of Canning. But what appears to have driven him more than any such patriotic motives was a belief that he could turn events to his personal advantage in a material way. The probability that he was an out and out charlatan is strong and, while the suggestion that he might in fact never have been to Mexico before Canning sent him is perhaps going too far,[1] there is no doubt that on returning to England he set out to represent himself as enjoying Canning's confidence and to have been that statesman's agent in negotiating a treaty. According to the Mexican newspaper *El Sol* of 28 February 1824, a Glasgow paper (unidentified and untraced in British archives) had carried a report in November of Mackie's arrival from Mexico and had learned 'from an entirely reliable source' that he had successfully completed a mission by concluding 'a very complete and satisfactory treaty of commerce with the Mexican Government on a basis of great advantage to our merchants'. He sent a warning of Iturbide's ill-fated attempt in the summer of 1824 to stage a come-back in Mexico in a personal letter to Victoria,[2] to whom he had also written from Vera Cruz as he left the country suggesting that he could get better terms for loans to Mexico than were being obtained by the Mexican agent there, Migoni.[3] And he managed for a while on his return, with the help of a Foreign Office clerk, William Broughton (who was apparently acting without authority, mesmerized perhaps by Mackie's plausibility) to deceive Migoni into believing that he could indeed do that, and to negotiate a cut of £12,500 for himself.[4] He also secured for himself a share in mining ventures (see chapter 12).

Mackie paid for his sharp practices, however, being cast into King's Bench Prison for debt in 1827 after losing a small fortune in his mining speculations. But even then he was as full as ever of his self-importance and fanciful ventures, explaining to the painter Benjamin Robert Haydon (who was also incarcerated there for a while for the same reason) how he had negotiated secretly in Mexico by arranging for Victoria to fain illness so that he could be visited by a doctor, and that 'Mr Canning was highly delighted & gave him great praise'. He was then 'planning steam coaches & talking of setting off for Mexico as soon as he was free – calm & undisturbed'.[5]

A particularly odd feature of Mackie's story is not only that he and Hall[6] were apparently unaware of each other's existence, even though they both claimed intimate connections with Iturbide, but that Mackie seems to have been unaware that Iturbide had taken steps to send his own agent to England; while this agent, also British, seems to have known nothing of Mackie.[7] A resolution was taken by Iturbide's government in January 1822 to send 'secret' emissaries to England, Rome and the United States.[8] The one chosen to go to England was Arthur Goodall Wavell. There are many obscurities in the story of this man's activities in and for Mexico, including his exact status when he reached England in November 1822; but at least his personal background, unlike Mackie's, is documented. He was the grandfather of Field-Marshal Earl Wavell (commander-in-chief of British forces in the Middle East in the early stages of the Second World War and later Viceroy and Governor General of India). He had been born in Edinburgh on 20 March 1785 and educated at Winchester College. He had joined the Bengal Militia in 1805 but had returned to England soon afterwards for health reasons. He had then begun a career as a soldier of fortune, first joining the Spanish army in 1810, being given the rank of lieutenant-colonel in 1811. He had fought with distinction during the Peninsular War, virtually losing the use of an arm when wounded at the battle of Barrosa but going on to win several Spanish decorations. He had left the Spanish army in 1817 and in 1820 joined the Chilean independence army as a colonel of infantry. According to his own later declarations (for which there is now no corroborative evidence), he rose to be major-general and deputy commander-in-chief.[9] The circumstances of his move to Mexico are unclear. He seems to have arrived some time in January 1822, claiming to be an official emissary from the Chilean government.[10] The Mexicans at first took this claim at face value, for on 12 February it was officially resolved 'to send an emissary to Chile to congratulate that Republic on its independence in reciprocity for having sent Brigadier Arthur Wavell to congratulate this sovereign Junta on achieving independence, although it has already officially communicated to the supreme Government of Chile the fact of our glorious independence and offered it our most sincere and fraternal friendship and embrace'.[11] But this resolution was never carried into effect, and the explanation may lie in Admiral Thomas Cochrane's recollection of certain events in November 1821 and January 1822.

Cochrane, later Earl of Dundonald, was one of the many British soldiers and sailors who, without the authority of the government (which had promised Spain its neutrality), had been assisting Chile and Peru to gain their independence (there was no such British participation in Mexico). Late in 1821 he was sailing north with his squadron to visit Mexico and while at Guayaquil in November, he

> met with two officers, General Wavell and Colonel O'Reilly, to whom the Chilean Government had given passports to quit the country, not estimating their services as tantamount to their pay … [They] had represented to the authorities at Guayaquil that they were ambassadors from Chile to Mexico deputed to congratulate the Mexican Government on their achievement of independence. Knowing this to be false, I requested them to show their credentials, which of course they could not do. Their passports were then demanded, and evinced by their dates that the pretended ambassadors had quitted Chile prior to the intelligence of the establishment of independence in Mexico.

When Cochrane got to Acapulco on 29 January 1822, he was surprised to find the Mexicans highly suspicious of him. According to Cochrane, Wavell and O'Reilly had discovered, on arriving in Mexico City, that the story of their contretemps with him at Guayaquil had preceded them. 'In revenge', as Cochrane put it, they had told the Mexican authorities that Cochrane had 'possessed himself of the Chilean navy, plundered the vessels belonging to Peru, was now on a piratical cruise and was coming to ravage the coast of Mexico'. This 'misunderstanding' was then cleared up, and Cochrane received a very warm letter from Iturbide.[12]

Not all that Cochrane later wrote about those days can be taken as the whole truth. He was a controversial figure whose exploits were as much for his own profit as for the benefit of Spanish-American independence, important though his contribution to that was. It could be that Wavell had knowledge of some of Cochrane's more dubious activities, disliked him and was eager to discredit him. But something happened to stop the Mexicans sending a reciprocal Mexican mission to Chile and it seems that Cochrane may well have had the last word. But in that case, how Wavell gained the confidence of Iturbide, who gave him the rank of brigadier-general, and later full general, in the Mexican army, is something of a mystery. Alamán had his own opinion in his later history of these times, referring to Wavell as 'no more than one of those many adventurers who at that time came from Europe to seek their fortunes amidst the revolutions in America' by whom 'Iturbide, too prone to welcome this type of person' was taken in.[13] But there is not the smallest jot of evidence that Wavell ever acted in any way dishonestly. On the contrary, he actually lost money through a combination of honesty and naïvety in his subsequent business dealings; and he did in fact render useful service to Mexico in his military capacity.

Wavell later claimed to have been sent to England by Iturbide with diplomatic status. He may have been given some document appointing him as an agent of the Mexican government, but there is no evidence that on arrival in England he attempted to claim such status: in 1823 he actually wrote to the Mexican authorities from London to ask for it.[14] When he sailed from Vera Cruz on 11 August 1822 he did so in the French barque *L'Azema* bound for Bordeaux, which would have been a curious way of reaching England had he been travelling with a diplomatic passport on an official mission to England. But this ship was attacked by pirates off Cuba and he lost most of his possessions and papers, so it is possible that among these was a written order from Iturbide. After the piracy, the ship sailed to Charleston, where he obtained passage in an English vessel, *London*, which brought him to Liverpool on 11 November.[15] When, some years later, he submitted claims against the Mexican government, he made out that his mission had been to persuade the British government to recognize Mexican independence. But, while Iturbide undoubtedly hoped for this, it seems that his main interest at that time was in making use of an Englishman with a certain social status and useful contacts to persuade British financial houses to invest money in Mexican mines. Certainly

Wavell at the time did not take upon himself the mantle of plenipotentiary, as Mackie did. And his first actions seem to have been to arrange his own business affairs. Shortly before sailing he had asked Iturbide for a grant of land in Texas (then still Mexican) 'in order to colonise it with settlers from Great Britain', a project in which his partner was the American, Stephen F. Austin (the 'father' of American Texas, after whom the capital of that state is named) to whom he later lent money.[16] He must have gone straight from Liverpool to London, for he wrote to Austin from there on 16 November. And by the 21st he was able to report to him that he had a business deal arranged to their advantage provided he could get early confirmation of the grant of land.[17] (He did not in fact get this until 1826 and then ran into a lot of legal problems. In the end his title was not confirmed and he had to give up his dream of settling permanently in Texas, which later became part of the United States.)

When Wavell first made contact with the Foreign Office is unclear. In a letter to the Mexican government in May 1823 he referred to having had an interview with Canning 'a few days after my arrival in the capital' and to having further communications with him 'and with several other important people at court' later;[18] but there are now no records in the Foreign Office files in London of any meeting there before June 1823. If he did have a meeting with Canning soon after reaching London, this would have been just before Canning finally decided to send Mackie to Mexico and could therefore have been the trigger for that decision. If it were, however, why did both Mackie and Wavell apparently remain in ignorance of each other and why was there no mention of Wavell's 'mission' in Mackie's instructions? On balance, it seems improbable that Wavell had contact with the Foreign Office before Mackie left for Mexico. But he claimed, in his communications with Mexico, to have been active at once in spreading propaganda favourable to Mexico in the press and by means of pamphlets. None of this has come to light, except for a pamphlet entitled 'Reflections on the expediency of a speedy recognition of the Spanish Americas' which, although undated and unsigned, is generally accepted as being his work.[19] But certainly by December of 1822 he had got in prospect a loan of $20 million to the Mexican government.[20]

Wavell found himself in a position similar to Mackie's when he learned, in July 1823, of Iturbide's fall and he then took steps to play down his role as the emperor's secret agent.[21] He wrote to the new men to say that Iturbide had not given him a diplomatic mission, but had merely asked him to use what influence he had in England to get British investors interested in putting capital into the mines; and he took this opportunity to report on developments in this matter, at the same time suggesting that it might also be possible to get British help in equipping the army.[22] He was then intending to return to Mexico at the end of that month, but did not do so. However, he was evidently successful in averting suspicion that he might be an 'Iturbidist', and when he did return, in January 1824, he remained *persona grata* for some years, giving advice on military matters and even being appointed to conduct an enquiry into the activities of some Mexican soldiers involved in robbing a British naval officer and murdering some Americans.[23] Meanwhile, he had taken personally to Planta in June a detailed memorandum on Mexico (and on Chile and Peru), most of which he had had to write from memory because of the loss of his papers by piracy.[24]

Of active attempts by Wavell to persuade the British government to recognize Mexican independence there is little evidence, and such as there is seems to have been in the context of the potential advantages to Britain rather than on behalf of the Mexicans. It was at this time that he became involved in the business affairs of Sir William Adams, who wrote to Planta that he was 'very warmly & sincerely interested in the success of the General's mission' because he was convinced 'that the trade & prosperity of England might be promoted by an intimate commercial alliance with the South Americas to an extent which the most sanguine speculator could scarcely venture to anticipate'.[25] Adams also wrote to the prime minister (the Earl of Liverpool), referring to Wavell as 'the envoy from Mexico' who had been

> second in command of the Chilean army, and virtually acted as Commander-in-Chief .... The General had been but a short time in Mexico before he manifested such superior talents that all the parties in the Mexican Government concurred in selecting him as the fittest person to send to England to solicit the recognition of the independence of that most extraordinarily gifted country .... He has most successfully exerted his influence with the Mexican Government in favour of the interests of his native country, in opposition to French and North American intrigues and hostility.[26]

Adams was presumably simply taking Wavell's own word for this; but even if 'all the parties in the Mexican Government concurred in selecting him' it was probably no more than an unavoidable endorsement at the time of the decision of a man, Iturbide, with whom few were likely to try disagreeing.

Adams was certainly an ally with influence. He was two years older than Wavell, whom he had known since childhood, a distinguished (and in some respects controversial) oculist who was appointed surgeon and oculist to the Prince Regent, and other members of the royal family, and knighted in May 1814 at the age of 31.[27] He was also interested in the development of steam guns, in which he had Palmerston's enthusiastic support.[28] Whether it was he who persuaded Wavell to get deeply involved in Mexican mining investment, or the other way round, is not clear; but for a couple of years after this they were close business partners – until things went wrong and they broke up with recriminations. But the connection at this time, in the summer of 1823, made Wavell more keen on developing business interests in Mexico than in promoting the idea of British political recognition of Mexican independence. It is true that in writing to Planta, after his meeting with him on 17 June, he referred to Mexico as 'a country which I hope & trust ere long Gt Britain will count amongst her most valuable *allies*'; but his main concern then was to secure a passage back to Mexico in a British man-of-war for himself and an agent appointed by 'a most respectable body of merchants' to accompany him 'in order to enter into some very important mercantile negotiations'.[29] He was not successful in this request, and according to a Mexican press report he eventually took passage from Falmouth in October 1823 in the merchant vessel *Sarah*, reaching Vera Cruz sometime in the first week of January 1824.[30]

Wavell found Adams to be an enthusiastic ally also in his amorous affairs. He was arranging to take a mistress with him to Mexico and Adams wrote to him at Falmouth saying 'I will do all you wish for your Dulcinea[31] & will give her *some good advice* before she goes off .... I shall expect full accounts from you of everything ... as also of how many children you get a year.'[32] Who this was is not known; but she did not stay long. In July 1825 his father wrote to him 'the woman you sent back says she has a Will *of yours* in her possession ... you know these things & I doubt not you will take care to leave no document of consequence in such hands'.[33] In another letter, four days later, his father wrote:

> In my last I mentioned to you the reports I had received respecting a Will of yours in the hands of a certain female I

> will mention to you a fact. Capt John Powell, when in the E Indies ... had made a Will in favour of a young woman, in a kind of bravado with other officers, on the eve of a battle and forgot it. He died many years after intestate, as was believed, his brother General Peregrine Powell administered to his property, when, soon after, this Will was produced and the family robbed of the whole fortune more than £30,000.[34]

Apparently Wavell took this advice: at all events, he entered into a respectable marriage in 1828, and there is no record of any subsequent problems over his temporary mistress.

Wavell was not the only person appointed by Iturbide to represent Mexican interests in Britain. Francisco Borja de Migoni had been resident there for some time as a merchant banker, involved in getting British capital invested in Mexico, when Iturbide made him the official agent of his government for raising loans. There is no sign that he was involved politically then in trying to persuade the British government to recognize Mexican independence: indeed, when he learned in September 1823 that Canning was preparing to send an official mission there, he merely offered his help in a general way.[35] But, despite this earlier connection with Iturbide, it was he who was later appointed to represent Mexico as diplomatic agent (Alamán's letter to Canning sent with Mackie). Alamán sent him copies of the records of Mackie's meetings with Victoria and instructed him to 'try to follow up this matter with the care its importance requires', but 'to take no active steps before [Mackie] arrives'.[36] He was meanwhile to keep himself informed, and report at once, on all developments of interest to Mexico 'not only in [England] but in the other countries of Europe, if necessary making contact with such governments as may seem appropriate to prevent any threats to our independence and freedom which may arise from political movements in Europe'. But he was to act throughout with great discretion and circumspection.[37] He was received at the Foreign Office by Planta on 24 November 1823, when he may have handed over the copies of the Mexican records of the discussions with Mackie which alerted the Foreign Office to that man's actions in misrepresenting his status.[38] But he failed in his attempts to be accorded diplomatic status. He informed Canning by note in December that as he was now 'Minister Plenipotentiary in this Court from the Mexican Government' he wanted the gift of cigars and chocolates he had arranged to have sent from that country to the

Spanish ambassador released by customs to him.[39] He got a dusty official answer. Canning was not prepared to grant diplomatic recognition to any Mexican emissary, however grandly he might be designated by the Mexican government, before he had taken some formal step to recognize that country as independent from Spain; and this attitude, correct though it was in diplomatic practice, was the cause of some offence over the next year or so.

In those days it was quite normal for all kinds of people to try to participate in international intrigue; but they had little or no effect on foreign policies unless it suited a great power to make use of them. Despite all the activities of the likes of Mackie, Migoni and Wavell, Canning was influenced by nothing more than his own perception of where British national interests lay when it came to deciding when to recognize the independence of Spain's colonies in America. Like Castlereagh before him, he knew the importance of ensuring that Britain could trade freely with them. As early as June 1822 Castlereagh had recognized the Spanish colonial flags for shipping purposes. In November of that year Canning had written to Wellington: 'Every day convinces me more and more that … the American questions are out of all proportion more important to us than the European and that, if we do not seize and turn them to our advantage in time, we shall rue the loss of an opportunity never, never to be recovered.'[40] Thus the sending of Mackie to Mexico was in no way a response to special pleadings, but rather a deliberate act in pursuance of a long term intention, even if at that time he could not make any overt act of recognition of independence. And by the summer of 1823, months before Mackie had returned from Mexico and Migoni had presented himself as the official representative of the Mexican government, he had decided that he should move more openly.

As explained in chapter 1, in April of that year Canning had had to deal with a new European crisis arising out of a French invasion of Spain. France had been determined to support King Ferdinand against the government there which had forced him in 1820 to accept a 'liberal' constitution in which the power of the monarch was severely limited. Canning had been unable to prevent this but had warned France of the possibility of war if she went further and supported military steps by Ferdinand to recover his American colonies; and he had made clear that Britain would recognize their independence when it suited her, without reference to other European powers or Spain. Having suffered a diplomatic defeat in failing to prevent the French invasion, Canning now decided, in July, to regain the initiative by making an overt move towards such recognition, which had already been granted by the United States, Sweden and Belgium. (In fact it could be said that *de facto* recognition had already been extended in 1822 when Castlereagh had arranged for the flags of the colonies to be recognized for shipping purposes in British ports.) He began to draw up plans for the despatch of official missions of enquiry to Mexico and Colombia and the establishment of consular posts, making no secret of his intentions. And he went further in regaining political initiative vis-á-vis France by persuading the French Ambassador in London, Polignac, to sign a memorandum (subsequently known as the Polignac Memorandum). This recorded the outcome of three days of discussions in which Polignac had agreed that it was hopeless to consider bringing the Spanish colonies back under Spanish dominion and had declared that France would never be a party to any attempt to do so. (Copies of this memorandum were circulated in confidence to the European powers and the United States but it was not made public until March next year.)

It is curious that in the course of formulating these policies Canning should have totally ignored Mackie. He certainly saw Mackie's reports from Havana sent in March and May, yet he sent no replies. The first had reached him in April when he was deeply preoccupied with the French interference in Spanish affairs, and as it told him no more than that Iturbide was dealing with a revolt, he may have felt that until he knew the outcome of the French action in Spain he was in no position to decide the line he should adopt in America and therefore what further instructions to send Mackie. Indeed, in this letter Mackie had reported that Santa Anna was optimistic about reaching an agreement with Iturbide which would restore proper constitutionality and keep him on the throne, so Canning may have thought that he would in due course simply continue with his fact finding mission. When in June he received Mackie's second report from Havana about Iturbide's fall from power (in which there was no request for further instructions), Canning had 'taken it for granted' that he was on his way home.[41] It seems that he may never have been shown the third letter Mackie sent in June (not received until August), in which he merely reported that he was leaving Havana to return to Mexico. Even if he had seen it, it was by then too late to stop Mackie taking the initiative he did. And it was in ignorance of this that Canning now took the first open step on the road that led to Britain's formal recognition of Mexican independence.

4

THE HERVEY MISSION TO MEXICO, 1823–4

Canning began in July 1823 to draft instructions for the official mission of enquiry he had now decided to send openly to Mexico. By September he had chosen its principal members and its existence had become public knowledge, but it did not set out until October. As First Commissioner he chose Lionel Charles Hervey who, after service in Bavaria, had been posted to Madrid in 1820 and had been temporarily in charge of the legation there for a period in 1821–2. Sir William à Court, when he took over as minister plenipotentiary, thought highly of him. Sending him back to London with despatches, he told Castlereagh that

> [Hervey's] opinions and mine … agree on almost every point, and I can pledge myself for the accuracy of the statements he will have the honour of submitting to you. I must be allowed also to take this opportunity of expressing my opinion that the country is under great obligation to him for the prudence and temper with which he has conducted the business of this Mission during very difficult times.[1]

He was not in fact a good choice for the Mexican mission, his judgement in the volatile politics of that country proving unreliable. So it was as well that Canning chose as Second Commissioner young Henry George Ward. Born on 27 February 1797, he was then only 26 and on the face of it no more than a useful work-horse to help the more experienced and older First Commissioner. Up to that time he had been merely attached to the diplomatic service, with no official salary and no sure career prospects. After education at Harrow he had been sent abroad to learn languages and had then obtained a post as attaché in the British legation at Stockholm. From there he went, in the same capacity, to The Hague in 1818, and to Madrid in 1819. These posts would have been obtained through influence. His father, Robert Plumer Ward, was a friend of Pitt's and, through his first marriage, well known to the 1st Earl of Mulgrave who had given him an under-secretary post in the Foreign Office in 1805 and then a seat on the Board of Admiralty, which he held until 1823. He was MP for Haslemere from 1807 to 1823 and was intimate with Canning. Young Ward himself knew that it was this background that had persuaded Castlereagh (Lord Londonderry) to give him his opportunities for diplomatic service which he hoped might eventually lead to a full career in that profession, and on hearing of Castlereagh's suicide he had written a very gloomy letter to his friend Charles Richard Vaughan, a professional diplomat who had been in Madrid for a while with him:

> I am terribly low and cast down about my prospects. Be Lord L's successor who he may, he can know or care nothing about a man whose only claim is having sacrificed six or eight years of his life to a profession, the uncertainty of which ought to deter any one who has not a competence of his own from entering it .... I know not what to look forward to.[2]

However, his talents had not gone unnoticed, and while in Madrid he and Hervey had been friends. Hervey himself may have suggested him for the Mexican mission. Both the Duke of York and the Duke of Wellington were aware of his qualities, having been shown some of his private letters from Madrid which they had found full of good sense.[3] Possibly his father's intimacy with Canning was crucial in giving young Henry this first officially salaried appointment; but whatever may have been the chance influences at work, it turned out to be an inspired choice of the greatest importance to the development of British-Mexican relations. During the next three years it was Ward more than anyone on the British side who kept negotiations from breaking down.

The third member of the commission was Charles Tadeau O'Gorman. Born in 1786 into a distinguished Irish Roman Catholic family, he had come to Foreign Office notice when, as a businessman in Spain holding a consular appointment, he had been involved as an unofficial agent of the legation in the negotiations for the settlement of British claims.[4] In January 1823 Canning had expressed his regret that it was not possible to make O'Gorman a member of the Mixed

Commission that was to meet in London, even though he was someone 'to whom the British claimants and His Majesty's Government are so much indebted for his zeal and assiduity in bringing this matter to a conclusion'.[5] But Sir William à Court made sure that Canning did not forget him. He sent him to London as his personal courier with important despatches in March of that year, writing to Canning:

> … for as he has been so greatly instrumental in bringing this business, as well as the arrangement of our money claims, to a successful issue, he has in my opinion a full right to be brought in this favourable manner under the notice of His Majesty's Government .... I should be wanting in justice if I did not avail myself of this opportunity of recommending him most strongly to your consideration and patronage.[6]

Canning, who was a strong supporter of Catholic emancipation, decided that he would make an admirable consul-general in a strongly Roman Catholic country, and so it proved. It was perhaps just as well that he did not then know that O'Gorman had fathered an illegitimate daughter in Madrid, leaving her in the care of his former clerk, to whom he was making annual payments for her maintenance, for this could well have ruled him out.[7] Ward, who of course had known him in Madrid, was none too pleased at the choice, finding him at first an unpleasant colleague whose head had become 'so completely turned by his new elevation that he has become one of the most disagreeable animals that ever existed'.[8] However, Ward later had reason to be glad of O'Gorman's influence in consular, and indeed political, matters, doubtless due in part to his being a Roman Catholic and marrying the daughter of a distinguished Mexican family.[9]

Included in this party was the consul designate for Vera Cruz, Charles Mackenzie. He may have been the Charles Mackenzie who in 1811 applied from Edinburgh to the then Foreign Secretary for employment in South America, referring to himself as 'son of an old but unrequited servant of the Crown'[10] (who may have been in some modest public service position in the West Indies[11]). It was quite usual in those days for people to apply for consular posts, and to do so in the hope not only of receiving a salary, but of being able to use their position for personal gain. To be successful they would usually require some kind of sponsorship. Mackenzie was known to Wavell's friend, Sir William Adams (who may have got him the job), and might therefore indeed have been 'based a physician' in the Peninsular War as he was described by Adams to Wavell (although there is no other evidence to corroborate this). Sir William was delighted at Mackenzie's appointment, writing to Wavell at Falmouth that he had promised 'to do everything in his power to promote our interests' and was

> a capital open hearted fellow & with yourself excepted as fond of the fair sex as needs be. This qualification I told him would greatly enhance him in your estimation .... His appointment ... is quite providential to our cause .... He looks beyond his present employment hereafter & is therefore most anxious to obtain the earliest and best information to send home .... You have only therefore to concert with Mackenzie how he should act & everything will be as you wish.[12]

Later, however, Mackenzie got involved with Wavell and Adams in mining business, with most unfortunate results for Wavell. Whether he was really dishonest, as Wavell (and even Lady Adams) believed, cannot now be fairly judged: he had the smooth charm that often goes with the art of looking after number one. But certainly he gave Hervey and his successor a lot of trouble as consul, even though, apparently, he was effective as a gatherer of commercial intelligence.[13]

The party also included a (genuine) physician, Dr Mair and, as secretary to the commission, Mr G.A. Thompson on loan from the Audit Department. Ward thought poorly of 'little Mr Thompson', who told the captain of their ship 'that he conceived that the whole business of the Commission was likely eventually to turn upon himself' because 'you see how soon the choice of Commissioners was made: Mr Hervey and Mr Ward were appointed long ago. The salary was the only thing there. You soon found people ready to touch it.[14] But a Secretary, Sir, that was the difficulty; and Mr C remained undecided about it to the last.'[15] Thompson certainly displayed a somewhat Uriah Heepish character in a letter he addressed personally to Canning shortly after arriving in Mexico. He was 'impressed ... most sensibly with the debt of obligation which I owe to you for the unprecedented liberality with which you were pleased to confer upon me my present appointment' and 'under the kind and liberal direction of Mr Hervey, my situation fully answers the expectation I had formed of it, and is in all respects as comfortable (excepting as regards my separation from my wife and family) as I could wish. I am, however, supported by the conviction that it is my sole interest to endeavour to fulfil to the best of my humble abilities the duties of the office which you have been so kind as to confer upon me, and to employ all my leisure in acquiring that sort of exclusive information which this extraordinary country is so calculated to afford'.[16] (It casts an interesting light on Canning's character that he should have bothered to keep this letter.) Nevertheless, Thompson was later considered to have been a useful member of the mission, and when, in February 1825, he wanted to return to England for family reasons, he was sent home carrying despatches for the Foreign Office, with this commendation: 'Mr Thompson, having mixed much in Mexican society, and being intimate with many of its leading members, his information will perhaps be found of importance'.[17] Clearly he had turned out to be that most valuable of junior members of a diplomatic mission, one who could blend with the locals, be liked by them and gather useful information. And after he had left Mexico to return home, an instruction was received from the Foreign Office to send him to Guatemala 'with directions to collect detailed intelligence respecting the present state of that country', so it is evident that Ward's early judgement was faulty.[18]

It is no longer usual for British diplomats to travel to distant posts by sea. As recently as the 1960s, however, it was still possible to join a 12,000 ton steamship to take up a posting to South America and enjoy a sense of adventure which cannot be experienced in a journey by air. But even that sense of adventure was but a shadow of what it must have felt like when embarking in 1823 in a naval sailing ship of only 1000 or so tons, for a voyage likely to last six weeks or more to a country of which so little was known as Mexico, and on a mission of such political significance. Hervey, who had been told by Canning that his reward would be promotion in the service to the rank of minister plenipotentiary whatever the outcome, and appointment as head of the new legation in Mexico if full diplomatic relations were established, was in a confident mood, exuding an aura of self-satisfaction and self-importance. His subsequent despatches reveal an abundance of self-assurance and belief in his country's superiority. Ward was far from feeling nervous, even though this was his first step in what he hoped would be a long career as a professional diplomat; but he was conscious of his own ignorance about the country to which he was going, of his good fortune in being chosen and of how much his future would depend on his performance. Also he had just become engaged to a girl he might not see again for many months.

The delay between the selection by Canning of the team to send to Mexico and their departure on 19 October 1823 had given Ward the opportunity, in September, to get the willing consent of Sir John Swinburne Bt (of Capheaton, near Newcastle upon Tyne) to betrothal to his daughter, Emily.[19] Ward had known Emily for some years but had felt that he could not ask for her hand so long as he had no prospects in the diplomatic service, lest it appear he was solely after her money.[20] His appointment to this mission gave him the necessary prospect, even though he still had only a very modest income of his own. He wrote to Sir John on the eve of sailing that he could not leave England

> without having thanked you once more for all the delightful hopes with which you have enabled me to do so. When I think of what would have been my feelings had you *not* been the most generous of men, I seem never to have felt properly before how immense my debt of gratitude to you must be! I had so very little right even to hope that you would consent to give your daughter to a man who has nothing but his profession to look to in the world, and to allow his attachment to her to outweigh the numerous disadvantages of so unequal a match! .... I am not fond of boasting, or of professions, but I do most sincerely hope that my conduct and my success in the world will hereafter be such as never to leave you room to repent of all that you have done for me, in consenting to receive me into your family.[21]

Nor did it: he went on to a distinguished career and a knighthood. But in the circumstances then it was only natural that his joy at his engagement should be tempered with some apprehension. Fortunately he took an instant liking to Sir John Phillimore, the captain of the roomy 38/46-gun frigate HMS *Thetis*, whom he found to be

> an odd, amusing man, which will be a great resource to us on the voyage. Among other odd fancies, he has taken an antipathy to the old colours of black and white, and he has had the Thetis painted brown and yellow. She now, among the sailors, goes by the name of the 'Chocolate and Barley Sugar Frigate'; but she is a beautiful thing in the most perfect order.[22]

Phillimore's choice of colours may have had something to do with the economies practiced by the Navy Board in the supply of paint, which once caused him to ask whether he was supposed to use his ration on the starboard or the larboard side of his ship.[23] But his eccentric humour may also have assisted him in getting his ship's company to cooperate in his experiments on the standard victualling system in use at the time. He had become convinced that sailors' health (and discipline too) was being undermined by the then grog ration of half a pint of 'ardent spirits' mixed with one and a half pints of water, served half at noon and half between 4.0 and 5.0 p.m. He halved this, the other half being added to pay, and in addition provided extra rations of tea, coffee or cocoa sufficient to make a full pint of liquid every evening. This new ration was officially promulgated throughout the navy in July 1824 when, thanks to Sir John's experiments, healthier food rations were also introduced to produce a more balanced diet.[24] But not all the company were happy with the experiments. The day they set sail for Mexico with Hervey's mission 'some of the inferior Petty Officers came aft to request the full allowance of spirits – the three months of trial having expired'.[25] The outcome is not recorded; but Phillimore was quite prepared to allow his passengers generous rations of wine. Hervey had requested it for his six servants on the ground that he had found it impossible to procure them without a promise of 'this indulgence', and Phillimore allowed them a pint of port wine a day. Hervey had promised to pay for this personally if the Foreign Office would not, but in the end Phillimore could not be bothered to work out the extra cost to him, which had not been included in the amount agreed between the Foreign Office and the Admiralty to be paid to him for conveying the party, 'this being' as the Admiralty later explained to the Foreign Office 'the first instance of any diplomatic officer desiring that his servants should be supplied with port wine in addition to the ship's allowance'.[26] This was characteristic of Hervey.

All in all, therefore, this group set off in good heart and found the voyage, thanks to the captain, agreeable enough. Ward, it is true, wrote with a touch of melancholy as they approached Funchal, where they stopped a few days:

> … there is something very formidable, even to a man as much accustomed as I am to absence from all I love, in the preparations for a long sea voyage and, above all, in the thoughts of being

> probably some months without the possibility of receiving a letter.[27]

But at least he suffered little from seasickness and he took his mind off separation by spending long hours reading up background to Mexico. By the time they were nearing Vera Cruz he was able to tell his future father-in-law that he was

> quite pleased at seeing how much I have got through since I left England. I have really been fagging very hard, and doing my utmost to turn every hour to account .... I have never turned my mind at all to American affairs before, and felt most thoroughly ashamed of my ignorance on a subject with which I ought to have been well acquainted in order to be fit for my present situation. .... For the last six weeks I have devoted nearly ten hours a day to the works which I thought best calculated to give me an insight into it. I have now, I believe, gone through everything of consequence that has been published respecting America.

By then he already knew that Hervey had decided to send him back as soon as possible with a report, so he was now looking forward to seeing Emily again sooner than he had expected:

> I am delighted ... with this prospect; for though nothing shall induce me to quit Mexico one hour before I am perfectly master of the state of the country, and sure of being able to come off with flying colours from all the cross examinations which I may expect to undergo on my return, yet nothing affords me so much pleasure as the idea of being able to effect this in a shorter space of time than I had calculated upon; and this of course must depend very much upon the more or less settled state of the country. We shall find a Yankee Party, and a French Party already organised there; but I trust that our Commission will bear down upon them with such weight of metal as will force them to quit the field.

And he thought

> that this temporary separation, however severely it may be now felt, will enable me to spare my dear Em a thousand risks and inconveniences, and to arrange everything for her, in the most

> comfortable manner, when she joins the party to Mexico next summer.[28]

In the event, however, it was nearly a year before they were together in Mexico.

After an uneventful passage of 54 days, including the stop of four days at Funchal, *Thetis* arrived at the anchorage off Sacrificios on the morning of 12 December 1823. When they had left England they had not heard of the open hostilities between Ulloa and Vera Cruz which had broken out not long after Mackie concluded his negotiations with Victoria, although this had been reported by Captain Roberts of HMS *Tyne* (in a despatch which only reached the Foreign office on 22 December[29]). Roberts had arrived at Vera Cruz on 20 September and found the town severely damaged by bombardment from the castle batteries with communications between the two cut. The Royal Navy was not inclined to allow such quarrels to interfere with its freedom of movement and, after seizing the opportunity of a lull in the firing, Roberts had anchored close to the castle and then made clear to both parties that he expected to be allowed to stay there unmolested. He had been assured by both Victoria, who had moved to Vera Cruz from Jalapa to take personal charge of operations, and the governor of the castle, General Le Maur, that neither would be the first to open fire again upon the other. The latter, however, three days later had peremptorily ordered Roberts to move his ship to Sacrificios because he 'was going to fire immediately and that I must move the frigate out of the way of shot or take any accident to my charge'. Despite his reluctance to expose himself to approaching 'nortes', Roberts had moved, although not without making strong protest. In the event the Spaniards did not immediately open fire; but when Roberts went ashore at the town on the 25th shortly before noon, he 'found great consternation'. At nine that morning the governor of the castle had given warning that in three hours he would start a bombardment unless the Mexicans bowed to his demands to evacuate Sacrificios and open up the port of Vera Cruz.

The bombardment began on time. Roberts returned to his ship to send a stiff letter to the castle explaining the purpose of his visit and that boats would come to the castle to collect specie from British merchants there 'with a flag of peace and the British colours flying', while he personally would go in the same way to the town. He expected the Spanish batteries to 'respect the British flag'. The governor replied that it was 'not possible for me to comply with your request, whatever may be my desire to respect the flag of His Britannic Majesty'. Roberts then decided not to risk being drawn into having to respond to an act of aggression against the British navy. But the British in Vera Cruz had been unable to remove themselves and their goods from the town and were consequently suffering damage to both from the bombardments. They considered that, having been compelled to pay duties to the castle on goods taken to the town, they were entitled to the protection of the governor, not bombardment, and they appealed to Roberts for protection. Roberts made this point forcibly to the governor, who simply replied 'you forget that protection can only extend so far as force reaches', and consequently those who voluntarily carried their goods beyond the castle could not expect his protection. He assured Roberts that those with property in the castle could expect it, but not 'those who have only placed their trust in the dissident government, for whose irregularities and aggressions no less impudent than unjust Spain can never be held responsible'.

Roberts had then tried diplomacy, offering to Victoria that he should negotiate a truce to enable British merchants to remove their goods to a place of safety. Victoria, while protesting that he had done no more than repel aggression from the castle and had done everything possible to help merchants get to safety, replied that if Roberts thought

> it your duty to treat with the Commandant of Ulloa respecting the interests of British subjects, you may do so, with the understanding that I shall neither open the port for him, nor abstain from replying to his fire: and all that I can do, as a mark of consideration for the great nation which you represent, will be to suspend my firing whilst the guns of the Castle are silent, and this only for the fixed period necessary for the removal in question.

Roberts tried unsuccessfully to persuade the Spanish governor to accept Victoria's conditions and agree to a truce for a specified period. He was clearly, however, exercising his neutrality in favour of Victoria. He threatened the governor with 'strong measures' and 'an adequate force' to protect British merchants if his request for a truce was not met, which nearly produced renewed bombardment of the town. Victoria, however, was not exactly helpful. Not only did his batteries fire on Captain Roberts' own boat 'flying the flag of peace', thus committing 'an affront to the English flag and to myself personally as mediator', they also fired on a pilot's boat from the castle, drawing the remonstrance from Roberts that a pilot's 'person in all countries throughout Europe is held sacred'. But Victoria contended that he could not trust the castle pilot because he had been detected landing soldiers on an American merchant vessel to force the captain to unload his supplies at the castle instead of the town. This had finally persuaded Roberts to give up his mediation attempts and to inform Victoria that his, Victoria's,

> good intentions have failed through General Le Maur's obstinancy of mistaken policy. And most deeply accountable will he be held by the British Government for such unprecedented folly .... I am satisfied you have done all that is required and could be expected by the English residents here in the present state of things: and I shall most assuredly express in the strongest terms to the British Ministry Your Excellency's feelings for the British nation.

Roberts had then sailed away, on 13 October, despite strong pleas by the British merchants to stay and protect them, bearing an anxious message from Victoria for answers to the letter he had sent to Canning by Mackie.

Sir John Phillimore's only warning of what he might find on arrival was that received from an American schooner newly out of Vera Cruz with which they spoke as they approached on 8 December. They therefore knew that artillery duels between Vera Cruz and the castle had been continuing, off and on, for some time; but they knew nothing of the exploits of Captain Roberts and were considerably taken aback by what they found. Soon after anchoring, Ward was instructed by Hervey to open communications with the Mexican authorities. There was no firing at the time and he was rowed the 2 miles to the pier at Vera Cruz, unaware that this was not in use. Once ashore he had some difficulty in persuading a soldier to open the gate in the town wall to let him in. Even though he had had some experience of urban war damage in Spain, he was shaken by what he saw. In the book he published five years later he described 'a town entirely abandoned by its inhabitants. ... When to this unnatural solitude are added the marks of recent warfare, houses riddled with shot, churches half in ruins, and flights of vultures congregating around the carcase of some dead animal in the streets, it is difficult to imagine a more striking picture of desolation'.[30]

By chance Ward's arrival coincided with Victoria's name day, which was being celebrated by his officers and troops with full Mexican vivacity. When the purpose of this British visit was discovered, these celebrations became even more enthusiastic. Victoria naturally assumed that the arrival of the Commission was a direct result of his dealings with Mackie, and declared that 'next to the independence of his country, his first wish through life had been to see an intercourse established with England; and that wish was at length gratified'. There were many toasts in honour of England and her king. There was even an unintended salute from the castle as Ward and his party were eventually seen off back to the ship:

> The last mark of attention with which they [the Mexicans] favoured us I should willingly have dispensed with, for wishing to honour us with a salute, on pushing off, they forgot that their guns were shotted and directed against the Castle, which immediately opened its batteries in return, so that for some time we had the pleasure of finding ourselves between two fires. The balls and shells passed considerably above us, but we saw more than one strike the pier which we had just left, and many others bury themselves in the sands near a bastion at the southern extremity of the town.[31]

Hervey himself went ashore to meet Victoria on 14 December and that night the whole Commission were guests at dinner at Victoria's house. '[The General's house] presented a curious scene; for although there was not a woman in Vera Cruz, we had the music of all the regiments playing in the patio, while the soldiers danced … until a very late hour'. Because a 'norte' had blown up they were unable to return to their ship until after breakfast next day, so had to sleep in beds made available by Victoria. Victoria had wanted to detain them until he could notify the executive in the capital and await their instructions; but Ward had persuaded him that they must press on.[32] Nevertheless, it was a slow business getting ready to set off for Mexico City. Because of the unpredictability of the bombardments from the castle, all the baggage had to be landed onto the open beach near Point Mocambo. Ward had to make several trips to see Victoria to get things organized. But Victoria and the civil governor were both 'doing their utmost to forward the preparations', and in the end they were able to set off with 50 baggage mules and all the three carriages they had brought with them, each drawn by 'seven wretched animals'. However, despite getting ashore by 6 a.m. on 17 December, it was four in the afternoon before they could begin their journey. Ward had to organize everything:

> None of our English servants were of the slightest use as, with the exception of mine who had been four years with me in Spain, they spoke no Spanish; but had they been perfect masters of the language, it would have been of little avail, for neither remonstrances, nor persuasion, nor abuse produced the least effect upon the lawless set by which we were surrounded … whilst with us they certainly acknowledged no superior but the Corporal of the escort, whose sword, the flat part of which was applied without scruple to their backs, sometimes accomplished what it was impossible for any other mode of treatment to effect.[33]

This early contact between Ward and Victoria had profound effect on the future development of relations between the two countries, for they became personal friends. Victoria, ten years older than Ward, was immediately attracted to this good looking young Englishman who spoke such excellent Spanish and displayed such friendly good manners. Here at last, in the rough, uncultured conditions of Vera Cruz at the time, was a man with whom he could converse freely on many subjects, to whom he could speak of his dreams for Mexico and his determination to gain European recognition of her as an important independent nation. For Ward, who had spent several years in a Spain rent by political turmoil, among a people for whom he had felt little affection,[34] it was heady to be so warmly welcomed by a hero of revolt against that country, from whom he learned of all the hardships undergone to achieve success. 'I like Victoria very much' he wrote in his letter to Sir John Swinburne, 'he is a sensible man, & altho' exceedingly quiet in his manner, becomes animated the instant the independence of his country is mentioned .... There are some monstrous fine men amongst [his] troops.'

5

HERVEY RECOMMENDS RECOGNITION –JANUARY 1824

Hervey and his party took 14 days to cover the 300 or so miles to Mexico City. This was not bad going given the very primitive roads, the altitudes they had to cross, a stop of three days at Jalapa awaiting fresh mules and the need to accept hospitality on the way. At Jalapa they were met a league outside the town by a deputation from the governor and they entered

> amidst the acclamation of the whole population, the ringing of bells and every demonstration of joy .... A dinner was prepared for us, as well as a house and every other accommodation. Our wish was to avoid these public testimonies of consideration, but we found it impossible to do so without offence and were therefore persuaded to accept the apartments prepared for us; and indeed, travelling through this country is attended by so many difficulties that a refusal would have subjected ourselves to much inconvenience.

So wrote Hervey in one of his early despatches.[1] Word of their journey had indeed spread rapidly, and they were fêted even in the smaller towns and villages through which they passed. For instance, 'at Santa Anna, a village about two leagues from Ojo de Agua' says Ward in his book 'we were received with great politeness by the Cura, an old man who came out to meet us in his sacerdotal dress. Such an instance of courtesy towards heretics was too remarkable not to be most gratefully acknowledged and we remained some time receiving and returning and returning compliments, to the great edification of by-standers, who regarded us with intense curiosity'. But they sometimes had to rough it. 'Two nights we came to a regular bivouac in the open air, with our servants, escort and about eighty mules and muleteers quartered in a wide circle about us.'[2] And it would have been cold at that time of year at those altitudes. Ward commented in his book 'that if this were a fair specimen of the introduction to American diplomacy, there would be few candidates for the missions to the New States amongst His Majesty's older diplomatic servants in Europe'.

Hervey had already taken one diplomatic initiative. Before leaving Vera Cruz he had tried to ensure that the Spaniards in the castle would not misunderstand their presence, but would respect British neutrality between Spain and Mexico. O'Gorman had known the governor, Le Maur, in Spain and had been sent by Hervey to call on him. He had found the general 'determined, whatever his political sentiments as an individual might be, to defend the Castle for Old Spain, let her form of government be what it would, against any force which might attack it'. But he seemed realistic in believing that there could be no hope of Spanish reconquest of Mexico, and that Spain would eventually decide to make the best terms she could by commercial treaties. 'In the midst of all his prejudice' reported O'Gorman 'he considers the Mexicans capable of becoming a great nation under a monarchical system, but that they require to be directed as well as assisted and protected for a series of years to come by some powerful State'. The general 'appeared to labour under considerable agitation & solicitude as to the projects of Great Britain upon the former possessions of Spain in America'. O'Gorman believed he had succeeded 'in allaying his fears by assuring him that Great Britain was perfectly neutral and had no projects of territorial aggrandizement … they were strictly no more than agents for the protection of British trade'.[3] He does not seem to have done so, for not long after his call the British merchant ship *Sarah* was boarded by 12 Spanish soldiers and made to anchor close to a Spanish warship until permission had been granted by the castle governor for her to proceed to Sacrificios. General Le Maur refused his permission, even preventing her sending a boat over to a British warship for water unless she first put to sea after paying $12 for pilotage.[4]

HMS *Thetis*, observing this incident, intervened by sending an officer and men to sail *Sarah* over to an anchorage by her, although her master was at the time in the castle. The redoubtable Sir John

Phillimore then sent a stiff note to the commander of the Spanish squadron saying that 'such conduct appearing to me to be contrary to the law of nations, for you to stop a British merchant vessel and take her to an anchorage to which she was not bound, I have to call on you to inform me what are the circumstances that you consider to justify your interference with this British vessel'. Phillimore had also, however, been asked by Le Maur to mediate with Victoria. Phillimore, in the absence of an interpreter, found this difficult, succeeding only in understanding that Victoria would consider only proposals direct from Le Maur himself. To this, Le Maur indicated that as he had been the last to make a proposal through Captain Roberts (the details of whose activities were not then known to Phillimore), he could not be the first to make another, but that as soon as Victoria ceased his regular morning and evening bombardment of the castle he would be prepared to regard hostilities as having ceased. Phillimore went so far as to make an unavailing appeal to Victoria in writing to accept his mediation 'for the sake of humanity'.

When Hervey heard about this, he rather surprisingly sent a mild reprimand to Phillimore. He had been sufficiently concerned about the attitude of Le Maur to have written to Phillimore from Jalapa on his way to Mexico City to ask him not to leave British merchants unprotected by sailing away from Sacrificios, and even asking that HMS *Carnation*, recently arrived, should stay there as well for this purpose. But when it came to the crunch he was all for caution. He wrote to Phillimore:

> We must take the liberty of suggesting to you the policy of not pressing the Spanish authorities at the Castle too hard in the present instance, as it might lead to the proclamation of a blockade on the part of the Governor and Admiral, which would be attended with the most serious inconvenience .... We must confine observations upon this subject to reminding you of the peculiar situation in which Great Britain is placed between the two contending parties; and we must, at the same time, take the liberty of pointing out the necessity of the greatest caution on the part of an officer of such high standing as yourself in H.M.'s Service, lest his eagerness to promote the interests of humanity should be construed into a violation of that neutrality which Great Britain has announced her intention to maintain, particularly if his efforts to restore a good understanding

> between the two Parties should extend to anything beyond verbal communications.[5]

This must have seemed pusillanimous to Phillimore. But Hervey was under strict instructions not to show favour to either Spain or Mexico in this mission of enquiry, and one can understand his anxiety to avoid any complication from a clash between British naval forces and the Spaniards in the castle. This, however, did not prevent his coming down firmly on Mexico's side in his formal report to Canning sent within three weeks of his arrival at the capital.

The mission reached Mexico City on the evening of 31 December 1823, eight days after leaving Jalapa. At the request of Alamán they had avoided Puebla, where the bishop, a dyed-in-the-wool Iturbidist, was giving trouble, and taken the more northerly and higher route through Huamantla. They found that the Mexican authorities had made preparations to receive them almost as though Hervey were the King of England himself. At the gates they were met by Alamán for a ceremonial entry in a stage coach which had belonged to Iturbide. They were then conducted to an imposing house on which well over £1000 had been spent in redecoration and repairs.[6] It had been 'fitted up with plate, linen, china, crockery, beds & everything that we could possibly want, by a subscription amongst all the principal families of the capital'.[7] Here they were to be lodged while they assessed the situation and could decide in their own time on more permanent arrangements.[8]

Clearly the Mexicans were out to impress this mission and put them in a position where refusal to recognize their independence and dignity would be churlish indeed; and it is equally clear that Hervey's opinion of them was coloured by the style and generosity of his reception – even though aspects of it must have tried his powers of endurance. They were guests of honour on 4 January at a banquet (which cost over £600) involving three hours of eating, drinking and speech-making, and included the recitation of some 'impromptu verses' by their author who described himself as 'a proscribed Frenchman, at heart and in soul a Mexican'. It was an address, in French, to the Mexican people and to the English envoys:

> Pursue your great work, good people of Mexico,
> Be free, independent; the English extend their hand to you

it began, continuing later:

> And you, dear Envoys from a generous people,
> Associate your radiantly glorious names
> With the names of the founders of this new-born Empire

ending resoundingly with:

> One does not always live in prosperity!
> Oh Englishmen! If ever the wind of adversity
> Should blow over you, count on America!
> You will always have brothers in Mexico[9]

which was a remarkable forecast, almost in the class of Nostradamus, of Mexico's action in coming into the Second World War on Britain's side when they did. But the banquet was not the end. Everyone then repaired to the theatre for a gala performance of *The Caliph of Baghdad*, translated into Spanish from the original French, during the intervals of which various verses were sung in praise of Great Britain. The theatre was packed to capacity with all society in glittering finery, and the performance lasted from 8.0 to 11.0 p.m. If Hervey and his colleagues were bemused and exhausted by all this, they may have drawn comfort from one local newspaper which felt that it might have been counterproductive. It published an ironical criticism of the whole performance, explaining that it did so in order to try to convince the authorities of the need to improve the standards in Mexico's theatres and so as to offer excuses to the visitors in the hope that they might pardon a country which only a bare three years earlier had been raised to the rank of nation.[10]

Impressive as this style of reception was, and clear as it made the feelings and hopes of those in control of the country, not all voices were as enthusiastically favourable to this British initiative. An article in the newspaper *El Sol* was noticeably pro-American and suspicious of British motives,[11] while the *Águila Mexicana* suspected that Britain was concerned only with her own commercial interests, not Mexico's welfare.[12] However, Hervey did not allow such criticism to affect his determination to send Canning a glowing report of what he believed to be the true feelings in the country. On arrival he had delivered a formal message from Canning to 'The Secretary of the Government of Mexico' telling him that King George IV had 'determined to take measures which may eventually lead to the establishment of friendly relations with the Government of Mexico'.[13] The reply referred to establishing 'an intercourse likely to lead to such relations of amity as may be highly beneficial to both countries'. He and Ward had a series of meetings and discussions with people they regarded as representative and influential, by whom they were given all kinds of assurances. But whatever they had said, it would have made little difference to the opinions Hervey had already formed. Before he had even arrived in the capital he had come to the conclusion that there were no grounds for delaying full recognition. He was a prolific writer of despatches and letters at this early stage (none of which, however, reached the Foreign Office before mid-March 1824). In an early personal letter to Canning from Vera Cruz he had reported that Victoria 'expects much from the instructions he sent to M. Migoni whom they have appointed their Chargé d'affaires in London & hopes that the immediate recognition of their independence on our part will be the result of his Mission'. Hervey urged upon Canning recognition with 'as little delay as possible ... principally because it will give us decided advantage over all other competition'.[14]

Ward was of like mind. In the letter to Sir John Swinburne which he completed at Jalapa he referred to the way

> men of all parties and classes ... [were] ... eager to answer all our questions, & to give us every information in their power. All seem to feel the importance of the step which Gt Britain has taken in their favor, and all hail it as the epoch from which they must date their independence .... A month will I fancy be the outside of my stay in Mexico, for there is such readiness to communicate intelligence on the part of all those in power, that we shall be as well able to form an opinion in the course of that time as in a year.

He had been impressed by Victoria's determination to remain independent from Spain and his conviction that this was certain. He wrote that Victoria had

> burst out on my merely hinting at the possibility of the French assisting the Spaniards in any future expedition against Mexico, and said that they wd never obtain a permanent footing in the country, as they wd sooner burn the Capital & all the great towns

> than allow any one of them to fall again into the hands of foreigners. This sentiment is, I understand, a very common one, amongst *all classes*, and as the threat came in the present instance from a man who passed fifteen months in a cave after his guerrilla party was dispersed, sooner than accept the 'indulto', or pardon, proclaimed by the Viceroy, one can have little doubt as to the probability of its being carried into execution.[15]

Canning, however, was expecting them to take time to formulate a properly argued recommendation which would carefully assess differing shades of opinion on important constitutional matters. When despatching the mission in October 1823 he had had no clear and reliable information, and to persuade his cabinet colleagues and his king to adopt any particular policy towards Mexico he needed unequivocal answers to a number of questions. As a staunch constitutional monarchist himself, he still hoped that the Mexicans might choose to go that way rather than down the road of republicanism. He even thought it possible that, with the experience of Iturbide's attempt at military despotism masquerading as a monarchy behind them, they might be disposed to want some form of union with Spain after all. If that was in mind, he had told Hervey.

> there is no desire on the part of Great Britain to interpose obstacles in the restoration of a *bona fide* understanding between the Colonies and the Mother Country. But it must be with that Mother Country really independent; not in any shape subjected or subservient to France, nor employing the intervention of French arms to re-establish its supremacy in the Colonies. So far from interposing obstacles to a beneficial arrangement between Mexico and Old Spain, on the principle of reconciliation and mutual advantage, you are authorized to transmit to your Government any proposal to that effect which the ruling party in Mexico may be desirous of having communicated to Spain[16]

Canning even thought it possible that 'the views of the Mexicans [might] be turned with pretty general concurrence to the restoration of a monarchy, in the person of one of the Princes of the Spanish race, but on the basis of Mexican Independence'. If this were so, and it were clear that they wanted Hervey's 'co-operation to bring about such a settlement, you will not hesitate to avow yourself ready to accede, with the certainty of obtaining the cordial approbation of your Government'.[17] But, he told Hervey, 'while you are to accept such a proposal, if submitted to you, you are not to attempt to prescribe to the Mexican authorities this, or any particular course of action'. This was just as well. Had they been presented with a positive proposal from England on these lines, it might have awoken all kinds of suspicions. Indeed, some of the Mexican press in early 1824 even believed that Britain wanted a member of her own royal family on the throne of Mexico.

Canning was willing, however, to recognize a republican Mexico, provided only that he could be satisfied on four points. First, had there been a public statement of a determination to remain independent of Spain, and to admit no terms of accommodation with the Mother Country? Second, was the government in full military possession of the country and able to defend it against any probable attack from Europe? Third, 'does it appear to have acquired a reasonable degree of consistency, and to enjoy the confidence and goodwill of the several orders of the people'? Fourth, 'has it abjured and abolished the Slave Trade'? If Hervey was able to answer 'yes' to all these questions and was confident that the future looked stable, he was authorized to suggest that the Mexicans send a confidential agent to London to enter into dialogue with His Majesty's Government 'to determine whether the time is ripe for the establishment of an ostensible political relation with Mexico, by the interchange of diplomatic Missions'.[18] He was to make clear that he would be the British diplomatic representative in Mexico, but he was not to assume that character until he had heard from Canning after the arrival of a Mexican agent in London. But, 'provided only that your reception [in Mexico] be amicable and that you shall not find the Government indisposed to friendly and commercial relations with this country' the consul general and consuls were to open their commissions immediately so that they could enter upon their duties. And he was to ensure that the Mexicans understood clearly that 'so far is Great Britain from looking to any more intimate connection with any of the late Spanish Provinces than that of political and commercial intercourse, that His Majesty would not be induced by any consideration to enter into any engagement which might be considered as bringing them under *his* dominion. Neither, on the other hand, would His Majesty consent to see them (in the event of their final separation from Spain) brought under the dominion of any other Power.'

Canning, of course, when he had drawn up these instructions between July and October 1823, had not known that the Mexicans had already taken the initiative (following Mackie's unauthorized negotiations) in appointing a diplomatic agent in London. When Hervey learned of this, he felt justified, in the light of his very warm reception, in getting proper consular relations established at once. But he still had to answer the four specific questions put by Canning. He had some difficulty over slavery. There was no specific Mexican law prohibiting it, but a belief on the part of the Mexicans that they were automatically bound by the treaty of 1817 between Great Britain and Spain which outlawed it.[19] However, it seemed to Hervey and Ward that there was no attempt to prevent the continued use by Spaniards in Mexico of 'servants' who had originally come as slaves and had not formally been given their freedom, or even the further import of such 'servants' by those already owning them. They at first succeeded in persuading Alamán of the need for a solemn act by congress outlawing slavery in any form; but Alamán back-tracked, arguing that as slavery was not permitted under the constitution, any British anxieties could be dealt with by an appropriate article in any bilateral treaty, a draft of which was offered. They made clear that this was wholly unacceptable, and indulged in a measure of bluff-calling. Hervey said that Ward would have to return to England with 'this unsatisfactory' answer, which would 'delay the establishment of more intimate relations'. It was explained to Alamán

> that it was not the wish of the British Commissioners, or of the British Government, to persuade or entice the Government of Mexico into the adoption of any measure which might be deemed prejudicial to their interests: that it was for the Mexican Government to decide whether it would be advantageous for them to postpone the probable public recognition of their independence by Great Britain, and the appointment of a British Minister, by persevering in their determination not to abolish the Slave Trade by a public & voluntary Act of Congress.[20]

This had the desired effect, and an appropriate law was passed on 15 January. It provided that 'The Commerce and Traffic [of slaves] is for ever prohibited in the territory of the Mexican States' and that any slave that might be introduced in defiance of this would 'become free from the mere act of touching the Mexican territory'.[21]

Although it appeared to Hervey from the start that the answers to the first three of Canning's questions must be 'yes', and now he could say the same to the fourth, he was cautious about putting his head on the block with a formal recommendation, in what would be a state paper, after so short a time. In the formal instruction from Canning it had been made clear that he was in charge and solely responsible for decisions: '… while you are to avail yourself, in any points requiring deliberation, of the advice and assistance of the gentlemen who accompany you, *your* opinion is that which is to prevail on any point on which there may happen to arise a difference of opinion between you'. But he had arranged to keep *Thetis* at Sacrificios for only a few weeks and he could not know when there would be another ship available to carry despatches to England. (In fact it had been arranged with the Admiralty that one would be sent from Jamaica in March for this purpose, but neither Hervey nor Phillimore seemed aware of this.) It was obviously tempting to use her to take his first report back, and indeed to send Ward with it so that he could supplement the written word and add persuasion to his urging for early recognition.

So he took the plunge and signed a formal report on 18 January,[22] beginning it, however, by 'expressing the anxiety which we feel in giving our opinion upon questions which may have so important an influence upon the fate of this infant nation, and which may so materially affect the interests and commerce of Great Britain, or, if erroneous, compromise the dignity of His Majesty's Government'. And he was less than fully confident in giving his opinion on whether the government had 'acquired a reasonable degree of consistency' and enjoyed 'the confidence and goodwill of the several orders of the people'. He referred to the consequences of 13 years of civil war, both material and financial, reporting that 'under this state of affairs, the country is overrun by robbers, the army is partially paid and clothed, the Government is ill-obeyed, and all confidence destroyed'. He thought that 'the partisans of Iturbide … the friends of Ferdinand, and those who are favourable to a monarchical form of government under a Bourbon Prince, either French or Spanish' might 'prevent the consolidation of the existing form of government'. But he believed that the British loan being negotiated would give the government 'as favourable a chance of success as any other which could be devised under existing circumstances'. However, he emphasized that 'many of the beneficed clergy, of the nobility, and also of the army are favourable to a monarchical form of government'.

This equivocation was evident also in an accompanying personal letter to Canning in which Hervey wrote that the members of the Mexican government were

> not by any means firm in their posts, & the country is far from settled. Indeed, altho' I have not stated it in my report, I very much doubt of their capability of governing themselves .... The clergy have great weight here ... their interests must I wd think lead them to wish for a monarchic form of govt, & I fear that recent events in Spain may again form a Party for Ferdinand in this country'[23]

The fact that a British banking house was prepared to lend a large sum of money to this new regime was of course evidence that hard-headed businessmen had confidence in its stability. Nevertheless, it is difficult to understand how Hervey could have believed that such a report from him would persuade Canning, let alone the cabinet, that conditions for immediate recognition were right. Yet he urged on Canning a formal alliance, having apparently been persuaded that without this the Mexicans, needing the backing of a maritime power to protect them against reconquest and provide security for their overseas trade, would be 'forced to throw themselves into the arms of the United States, already opened wide to receive them'. He emphasized that the Mexicans were

> willing to form an exclusive alliance with Great Britain, and to grant her the most extensive commercial privileges. Our arrival has produced already beneficial effects, but it has also excited strong expectations; and if His Majesty's Government be not prepared to go further than a simple recognition of Mexican independence, we fear that that protection will be sought elsewhere, which Great Britain shall decline to afford, and that the glory and advantage of supporting and fostering to maturity this infant Province of a great and flourishing Empire, may be wrested from us to stimulate the industry and adorn the annals of some more enterprising nation.

Hervey was quite wrong in this, as events proved. Despite the subsequent delay of a year before open recognition of Mexican independence was forthcoming from Britain, and of an even longer one before this was formalized in a treaty, Victoria held out against American attempts to become Mexico's 'protector'. Hervey showed himself to be a poor judge of political realities, and one cannot but wonder whether he was not influenced by the expectation of soon having his own diplomatic mission there. His hopes, as he sent Ward off to England with his formal report on 19 January,[24] must have been high, and must have sustained him through the next few months of waiting for Canning's response. When this came, however, he was disillusioned, and his career in fact ended in ruins.

6

HERVEY FACES PROBLEMS – JANUARY TO SEPTEMBER 1824

'Men used to say the world was divided into men, women and Herveys – for that they were unlike every other human being.' So said Lady Hester Stanhope when referring to the Countess of Liverpool.[1] So far as is known, Lionel Hervey was not a close connection of the Herveys to whom Lady Hester was referring, but he was certainly a man of some idiosyncracies and independent views. His humour tended to be ponderous, and he was inclined to take himself somewhat seriously, even pompously. The style of his despatches often went well beyond even the rather heavy verbiage which was customary in those days. A good example is in one he wrote very soon after arriving at Vera Cruz, which included this:

> It is not extraordinary that some confusion and difference of opinion should exist in a country just emerging from the thraldom of the Government of Old Spain, under which she had groaned for more than three centuries. Nor is it astonishing that the vices & corruption of such a Government should, like the deadly shade of the Upas Tree, which blasts and empoisons every thing around it, have blighted this fair country, and have inoculated her inhabitants with its deadly venom.[2]

It speaks well of Ward that he was able to work happily with someone with such a way of expressing himself. When he had first met Hervey at Madrid in 1821, he had described him as 'not by any means a difficult man to live with', and they apparently lived harmoniously in the bachelor quarters there, unaffected by a considerable difference in their ages. But he was tolerant by nature and had added: 'I never met with any man yet whom I found it impossible to get on with.'[3] It is doubtful, however, if harmony would have lasted a spell of a year or more together in Mexico. Their ways of doing things were very different. Not that Hervey was without merit. He had his faults, and it was his belief in his own infallibility which led to his downfall not many months later. But he did in fact succeed in laying foundations on which others were able to build, and in circumstances which were by no means easy either politically or practically. Left as it were in limbo while the future of British-Mexican relations was decided at leisure in London, his very self-confidence as he set about establishing a British presence before this new nation was what enabled him to overcome obstacles.

Although the Mexicans treated Hervey as though he were the full diplomatic representative of a great power, he had no such status as of right. He was merely a commissioner making enquiries, under instructions to avoid any actions that might seem partisan as between Mexico and Spain, or as between political factions within the country. The Mexicans were expecting great things from his mission, and soon; and there were many only too ready to use any delay in seeing results as proof that Britain should not be trusted. Hervey was separated from his masters by 6000 miles of ocean, across which an exchange of despatches took at least four months at best, usually a good deal more. He was dependent upon the navy for these communications, and he did not always find them fully cooperative in his efforts to speed them up. Establishing an effective network of consular posts in a country with an unhealthy coast, atrocious roads and widespread banditry, and among people who were not accustomed to consular practices, was no easy matter. He himself, of course, strictly speaking, had no authority to act as a protector of British subjects and interests: this was a matter for the consul general, O'Gorman. But he had to present an image (to use modern terminology) of imperial dignity and power, and keep Mexicans regarding Britain with respect.

One of Hervey's first steps in image building was to rent an imposing palace as his residence. He chose what is now the Museo de San Carlos housing an impressive collection of paintings from the late fourteenth century right up to the early twentieth century. Situated in the district of San Cosme on the edge of the city as it then was, a little less than a mile west of the house in which the mission had been put up on their arrival, it had been built at the beginning of the century as a palace for the Count of Buenavista, who never lived in it. Among the occupants before Hervey took it had been the Iturbide family. It is a huge building, entered through a vast oval courtyard flanked by imposing pillars reaching up two floors. It had an extensive garden (now mostly built over, but partly a small public square) and a flat roof, or azotea, with what in those days was a splendid view over the city towards the dormant volcanoes of Popacateptl and Iztaccihuatl. He had a quantity of furniture locally made specially for it.[4] It was a grandiloquent way to 'fly the British flag', and it was a couple of years before the Foreign Office awoke fully to what it was costing and demanded a move to something more modest. But it certainly played an important part in winning Mexican respect.

Perhaps only a Hervey would have made such a gesture in choosing such a residence before he knew what Canning's next step would be. But he was a man not afraid of grand gestures, even in politics. Only a few days after Ward had left for Vera Cruz to return to England, he made one during an attempted coup against the legitimate authorities. On 23 January 1824 General Lobato, commander of the troops assigned to guard Congress, and some like-minded officers, with some 2500 troops prepared to support them in their demands, mounted a threat to public order. There is some dispute now as to exactly what Lobato's intention was and who were secretly in agreement with him. At the time, Hervey believed that his main, possibly only, interest was in cleansing the country of all Spaniards who had been kept on in the public service – like those in former Rhodesia who objected to Mugabe keeping on whites after the country became independent Zimbabwe. At first, however, the government appeared to be doing nothing and Hervey tried to convince Alamán of the need for firm action. Alamán said he himself could do nothing and invited Hervey to write to him to demonstrate the harm that could be done to relations with Britain if the situation continued. Despite having instructions not to interfere in Mexican internal affairs, Hervey decided to do so, in a private and confidential letter in which he stressed that he did not wish to meddle in their internal affairs but nevertheless expressed the fear that if strong measures were not taken 'all the Europeans who have something to lose will be obliged to leave a country where there is no military discipline and consequently neither law nor government'. Alamán's reply was uncharacteristic in its tone of near panic – he was 'desolated' to have to tell him that the government did not have the means to deal with the situation and he invited Hervey to 'pity this miserable nation which is going to be the plaything of the most infamous factions'. Was he perhaps deliberately trying to play on Hervey's feelings in order to get him and therefore Britain irrevocably embroiled? Hervey believed that his letter was shown to leading members of Congress and he claimed, when reporting these events to Canning,[5] that it was because of this that Alamán had been able to tell him next day that Congress had decided to stand firm against Lobato's demands, although they might have to withdraw to Guadalajara where they knew they would have popular support. It seems unlikely that Hervey's letter was really the direct cause of this, but Alamán had succeeded in embroiling him, and he then replied:

> I am convinced that it never pays to yield to the orders of soldiers who have forgotten their duty and attempt by force of arms to impose measures which they judge suitable. Be assured that my desires are limited to the establishment of tranquility and prosperity for Mexico. Should Congress feel obliged to leave Mexico City I shall not hesitate to accompany them.

In fact the whole affair fizzled out. Lobato's supporters accepted an amnesty offered on the 25th, and Lobato himself was arrested two days later, the subsequent sentence of death on him being commuted to life banishment. But Hervey was now hooked. One of the results of the Lobato incident was an appeal by the Mexicans to the British merchants in the city for financial help to enable them to create a more reliable army. The merchants were prepared to offer a loan of two or three hundred thousand pounds provided they could be sure of its repayment. Among them was the firm Staples y Cía, and Robert Staples, who had been appointed one of the consuls in Mexico by Canning, asked Hervey if he would recommend HMG 'to countenance' such a loan, which was to be sanctioned by an act of Congress, 'and even guarantee the eventual repayment'. Hervey grandiloquently promised 'on the part of the British Government' not only that such a loan would be approved of, but also that 'any political influence which Great Britain may acquire in this country shall be executed for requiring the eventual liquidation of the same'. Blandly assuming that Canning would view his actions in the same light as he did himself, Hervey explained to him that

> the danger of the dissolution of the Government was so great owing to the want of money, which is not to be obtained without some kind of approbation by the Commission, that I did not

> think myself justified in keeping altogether aloof. I do not entertain the slightest apprehension that the British Government will be called upon for its intervention, but should any difficulty arise, I hope you will not think that I have exceeded my instruction or committed His Majesty's Government. The timely aid thus afforded to the Congress has enabled them to stifle discontent, and has had a salutary effect both upon the tranquility of the country and upon the establishment of British influence.[6]

It may be questionable whether Hervey's intervention in the Lobato affair was as significant as he believed, but there can be little doubt that in virtually guaranteeing this loan he must have considerably enhanced his standing with the Mexicans. That it caused his subsequent dismissal by Canning was his misfortune (see next chapter); but for the present it gave him some helpful credit when Mexican sensibilities were otherwise ruffled. And he needed this in March when the navy acted with uncharacteristic discourtesy towards the man being sent to London as the Mexican government representative. With the arrival of the Hervey mission and the invitation from Canning to send a confidential agent to Britain to discuss the possibility of establishing full diplomatic relations, the Mexicans decided that it would be inappropriate simply to rest on the presence there of Migoni, with the political brief given him after Mackie's discussions. They realized that a gesture of more substance was now required, indeed that they needed someone of clear political standing to represent them in London. The first choice was Pablo de la Llave, who declined the honour, later becoming Minister of Justice. They then chose José Mariano Michelena. He had been one of the early supporters of Iturbide, but Hervey believed him now to be 'a decided enemy to the Bourbon interest and to Iturbide'. He did think that someone different would have been preferable, 'particularly as we believe that M Michelena has a great fondness for intrigue' (a belief which was borne out later); but he considered him to be 'not destitute of abilities' and reported that he was being 'entrusted with almost unlimited powers'.[7] Michelena was to be regarded as Chargé d'affaires and was to have as first secretary Vicente Rocafuerte, described by Hervey as 'Colombian by birth and possessed of considerable talent' and well known in both London and Paris. As Second Secretary they appointed

Tomás Murphy. Both these spoke French and English, but Michelena was 'almost entirely ignorant of these languages'.[8]

Because Ward had left for England earlier than the Foreign Office had anticipated, and had been able to return in the same ship that had brought them out, there was now available HMS *Valorous*, under command of Captain Murray, which had been sent from Jamaica at Foreign Office request to convey Ward home. Hervey therefore arranged that Michelena and his party should be given passage to England in her. This suited Murray very well, for he was able to get the Mexican government to pay him the equivalent of £2000 for the service. But even after extracting this exorbitant price, Murray had no intention of letting it interfere with his own plans. He had come up to the capital (without an invitation) and was determined to remain there as long as it suited him, despite the clear desire of Michelena to set sail by 25 March. The trouble was that Murray, in accordance with the naval custom of the day, was busy trying to collect orders from British merchants to convey goods and specie to England, for which he would be paid, and by 22 March he had still not left for the coast, although Michelena and his party had already done so. Hervey had tried a mixture of threat and flattery in a formal letter to Murray, in which he said he was convinced that his 'zeal for the public service will induce you to land Mr Michelena in England as soon as the uncertainty of the elements will permit, and I shall therefore have no hesitation in announcing to His Majesty's Government through other channels the departure of the Mission for England'; to which Murray, not to be outmanoeuvered, replied that he would 'make no further delay than is consistent with the orders I have received … which orders I have no doubt will admit of my landing His Excellency before you can possibly announce to His Majesty's Government his departure from this country'. Hervey then tried a different tactic, inviting him to dinner with leading Mexicans, from whom Murray apparently extracted an assurance that he would be adequately escorted to the coast. According to his own later statement, they had assured him 'that they would render me every thing requisite, and that I might carry the escort as far as Vera Cruz if not properly relieved at Puebla'. With this he finally condescended to set off.

Disaster, however, lay in wait for Murray and his companions (among whom was John Hall). On the 29th he wrote to Hervey from Perote (some thirty or so miles short of Jalapa) to report that the governor of Puebla had refused to allow the escort to accompany him further, even though they had 'volunteered to proceed with me'. Instead, the governor 'sent me an escort consisting of an officer and thirteen men so badly mounted & armed that it was impossible for them to afford us any protection'. As a consequence, he and his companions had been attacked and robbed the previous day, two civilians with him (one an American) actually being murdered. He reported that the escort was 'not even in sight, and did not appear till four hours after our arrival at Perote'. He blamed Hervey, indirectly, by claiming that the Mexicans had urged him to postpone his departure from the capital for a few days, for his better safety, but that he had been 'hurried off in order to do what I considered my duty'. Hervey received this on 3 April and immediately replied in great concern, and with an assurance that everything would be done to find the culprits. But he did not take Murray's strictures lying down:

> Having assured you of the support & protection of the Government and of HM's Commission, I shall not advert to many acts of impudence on your part which, I think, led to the catastrophe so much to be deplored; but I must remark that the Government, so far from wishing you to delay your journey, were extremely anxious that you should leave Mexico with as little delay as possible … [and I cannot] … avoid stating in the most official manner … that, so convinced am I of the detriment which must ensue to the interests of HM's Government from the arrival of individuals in Mexico [City] who are bent upon the advancement of their own private interests, without any regard to the opinion of HM's Ministers or public servants, acting upon official instructions, that I shall certainly do every thing in my power to prevent the Captains of HM ships of war who may arrive upon the coast from penetrating any distance into the interior.

In reporting this whole affair to the Foreign Office, Hervey expressed himself with bitterness, referring to Murray as having 'availed himself of every expedient, even to the detriment of His Majesty's Service and the personal inculpation of myself, to obtain additional freight', and protesting at 'the evils of the system of freightage when not controlled by the moderation and good sense of the officer who is thrown in the way of the temptation'.[9] But Murray still had a shot in his locker. When he eventually caught up with

Michelena at Vera Cruz, he announced that he would be sailing to England via Tampico and Havana. Not only would this delay the arrival in England, it meant that a diplomatic representative of Mexico would be exposed to embarrassment, if not worse, from the Spaniards still in possession of Cuba. At this, Michelena protested, through the Foreign Ministry, to Hervey, who did his best by writing to Murray to say he was sure that he would 'see the impropriety of putting into a Spanish port with a Minister from the Mexican Government on board' and inviting him to 'comply with M Michelena's wishes and proceed straight to England'. At least Murray was persuaded to pay the proper official courtesies to Michelena and his party when they came aboard *Valorous*, and Michelena, despite the annoyance he must have been feeling, chose to write a formal letter to Alamán (subsequently published in the local press) saying that he

> must attribute to the influence and good will of Mr Hervey the reception given me by the Captain in showing the greatest consideration to the Mexican flag and paying me all the honours which British regulations lay down for Ministers Plenipotentiary accredited to His Britannic Majesty. This is the kind of public recognition which presages a happy outcome for our just hopes. Thanks to the private and public recommendations which Mr Hervey has given to the Captain of the frigate, who for his part has executed them with the greatest willingness, I believe it my duty to write to Your Excellency to bring this to the notice of the Supreme Executive so that if it is judged appropriate it may show its approval and gratitude for such benevolent arrangements.[10]

Thus did Hervey reap the political reward for having shown his earlier support for the government. But Michelena must have wondered whether he had done right when Murray, after being delayed still longer by a 'norte' so that they did not finally sail until 21 April, still insisted on going first to Tampico, where he stayed a week so that he could take on more cargo to his personal profit, and then to Havana. In the event, however, the call at Cuba passed off without incident, and Michelena was actually able to make use of his three days there to contact people sympathetic to Mexico, and to correct false rumours about conditions in his own country.[11] But Murray paid for his obstinacy. When Canning heard of it he insisted upon paying back to the Mexicans the £2000 'so indecorously received' by Murray, and he called upon the Admiralty to get him to refund the difference between this and the £895 he was entitled to for performing this service. The Admiralty told Canning that this would not cause Murray hardship because 'he made a considerable profit on the freight of money which he brought home & the prospect of which profit seems to have had no small effect on his proceedings'.[12]

These experiences with Captain Murray were a bad start to Michelena's mission to London and must have contributed to the rather bitter tone of his reports from there. But before his somewhat jaundiced views could have any influence on attitudes in Mexico towards Britain, Canning had taken action to ensure that the former colonies understood his policies. On 9 April he circulated[13] to the British missions in Buenos Aires, Chile, Peru, Colombia and Mexico reports of the proceedings in Parliament in March when these had been explained.[14] This reached Hervey on 18 May just after he had received an earlier letter from Planta[15] sending him a copy of the Polignac Memorandum.[16] Hervey was instructed not to communicate the memorandum 'in any official form', but to use the substance 'to show how early and how anxiously Great Britain had declared against any project of bringing back the late Spanish colonies under the dominion of the mother country by foreign aid'.[17] Whether it was action by Hervey, or simply the result of receiving information from a correspondent in England, the newspaper *El Sol*, in its issues of 20 to 24 May, carried full reports, taken from the *Morning Herald* of 16 March, of the proceedings in the Lords and of the Polignac Memorandum.

With the revelation of Canning's understanding with Polignac, and the explanation of British policies made available to them in May, the Mexicans were feeling more sure of receiving the support they were looking for from Britain. They therefore responded without rancour, and as reasonably as they felt able, to the rather difficult instructions which reached Hervey at the end of June 'to claim for His Majesty's subjects from the Government of Mexico not only all civil privileges, but all immunities relating to religious worship.'[18] Given the long background of fierce Catholicism in Mexico under Spanish rule, and the consequent suspicious, not to say hostile, attitude of many to Protestant 'heretics', this was obviously not something that would be readily granted, even though Hervey could point to Canning's known support of Catholic emancipation in England and the appointment of a Roman Catholic consul-general. In carrying out his instructions, however, Hervey showed delicacy, not only in his choice of language, but also in putting the request in a consular rather than purely political context, by making it jointly with O'Gorman. Their note to Alamán dealt first with civil privileges, requesting freedom of property and persons 'against any act of the Government which may arise out of its political relations with other countries, or out of political dissensions which may unfortunately occur amongst the Mexicans themselves'; exemption from military service; and exemption from 'any peculiar taxes or contributions not borne generally by the community'. Only then did the note turn to requesting an assurance that the practice of the Protestant religion by British subjects in Mexico would not lead to trouble:

> There are likewise religious immunities no less necessary for the satisfactory domiciliation of subjects of one friendly State in the territory of another than indispensable to the comfort and well being of the members of Christian communities, such as the toleration of their religious opinions, the unmolested exercise of their religious worship and the decent celebration of the rites of sepulture according to their own persuasion … [British subjects] will be enjoined to avoid any offensive or ostentatious display of their religious worship and ceremonies, and to conduct themselves in all things not only in a peaceable and orderly manner, but with due deference and submission to the Government under whose protection they live, with strict obedience to law and with the most scrupulous respect to customs, usages and institutions, civil and religious, of the Mexican people.[19]

Alamán obviously appreciated the delicacy of Hervey's position and the tact with which he was approaching this matter; and, even though Britain had as yet done nothing concrete which might entitle her subjects in Mexico to special consideration, he recognized that his response would to some extent be taken as a test of Mexican sincerity and readiness to behave in a manner deserving of political recognition. He therefore gave his formal assurance that the laws of Mexico provided all the rights and protection that British subjects expected, but explained that there was a problem in the matter of religious freedom:

> By the 4th Article of the Constitutional Act, which is the fundamental law of the Republic, the exercise of any other religion but that of the Catholic, Apostolic and Roman is prohibited, and … consequently it is not in the power of the Government to accede to your wishes in this respect; being, moreover, under the disagreeable conviction that, looking on the actual state of the nation in as far as regards its religious opinions, they could not adopt the proposed measure without notorious scandal and great danger.

This indicated that those in high places were personally inclined to be pragmatic towards Protestant 'heretics' but that they dare not be so publicly because of the continuing influence of the Catholic clergy and the inbuilt feelings of the ordinary people. But Alamán was able to give one concession. He said that instructions were being sent to all state governors to set aside burial places for Protestants, whether British or not, in consultation with consuls, who would then 'have power of doing whatever they may deem proper for the decent sepulture of the persons in question … it being understood that, with respect to the rites of such sepulture, none other shall be practiced in public than the mere inhumation of the bodies'. (In the instructions to the state governors they were required to secure 'that decency of interment which the remains of mortality properly deserve'.) And Alamán added for good measure that

> the Government feels itself fully satisfied with the excellent comportment of the British residing here; and that it does not doubt that they will pursue the same conduct so long as they remain within the Republic; and the Government, in return for such good and laudable conduct, pledges to them its special protection and the guarantee of its laws.[20]

It is unlikely that there were many of those in temporal authority in Mexico at the time who felt strongly enough about religion to wish to object to such a reasonable concession; but there can be no doubting the high feelings that were liable to inspire the ordinary people, and Hervey very sensibly suggested to Canning that 'it will not be prudent at present to push the question of free exercise of our religion'.[21] The wisdom of this was shown when an unpleasant demonstration of bigotry occurred at the end of August. An American subject, a shoemaker, was sitting in his shop in the capital when a funeral procession passed by. A Mexican asked him to kneel before the Host, which he did, but on a chair. The Mexican insisted that he should kneel on the ground, and when he refused to do so he was immediately killed. Fortunately the officer of the nearby guard managed to prevent this developing into a serious riot, but it greatly disturbed the authorities. Alamán, anxious to demonstrate to Hervey that his words had not been empty, hastened to report it to him before he could react, and to assure him that firm action was being taken against those responsible. 'A crime of such magnitude' he said in his note 'cannot be suffered to pass with impunity or be regarded with indifference by a nation which has so just a sense of the respect, consideration and deserts due to other nations that are in friendship with her, and with whom it is ever her desire to fulfill all the duties which justice may dictate.' Nevertheless, he thought it necessary to sound a warning and

> to intimate to you that, in order to avoid for the future so disagreeable an occurrence from any similar altercations ... it would be very desirable that you should recommend to those individuals of your nation who may find themselves in the Republic that, whatsoever may be their religious opinions, they should conform with those of the country in the practical observances of the religion we profess.

There was worse to follow, however. Those who attended the funeral of the unfortunate shoemaker were 'insulted and stoned by 5 or 600 of the lowest populace and there were evident symptoms of an intention to raise a cry of heresy'. Hervey and O'Gorman became convinced that no real effort was being made to discover the murderer, and they organized a subscription among 'the different strangers in Mexico' to offer a reward for his identification. And they were certainly not prepared to let Alamán's lecture about religious observance go unchallenged. 'This crime, if it should remain unpunished,' they replied 'will strike at the root of all the intercourse between Mexico and the inhabitants of those countries which do not profess the Roman Catholic religion .... There is no doubt that individuals of all persuasions must conform to the rites, ceremonies and observances of the Roman Catholic religion if they should voluntarily assist at the public exercise of that faith; but no individual can be compelled to participate in the adoration of a particular symbol when he involuntarily meets and wishes to avoid it.'[22]

Perhaps this robust line had some effect. The matter of religious toleration continued to be a stumbling block in the establishment of full relations between the two countries for some time to come, but the Mexican authorities did try to remove irritants so far as possible. O'Gorman was able to report on 1 November (a most suitable date for such a report) that all consuls had by then negotiated successfully for burial plots with local authorities, although authorization was still needed from London to meet the costs of rent, and of enclosing and maintaining them. Hervey had suggested meeting this by voluntary subscriptions from 'British subjects and other foreigners', but O'Gorman thought this would be unsuccessful 'excepting perhaps in [the capital] which has repeatedly promised to make over to me, *gratis*, a piece of ground for a cemetery'[23] – which they eventually did.[24] And later, during the treaty negotiations in 1825, there was a fine demonstration of the kind of broad minded attitude that could be taken. During one of the debates in the Senate on the subject, Senator Juan de Dios Cañedo 'perfectly agreed with his worthy colleagues in principle' when they objected to the solemn burial of 'heretics'; but he saw practical difficulties in persisting with this objection:

> The melancholy influx of foreigners could not be denied, nor was it to be expected that amongst so many some should not be summoned, during their residence in the Republic, to receive in another world the penalty of their unbelief in this. What, then, was to be done with the bodies? He saw but four modes of disposing of them; namely, to bury, burn, eat or export them. To the first, his reverend colleagues seemed to object: the second might prove inconvenient from the scarcity of fuel: in the third he, for one, must decline any participation: and as to the fourth, dead heretics not being included amongst the exportable commodities mentioned in the tariff, he feared that such an innovation might seriously embarrass the custom house officers on the coast. He should, therefore, upon the whole, incline for burial, as amongst the four serious evils it appeared to him to be the least.[25]

At the same time as Canning was seeking religious toleration in Mexico he was also increasing his pressure on Spain to recognize her independence, and it was therefore helpful to Hervey now to receive further news of this to pass on to Alamán. Canning had already warned the Spanish government that, although the British government had no desire to recognize the independence of the American colonies before Spain herself did so, unless Spain gave some sign of moving in this direction Britain would have to act independently; but he had promised to give notice of such a step. He had sent a copy of Hervey's formal report (brought home by Ward) to Madrid, not for communication to the Spaniards, but with instructions to à Court to make one last effort to persuade them to make some concession to Mexico. They were to be warned that once the official agent of the Mexican government reached London, while it did not

> follow of necessity that we must acknowledge the independence of his Government by the immediate reception of this gentleman in the public diplomatic character with which he is invested, it does follow that the question of that acknowledgment must be brought to a point during his stay here, and that decision can be postponed only so long as there is a hope of bringing Spain to consider fairly and reasonably of the expediency of leading the way in such acknowledgment .... A refusal on the part of Spain to … propose any distinct terms of accommodation with Mexico must be considered as discharging us from the obligation of any further references to Madrid.[26]

In sending Hervey a copy of this instruction, Canning explained that his original intention had been to await a Spanish reply to this *démarche* and then send Ward back to Mexico with instructions on the action to be taken in the light of it. Ward, however, had urged upon him the danger of keeping the Mexicans in suspense, and so he gave Hervey discretion to let them know of the instructions to à Court. If he chose to do so, he was to explain that His Majesty's Government were 'entirely and sincerely convinced that we shall render the greatest service that it is in our power to render to the Mexican Government if we can succeed in persuading the Cabinet of Madrid to treat with them on the basis of an acknowledgment of Mexican independence'. Compared with that, formal recognition by Britain would be 'of trifling benefit'. Hervey was also to invite the Mexicans 'to soften [Spanish] animosity and encourage concession on the part of the mother country' by emulating Buenos Aires which had been prepared, not long since, to offer Spain 'a large pecuniary subsidy as the price of an acknowledgement of their independence'. At that time Spain had been at war and therefore in financial straits (partly from the lack of the income she had previously been able to count on from her colonies); but, Canning emphasized, 'the fiscal wants of Spain are not less urgent at the present moment … and the credit of the Spanish Treasury is even worse than it was at that period. Might not the offer of pecuniary assistance from Mexico tempt the poverty as well as soothe the pride of Spain?' He also wanted Mexico to offer special trading concessions (for a limited time) if this would induce Spain to extend recognition.[27] And in a separate private and personal letter he wrote:

> If you can bring the Mexicans to originate a reasonable proposition, the game will be greatly in their favour. You must not lead them to rely upon us for assistance of that sort which we have so loudly proclaimed our determination not to allow the powers to furnish to Spain. We cannot give it and Mexico, if they play their game properly, will not want it.[28]

To suggest that the Mexicans might actually buy Spanish recognition shows that Canning had understood neither Spanish pride nor the feelings of Victoria, by now back in the capital as a member of the Supreme Executive and beginning the electoral campaign which led to his election as president in September. Neither he nor Alamán saw good reason why Mexico should, as it were, go on bended knee to beg Spain's recognition – and Hervey's immediate reaction was that there could be no question of Mexico's offering financial assistance to Spain, although the offer of commercial privileges was perhaps a possibility.[29] This opinion was later confirmed by Michelena, who told Planta[30] that he had received instructions, following Hervey's explanation of Canning's hopes, to say that Mexico welcomed the continued British attempts at mediation, that the Spaniards could certainly be told that Mexico was prepared to respond to recognition by granting special trading privileges, but that an offer of financial help was out of the question.[31] By then, however, Canning had lost patience with Spain and these exchanges with Mexico had become largely irrelevant, thus once again illustrating the great difficulties in trying to conduct diplomatic dialogue at that time over such distances.

Victoria himself had not been very happy at the proposal that Canning should be authorized to let the Spaniards know that the Mexicans were prepared to offer commercial privileges in exchange for recognition; he could not understand why Britain should hold back her recognition in order to give Spain a chance of getting in first. But he had been persuaded by Hervey that Spanish recognition would be of inestimable value to Mexico and had reluctantly agreed that the offer should be made on their behalf by Britain.[32] His suspicions of British motives were deepened, however, when Hervey spoke to him about Mackie's activities. Canning had feared that Mackie might have been indiscreet and that his actions might have come to the notice of the Spaniards. He had therefore instructed à Court to explain the nature of Mackie's mission and that his actions had been disavowed, and the nature of Hervey's mission.[33] And Hervey was given discretion to do the same in Mexico, being careful, however, not to prejudice Victoria's own position in case he had negotiated with Mackie without authority.[34] Hervey chose to speak directly to Victoria about it and reported[35] that he was 'much mortified'. Interestingly, Victoria told Hervey that Mackie had been wrong to report that he (Victoria) was at the time offering Spain a trading monopoly in Mexico: he had offered only some privileges if they would recognize Mexican independence and give up Ulloa. But he claimed that he had indeed broken off negotiations with the Spanish commissioners because of Mackie's protest. (That, of course, is not borne out by the contemporary Mexican documents already referred to in chapter 2.) Hervey took the opportunity when reporting all this to Canning to say: 'I wish that something would be done to manifest on the part of His Majesty's Government their sense of the devotion of General Victoria to the British nation, for he is a staunch friend to us and may eventually prove of the greatest utility to our interests.' Prophetic words!

On the whole, during the months they were waiting for news of the decision in London whether to recognize Mexican independence, Hervey and O'Gorman managed to avoid serious difficulties in their relations with the Mexican authorities. Their problems came more from the Spaniards in Ulloa, from slow communications with England and in trying to establish an effective consular network. For instance, there was another attempt in July 1824 by the commander of the castle to interfere with British trade by forbidding ships from anchoring at Sacrificios, which he claimed as Spanish territory, and insisting that they discharge passengers and goods at the castle, paying 8 per cent duty on goods. Hervey invited the admiral at Jamaica to make it clear that the navy would not allow such interference, and advised the captains of merchant ships to respond with force if force was used against them, or seek assistance from any naval ship in the vicinity.[36] This time he had no trouble with the navy: on the contrary, Admiral Sir Lawrence Halstead responded by sending a firm note direct to Ulloa:

> The roadstead of Sacrificios is out of gunshot of the Castle, consequently you cannot give that protection which is to be expected to vessels that pay port and harbour dues; whilst on the other hand the place where the British vessels anchor that trade with the Mexicans is certainly part of the same roadstead but close to their batteries which, if necessary, can protect them .... Your observation ... relative to the extent of your jurisdiction being established by the distance a gunboat or launch could go from and return to the Castle in a given time, is to me so extraordinary that I must beg of Your Excellency not to enter into the merit of such a rule.'[37]

The Spaniards, in face of this, quietly dropped their demands, and no doubt the Mexicans derived much quiet pleasure from the incident, and felt that the British were proving themselves already to be friends worth having. But the navy continued to prove less than obliging in the matter of communications with England. There was of course nothing anyone could do to overcome the intrinsic slowness of sail in covering the 6000 miles of ocean; but the lack of a regular direct service of mails between the two countries was an added inconvenience. There was a monthly packet between England and Jamaica (which managed on the whole to be remarkably regular), but only *ad hoc* arrangements between Jamaica and Vera Cruz. The Foreign Office did ask the Admiralty to provide a naval vessel every two months from Jamaica to enable Hervey to send confidential despatches direct to England, but Halstead, on receiving instructions to meet this request, begged Hervey not to take advantage of them without pressing need because he did not want to be thus deprived of ships from his squadron.[38] And Hervey suspected him of not even arranging to send a ship over to Vera Cruz immediately the packet from England arrived in order to forward to him despatches received in it from the Foreign Office. He complained at the end of March, for instance, that local merchants had by then received letters and newspapers from England with dates as late as 12 January, whereas he had had nothing from the Foreign Office later than 5 December.[39] It was a considerable time, and long after Hervey had left Mexico, before things improved, and this extremely slow, and indeed unreliable, method of communication was a cause of many misunderstandings over the next couple of years: there were many occasions when instructions from London based on reports from Mexico crossed with further reports which made them less than appropriate when received.

As regards consular arrangements, Canning was very insistent that consular officers were not to

> levy any fees whatever upon the trade or shipping frequenting the ports of your consulate. The only fees which you are to be permitted to levy are those which are purely and strictly notarial: and these you will place on the most moderate footing. Your consular duties will be performed by you for the benefit of His Majesty's commercial subjects, without any other gratuity than the sum which His Majesty has been pleased to grant you by way of salary.

A consular officer was also required to abstain rigorously from participating in any commercial dealings, and to

> be most careful to avoid mixing in any way in political discussions & giving offence to any one. He will recollect always that his character is purely a commercial one & his object expressly of a conciliatory nature. He will give his best advice when called upon, and his assistance, to His Majesty's trading subjects, quieting their differences, promoting peace, harmony and good will among themselves, and conciliating as much as possible the subjects and citizens of the two countries on all points of difference which may fall under his cognizance .... He will at the same time be careful to conduct himself with mildness and moderation in his transactions with the public authorities.[40]

This was part of the extensive reforms of the Foreign Service which Canning introduced and was a deliberate attempt by him to clean up the old system under which consuls expected to make the most of their living by indulging in private business deals and charging whatever fees for their services they could get away with. But, although they were now guaranteed a reasonable salary and some allowance for expenses, together these did not necessarily meet expectations, particularly in a new territory where there was no previous experience of costs to use as a yardstick.

In Mexico there was particular trouble in this respect with Mackenzie, who was supposed to be consul at Vera Cruz. He showed the greatest reluctance to live in the generally unhealthy climate there or even to leave Mexico City (where he no doubt found it easier to engage in the private business he was determined to develop, despite the strict rules against this). He was eventually persuaded to move to Jalapa, but even before he left the capital he was writing to London to ask for more money because the restrictions placed on charging fees meant that he could not pay even a 'common clerk'; while he contended that the smallest establishment in Vera Cruz cost at least £800 a year *excluding* rent, servants and 'every kind of personal expenditure'. He said that unless his revenue were increased he

> must every year become deeply involved in debt and all its concomitant horrors .... I lay no stress on the separation from every thing like civilization or intellectual intercourse ... as I consider every public servant bound to make some sacrifice. But I cannot refrain from observing that the only inducement to a man of integrity and character to remain in a situation such as I have described are the possession of means adequate to his indispensable expenditure during a limited term of service, and the certainty that he will not be left destitute at the expiration of that term when in all probability the ruined state of his health (if he survive) will render him incapable of further exertion.[41]

Not surprisingly this called forth a sharp rebuke from Planta:

> Mr Canning presumes that you were apprized of all these circumstances (as all the world was) when application was made by you, and on your behalf, for a Consulship in Spanish America .... [He] cannot listen now to any representations founded upon circumstances essential to the destination which you have sought, and inseparable from it. Should they prove more inconvenient in effect than they appeared in contemplation, you are of course at liberty to resign your appointment .... Mr Canning is beset with applications for consular situations in Spanish America.[42]

At this, Mackenzie, now in Jalapa, felt he had to grovel:

> The almost unbounded admiration I entertain of the talents of Mr Canning; the respect with which I look up to him as my official superior and protector; the consequent deference I feel for his opinions; my perfect confidence in his justice; and the gratitude which has naturally been produced in my mind by his having named me to the office I now fill, would under any circumstances make me keenly alive to any censure which he might think it right to apply to me.

Nevertheless, he persisted in his plea for more money, explaining that he had to pay £239.13.9d a year for the rent of three unfurnished rooms, and £56 a month for housekeeping even though living 'with niggardly economy having only two servants', which did not include 'wine, beer, clerk's salary, servants' wages, clothing and all incidental expenses'. To travel to the capital cost more than £50 a time (one coach and horse). He contended that it would cost even more to live in Vera Cruz and explained that his original intention had been to refuse the offer of the consular post there 'notwithstanding many circumstances [which] rendered employment necessary', but that a friend [possibly Sir William Adams?] had urged him to accept. He was still in need of employment, but the debts he was incurring 'by no means lightened' the circumstances making this necessary. It was therefore obvious that resignation 'before I know whether or not [the post] will afford me the means of living with decency and respectability would be an act of insanity'.[43]

Hervey knew nothing of Mackenzie's complaints to the Foreign Office until he received a letter from Planta in July. Having by then managed to get Mackenzie to establish himself in Jalapa, from where he could at least have reasonable contact with Vera Cruz itself, he probably wanted to be spared any further bother over this tiresome consul, and he replied to Planta by supporting his pleas:

> I can assert from experience that the prices at Vera Cruz are extravagantly high, and although accidental causes may have rendered them so, yet I believe the city was always famous for its dearness owing to the great influx of wealth and the unbounded luxury of its inhabitants. I have no hesitation in saying that I

> consider the salary of Mr Mackenzie at present as insufficient to enable him to live with comfort and respectability.[44]

Mackenzie was not, however, going to let this set-back ruin him. He managed to persuade all concerned that he needed to return to England for 'surgical assistance', and he sailed in HMS *Pyramus* on 23 March 1825, reaching London in early June. And because he was asked to carry official despatches he was able to get the cost of his passage met from public funds.[45]

Wavell had cultivated Mackenzie, who agreed to act as his attorney while in England; and somehow he managed to convince the Foreign Office that he should not return to Mexico. He then busied himself with the Adams/Wavell mining affairs, and in the process he succeeded in putting everyone against everyone. Whether he acted dishonestly to line his own pocket must rest not proven. Lady Adams (by now Rawson; see note 27, Chapter 3) was immediately suspicious of his intentions and said as much in writing to Wavell, referring to him as 'not a man of truth'.[46] He seems to have been responsible for sowing discord between Adams (Rawson) and Wavell, for Lady Adams (Rawson) wrote to Wavell in September complaining that he (Wavell) had not been honest with her and Sir William,[47] and Sir William actually informed Mackenzie that he was withdrawing the power he had given Wavell to act for him in Mexico. Meanwhile, Wavell was concerned that he was not receiving from Mackenzie money he thought due to him and believed he was being cheated. He got his father involved on his behalf, and by July the latter was writing to his son that he had been thrown by his friend Sir William 'into a den with as unprincipled a set of rascals as the earth is cursed with – Sir William is guided solely by his own interest .... This man has disgusted me more than I can express .... He is, I am persuaded, a sordid, selfish, cunning fellow ... and *Madame*, as he calls her, is as adroit in her machinations as Sir W himself.' Wavell's father had also met Dr Mackie, whom he thought 'a kind of parasite'.[48] But Mackenzie evidently had a way with him, for Wavell's father in January 1826 still considered him 'a very pleasant gentlemanly man' and actually invited him, as his son's supposed friend, to be a sponsor at the baptism of his latest grandson.[49]

Not long after this, however, Sir William and Wavell senior joined forces again to try to stop Mackenzie disappearing to Haiti, where the Foreign Office had appointed him consul. Their approach to Planta (supported by Lords Ebrington and Fortescue) induced the latter to request an explanation from Mackenzie of his activities.[50] He was satisfied with the answer and Mackenzie, to the fury of his self-claimed creditors, departed. This fury was fuelled by the very intemperate language used by Mackenzie in writing to them. To Sir William he had written to give him 'fair warning that if you indulge in liberties with me, I shall teach you, unless you be as deficient in manliness as you are in gentlemanly feelings, that there is less security in unblushing falsehood than you imagine'.[51] And to Wavell's father he wrote, after Planta's enquiry, that 'altho' your grey hairs may save you from personal chastisement, they shall not from the punishment which the laws will inflict on every infamous calumniator [*sic*]'.[52] There is no evidence that Mackenzie ever followed up any of these threats, but he was obviously a touchy and even arrogant man. Wavell's father told his son that Mackenzie's 'conduct when we saw him was so fair, so conciliating, his promises so strong and apparently sincere that the devil himself when tempting Eve could not have been more alluring or seductive .... I confess I was at first much pleased with him. I however regret my folly and gullibility, yet I never met a man who would lie with so good a grace.' And he pleaded with his son 'when in future you select a friend, be my dear boy a little more cautious'.[53]

Such evidence as there now is suggests that both the Wavells were somewhat gullible and that Sir William did not play entirely straight with them.[54] But speculators, however honest, risk getting their fingers burned. Mackenzie may have been plausible and unreliable – one of the financial houses involved had 'added a very particular caution as to money transactions [with him] .... I believe he always intends what is honourable but … he is most recklessly extravagant and would probably always outrun his income however large, and is besides very speculative';[55] but there is no proof that he actually profited at the expense of either Wavell or Sir William, although, through incompetence and rashness, he may have caused them losses.[56]

None of this, however, except for Mackenzie's reluctance to go where he was told and his complaints about his conditions of service, affected Hervey or made more difficult his task of establishing adequate consular representation in an entirely new country, and in conditions of which no one in London had any experience. Hervey's was not an easy assignment. Not only had he to set up the infrastructure in a new country for what was expected before long to be a full diplomatic mission, he had to maintain Mexican confidence in the good intentions of a government from which he continued for many months to receive no firm news. He tackled it with confident energy, showing no sign of anxiety. His possibly overweaning confidence in his own wisdom and judgment was his shield against all adversities and, whatever may have been his faults, it cannot be said that he shirked the challenge: indeed, so far as establishing a good basic understanding with the Mexicans went, he appears to have done a good job; and so confident was he of soon representing Britain as a fully accredited minister plenipotentiary, that in September he began to tour the provinces to make himself known more widely and gather material for further reports.[57] But it was while doing this that, out of the blue, he received a blow which put an end to his diplomatic career.

7

HERVEY IS RECALLED – OCTOBER 1824

Ward had reached London on 20 March 1824 with Hervey's formal report on conditions in Mexico, and all his other despatches and letters up to 18 January, bringing also gifts for Canning of seed, wine and oil from Alamán. Canning was delighted at his news. 'Here is Ward arrived from Mexico' he wrote to his wife in the country, 'they would give us anything we asked; but we asked nothing but the abolition of the Slave Trade, & they immediately proposed a law abolishing it, requesting our mission to be present at the discussion. They were present & the law was passed. The country is magnificent, but the state of it wretched beyond any thing that could be imagined', and he added that Ward had described Alamán as 'certainly the most efficient individual in the Govt and a clever man in any country'.[1]

This was Canning's first chance, since his interview with Mackie 18 months earlier, to hear at first-hand about a country of which he knew very little. He was sufficiently impressed by Ward's enthusiasm to wish to move quickly to recognition; but he still wanted Spain to do so first. His immediate thought was that he should show Hervey's despatch to the Spaniards as proof that Britain would not be justified in holding back its recognition any longer. Wellington, however, who did not share Canning's enthusiasm for supporting what he saw as dangerous republicanism, advised caution. He suggested to Canning that it would be foolish to rest Britain's case on a despatch written after so short a time in the country and 'in such a tone and temper as to do but little credit to the Government'.[2] He even recommended that Ward should be sent straight back to Mexico with instructions to deepen the enquiries and thus perhaps enable them to have a fuller and more accurate picture before any Mexican envoy could arrive.[3] The outcome of this was the decision, explained in the preceding chapter, simply to get à Court to make a *démarche* in Madrid in the light of what

Hervey had reported and to instruct Hervey to let the Mexicans know what was happening. But, on further reflection, and after questioning Ward even more closely, Canning decided that he must remonstrate with Hervey over the speed with which he had reported. He told Hervey that he was compelled to

> greatly regret that [your report] was framed so soon after your arrival, and before you had allowed yourself time to form a mature judgment upon many circumstances of the utmost importance. A fortnight's or three weeks' experience could hardly supply even the most active and intelligent observers sufficient opportunity for estimating justly the state of things so new and so extraordinary.

He specifically criticized Hervey's failure to mention the attempted coup by Lobato, of which he had heard, but of which even Ward could give only incomplete (and inaccurate) information. Canning felt that Hervey had not properly addressed the question of whether the Mexican government really 'possessed a character of stability and the confidence of the several classes of people'. He was concerned about 'the opinions and authority of the superior clergy' and thought that Hervey could only correctly estimate this 'by some degree of personal intercourse with individuals of that description'. And he criticized what seemed to him to have been a failure in this respect:

> By Mr Ward's account it appears that you have rather avoided than sought opportunities of such intercourse, as if you conceived that your seeking it might give umbrage to the ruling party. This may be the fact; but if it be so, it is a material fact, and one which should have been distinctly stated in reference to this head of enquiry. The higher clergy cannot be other than a powerful body in Mexico, a country in which, however ardent the principles of civil freedom may be, those of religious bigotry are not supposed to be extinct among the mass of the people. Spain relies mainly on the influence of this body. Is her reliance vain? and is it vain because the clergy are not as friendly to her interests as she believes? or because, however friendly in disposition, they have not the means of befriending her in practice? Whatever be the answers to these questions, the questions themselves are too important to have been overlooked.

It is interesting that Wellington expressed his misgivings to Canning about the refusal of Hervey to have 'communication with the persons comprising the hierarchy' in Mexico,[4] and it seems that Ward may not only have told Canning about Alamán's request that they avoid Puebla on their way to the capital from Vera Cruz, but may have shown that he himself felt that Hervey had been too ready to avoid giving offence to the party in power in choosing his contacts from whom to gather local feelings and opinions. Canning told Hervey that in comparing what he had written with Ward's verbal reports, he found the former's

> inferences various and contradictory. Mr Ward speaks highly of the influence of the parochial clergy, and but lightly of that of the superior orders of that profession .... You state that Spain has no partisans. Yet in your general report you mention the 'friends of Ferdinand', and foremost amongst them you rank (as might be expected) the dignified clergy.[5]

Canning's critical comments are understandable. Hervey's reports did not add up to the clear picture that a foreign secretary is entitled to expect; and, given his own difficulties in persuading his cabinet colleagues and the king to look favourably on Spanish-American independence, Canning would have been particularly anxious to receive something which might convince them that he was moving in the right direction. But was he entirely fair? Did Ward make matters worse with his own comments, taken by Canning to indicate that he had doubts about the value to be placed on Hervey's views? Was Ward being disloyal to Hervey and trying to advance his own career by shifting his own ground on sensing Canning's reactions? There is nothing in what is known or can be deduced about his character to justify such a supposition; and what he actually said may not have been as damning as Canning's despatch suggests. Moreover, he had left from Vera Cruz with no authentic knowledge of the outcome of the Lobato revolt: Hervey's report on this did not reach London until 6 June.

Hervey, equally understandably, was hurt by these rebukes, which he did not receive until 29 June. 'We are at a loss' he then wrote 'to account for the insinuations of Mr Ward that we rather shunned than courted an intercourse with the superior clergy.' He explained that, in referring to 'many beneficed clergy, of the nobility and of the army' as being in favour of a monarchical form of government, he had meant that they favoured not Ferdinand but Iturbide 'or any Prince of a European royal family who might secure the independence of Mexico'. And he firmly stated that six months later his opinions had not changed. He explained that he had not sent his report on Lobato with Ward because while that revolt was in progress he could not send a courier to Vera Cruz, and he had assumed, incorrectly as it turned out, that Ward must have sailed before anything could reach him once it was again possible to despatch a messenger (see note 25 to chapter 5). But he did offer an apology of a sort, in his usual heavy style:

> Our anxiety for the public service makes us feel most sensibly the embarrassment which we have occasioned to His Majesty's Government by the untimely arrival of Mr Ward with our report … and our unbounded admiration of the wisdom and talents displayed by His Majesty's Ministers in their administration makes us feel more acutely the censure conveyed to us upon omissions & contradictions in that report .... But, although always disposed to kiss the rod of correction when displayed in such hands, we must nevertheless consider ourselves as in some measure the victims of a change in the political aspect of the four great Powers, which has indeed made a corresponding alteration in the views and intentions of His Majesty's Government.

And he excused himself further by saying he had understood that he had been required to report as soon as possible.[6]

This explanation from Hervey did not reach Canning until September. By then, although the pompous, not to say impertinent language used might have in itself justified a sharp response, Canning had already found another reason for administering a rebuke – indeed one of the utmost severity. In June he had received Hervey's reports on the Lobato revolt and of his actions in guaranteeing the special loan requested by the Mexicans after that, as well as a despatch about the swearing of the Constitutional Act on 5 February. In the latter Hervey had reported that there was

> no enthusiasm for the constitution. The cry against the Old Spaniards is still very strong, and I have no doubt that eventually they will be excluded from all situations of trust and responsibility .... I will not again insist upon the expectation which our arrival in this country has excited, and upon the

> necessity of not abandoning the Republic at present to its own resources, lest I should be considered as offering obtrusive advice to His Majesty's Government; but I am sure that the observations which we had the honour to make upon this subject in our report and their bearing upon the present state of Mexico will not escape the penetrating scrutiny of His Majesty's Ministers, and that, if our judgment be deemed incorrect, our motives will not be condemned or misconstrued.[7]

No doubt Canning would have been irritated in any case to receive yet another piece of advice based on equivocal grounds; but it was the news of Hervey's action over the loan that was the last straw. Before he received Hervey's letter there had been a report of his actions which he had not believed could be true. On 2 July two London papers, *The Courier* and *The Morning Chronicle*, had carried the text of part of his letter to Staples although the former had said that it could not believe that it was genuine. This evidently embarrassed Canning, particularly as *The Morning Chronicle* was running a campaign for immediate recognition of the former Spanish colonies and implied that Hervey must have been acting with authority. So when he got Hervey's own report of what he had done he was furious. On 20 July he fired off a broadside:

> On what possible construction – I will not say of your instructions, for in them there is not a word that is susceptible of being interpreted as giving the remotest sanction to any such proceeding – but of the general duties and discretion confided to you as chief of the Commission, you can have thought yourself authorised to take such a step, I am utterly at a loss to imagine.
>
> I am astonished that it should not have occurred to you that, whether as between Spain and Mexico, or as between contending parties in Mexico itself, nothing could be more directly adverse to the neutral position which it was the study of your Government to occupy, than the thus committing its faith, whether directly or eventually, in a transaction for the supply of pecuniary aid.
>
> The whole spirit of your instructions went to caution you against mixing yourself in the internal concerns of the country … your participation in this transaction must be plainly and totally disavowed. After such a disavowal you will I am sure feel that you

could not continue, either with satisfaction to yourself or with advantage to your Government, to conduct the affairs of His Majesty's Commission in Mexico.[8]

And he informed Hervey that he was sending out someone to replace him, who would be carrying this letter, and that he, Hervey, was to return in the ship bringing the replacement. Canning also sacked Staples at the same time:

> It cannot be necessary to argue that money dealing is of all the forms of commercial adventure that in which it is most unfit that a public officer, to whom *all* trade is interdicted, should engage .... It is not to be supposed that you embarked in this transaction without some view to benefits, justly the object of a commercial man, but entirely unbecoming the character of His Majesty's Consul[9]

Hervey received his notice of dismissal on 30 October, while he was on tour at Guanajuato. It was hardly the kind of response he had been looking for when only a few weeks earlier he had written privately to Canning saying he 'shd wish very much to return to England for a few months in the spring of next year.'[10] It was bad enough to find he was being recalled: it was worse to find that his successor was already in the country. He had anticipated the possibility that his action over the loan might have to be disavowed ever since he had learned that what he had supposed was a secret matter had become public. As he put it to Canning:

> The extraordinary error of judgment which could induce the individual most concerned in the transaction to commit an act of felony upon himself, and to send a copy of a most important private letter to England without reserve or injunction of silence, will remain forever to me a mystery in the history of human foresight and calculation.

But he refused to repent of what he had done. He maintained that it had been 'the only measure which could save the country from the scourge of faction or from the desolating effects of a renewed Civil War'. He acknowledged that his instructions did not authorize his action and that when he took it he realized that if it resulted in committing His Majesty's Government it would have to be publicly disavowed. But, he wrote, 'as there are different modes of conferring favors, so there are various forms for conveying censure, and I am sorry to be obliged to observe that you have not chosen the most mild nor the most merciful. With a strong hand you have dragged the victim to the altar and have sacrificed him unannointed and unprepared.' He added that he assumed he was not being accused of gaining financial advantage for himself, since had he wished to do so he would hardly have confined himself 'to the moderate speculation of a premium upon a temporary loan for three months of £300,000'.[11]

One cannot but sympathize with Hervey even while regretting the style of his reply to Canning.[12] He had been in the position (faced often by diplomats abroad) of seeing the local situation with a degree of clarity not shared by those at home and trying desperately to get the home government to understand what he felt the issues to be and how Britain's interests locally could best be served. Faced with long intervals between receipt of instructions, London's receipt of his reports and recommendations, and his receipt of their reactions to them, the man on the spot had to decide for himself what action to take; and he had to take the risk that he would be disowned. Certainly his position in Mexico would have been difficult after being disowned over that one act; but he was respected locally and it probably would not have made a great difference to his general effectiveness. Indeed, Michelena, in an interview with Canning on 31 July (in the presence of Hervey's successor), expressed great regret at the news of Hervey's recall and the reason for it. Without putting it in so many words, he suggested that it was not exactly complimentary to his country to sack such a distinguished diplomat for an action which had been positively helpful to Mexico at a time of urgent need.[13] Considering the distinction with which Hervey had served in Spain, and the hard work he had put into laying down a sound basis for the development of British-Mexican friendship and successful British commerce with that country, he was surely treated somewhat harshly. And after the unsuitable outburst in his immediate reaction to his sacking he showed admirable restraint and dignity in his valedictory despatch before finally leaving Mexico City on 19 December 1824 to return to England on board HMS *Diamond* commanded by Lord Napier:

> If the testimony of the Mexican nation and subsequent events shall prove that we have not toiled in vain, I shall never regret

> having crossed the Atlantic on such a service: nay more, I may perhaps glory in having been placed by the gracious favour of His Majesty at the head of a Commission which shall have obtained this desirable result: although as far as my personal interests and feelings are concerned, I must ever deeply lament the circumstances which immediately subjected me to the recall.[14]

It was perhaps the publicity given to Hervey's action over the loan that forced Canning to 'drag him to the altar': he might not have reacted so violently had it been possible to keep it quiet. And he may not then have intended this to be the end of Hervey's career. In reply to Michelena's remonstrance he had said that Hervey would actually receive promotion on his return. But in the end this was not forthcoming, and Hervey was retired. There are many reasons to suppose that Hervey would not in fact have been the right person to complete the job he began in Mexico. It was unfortunate, however, that for the second time in little more than a year Canning's efforts to establish contact with Mexico should have gone wrong. Fortunately, Victoria and Alamán attached such importance to getting Britain's recognition that they were prepared to be patient while yet another commissioner set about examining their condition and reporting to Canning. But Hervey's successor had his difficulties too.

8

HERVEY IS REPLACED BY JAMES JUSTINIAN MORIER – 1824

Soon after arriving in Mexico, Ward had decided that on his return to England he and Emily must get married. He was assuming he would have to go back to join Hervey after only a few weeks, and that he would then have to remain there possibly for several years. In his first letter from Mexico to Sir John Swinburne he wrote that he had 'been thanking heaven ever since I set my foot upon the shore that Emily is not with us. I can laugh at difficulties which only regard myself; but I should feel very uncomfortable indeed if she were of the party'.[1] But the thought of further long separation was too much. He could now offer the prospect of a secure career and income, and he was confident that Emily would be ready to share with him the challenge and excitement of living in this new country. So he had ended this letter by asking

> that to all that I already owe you, you will add the last and greatest favor of all, your consent to make Emily mine as soon after my arrival as I can persuade the dear girl to fix her day. I have checked myself whenever I thought it would be selfish to be impatient, or that the gratification of my wishes might expose her to risks, or even to inconvenience. But you would do me but little justice if you imagined that my prudence arose from any want of all that the most ardent lover can feel for a woman on whom he has fixed his hopes for years. I shall be as impatient, on my return, to call her mine as I have been hitherto averse to pressing it while I thought a little self denial might enable me to add to her comforts afterwards. You have been too generous, dear Sir John, for me to apprehend much opposition on your part, & as to Emily

she has promised me already (let her deny it if she can) that delays shall not originate with her.

Sir John told Henry's father that he was very willing to agree to this request. Henry's father was equally keen 'that everything should be prepared for this dear union the moment it can properly take place'.[2] But he was embarrassed at not being in a position to match Sir John's proposed generous settlement on the couple. Fortunately one of his brothers decided to help out and the necessary arrangements were made in time for Henry to be able to tell Sir John within a week of arriving in England that he could make an adequate contribution and to ask for 'an early – a *very* early marriage. My stay in England depends too much upon circumstances to be at all settled; Planta, tho' he foresaw no probability of my being wanted immediately, strongly recommended that no time should be lost'. He reminded Sir John that he had 'been for *five* years looking forward to this moment'. He explained that his father was placing his country home, Hyde House near Chesham in Buckinghamshire, and servants at their disposal for the short time they expected to remain in England, and that as Hervey (not aware then of his forthcoming dismissal) had proposed leaving Mexico as soon as he returned, he would be able to move with Emily into a 'Govt house, and [with] so large an addition to my salary as will enable me at once to make her very comfortable'.[3]

Henry and Emily were married (by special licence) on Thursday 8 April 1824 at St George's Church, Hanover Square in London. From Hyde House Emily wrote to her father on the 12th to tell him of her happiness at having been given a husband 'good & kind to me far beyond what I can deserve'; to which Ward added that 'every day & every hour make me more grateful for the blessing which you have conferred upon me'.[4] But the return to Mexico did not come as soon as expected. Indeed, they then had to endure several months of order and counter-order. Ward was told by Planta early in July that Canning had decided to recall Hervey from Mexico and that he, Ward, would be needed to accompany the replacement commissioner, Morier, who would be setting out as soon as possible. Ward immediately 'went round to all my different tradesmen and gave orders for all our things to be ready and packed up in ten days' and returned to Emily in the country. On 10 July, however, he was summoned again to London. On arrival at Blake's Hotel, after a fast ride of thirty or so miles on horseback, he was handed a letter from Planta telling him 'as a piece of *good* news' that Canning had decided not to send him back to Mexico after all. Reporting these developments to Sir John, Ward said he was sorry for Hervey, that he would 'regret him as an old friend', but that 'after such a tour d'écolier as this, one cannot say that he is hardly treated'. He confessed, however, that he was glad not to be travelling out with Morier, even though he found him 'a very quiet, sensible, pleasing and gentlemanlike man, and if I join him later, I am sure we shall get on admirably together' (as indeed they did).[5]

Ward then enjoyed another two weeks of leisure with Emily at Hyde House before again being summoned to London. This time he took her with him to Blake's Hotel, and on Sunday 1 August he wrote to her father to explain that he had now been offered the post of Secretary of Legation at Madrid 'if I preferred it to Mexico'. He had been told that 'Mr C particularly wished to send me there as he thought my knowledge of the language, & of the bearings of the American question in particular, might be of use to Mr Lamb, who is going to replace Sir William à Court as Minister.' Ward had accepted with alacrity:

> My appointment is just all I could wish. It gives me £700 a year, puts me over the head of twenty men of much older standing than myself in the line, as Madrid is our first *Mission*, and keeps me in the *Spanish* line too, which is an object, as I am far from losing sight of the opening which America may hereafter afford .... For dear Emily's sake, and yours, I am glad of the change. Spain seems nothing after Mexico. We shall have messengers regularly once a week, & bad as the country is, it is infinitely better for a woman than Mexico in its present unsettled state.[6]

Ward expected to leave for Madrid in about three weeks, and Emily hoped they would have time to spend a few days in Paris on the way. She wrote to her father, suggesting that he and her two older sisters, Elizabeth and Julia, should 'embark in the Steamboat at Newcastle, & meet us at Calais .... It would be quite right for Julia to see the Biennial Exhibition, which will be open, & for such a *Patron* of modern art as thou art never to have seen one is really too bad.'[7]

All these plans came to nought, however. On 5 August Ward was told that Canning particularly wanted him to set off on the 10th for Madrid as a courier with à Court's Letters of Recall, leaving Emily behind until, after Lamb's arrival six weeks later, he could return to fetch her. This was bad enough; but next day he was told that his posting to Madrid had been cancelled. Canning had mentioned it to the Spanish minister at a social gathering, and the latter had immediately expressed the view that King Ferdinand would be most reluctant to receive a man 'transplanted from *one of the rebel colonies* to his Court, particularly as this man had ... passed four years in Spain during the Constitutional System, & was consequently connected, almost exclusively, with a Party, every member of which was now considered as a suspicious character'. (Ward had been attaché in Spain during the period when the 'liberal' government was in opposition to Ferdinand, who had been restored to power only by French intervention. It was at least some consolation for Ward to be told that

> neither [Canning's] opinion of me, nor his determination to employ me were in any way affected by [his decision]; and that I might trust to him, without being under the slightest uneasiness with respect to my future prospects .... C only felt my claim to be the stronger from the fact that one of the objections to my being received in Spain originated in my having been employed on a Commission which he himself had given me (Mexico) & that I might depend upon his taking the very first opportunity to convince me by *as good*, or perhaps a *better* appointment, of his wish to take me up.[8]

Meanwhile he was to be allowed to go on drawing his allowance as a commissioner.

In fact neither Canning nor Ward had been taken wholly by surprise by this development. Canning, in conversation with Ward's father even before telling Ward himself of the proposed posting, had thought that his son's 'having been in Madrid *might* make it not palatable to the Sp Government'.[9] And Ward himself told Sir John that he had 'anticipated something of the kind as soon as my appointment was known in Spain, & had hinted as much to Em'. He even felt that it was as well the appointment had been cancelled so quickly, 'for to have been stopped on the frontier, or insulted by a Royalist mob on the road, would have been much more serious, as it would have brought my name forward all over Europe in a most disagreeable manner'. Wondering where he might now be sent instead, he said he 'must trust in Providence & Mr C. I shall accept whatever he offers, altho' inferior to Madrid, just putting in a little word, however, if this shd be the case, to make him recollect me later shd anything better turn up.'[10]

So James Justinian Morier had to set out alone. He was a curious choice as replacement for Hervey. He had earlier distinguished himself as a young diplomat, but his service had been in Persia. Although a linguist, he laid no claim to Spanish and had no direct experience of Spanish affairs, or even of European politics. He had been born in Smyrna in November 1782, the second son of Isaac Morier (a Swiss who had become naturalized British in 1773) and Clara Van Lennep (whose sister Cornelia was the wife of Admiral William Waldegrave, 1st Baron Radstock). He had been educated in England, being brought up to speak English and French with equal fluency. He had joined his father's business in Smyrna and in 1806 had met Sir Harford Jones in Constantinople and been invited by him to travel in his coach to London. Sir Harford had then taken him onto his personal staff when he went as Britain's special envoy to Persia to negotiate a preliminary treaty of friendship and alliance 'to become a basis for establishing a sincere and everlasting definitive treaty of strict friendship and union'. Sir Harford attached him as personal aide to Mirza Abul Hasan Shirazi, the Persian special envoy who in 1809 took the text of this preliminary treaty to Britain and in 1810 concluded the definitive treaty which led to the establishment of full diplomatic relations between the two countries. Abul Hasan found Morier an admirable aide and made this clear to the Marquess of Wellesley, then Foreign Secretary. Wellesley told Abul Hasan: 'As for Mr Morier, it is his good fortune to have served you, for he has gained in reputation thereby'[11] and acceded to his request that Morier should return to Persia on the staff of the embassy to be established there. He remained in Persia until 1815, being Minister *ad interim* in charge of the embassy for his last year. He then left the diplomatic service with a pension and in 1818 published his second book about his travels (the first having been published in 1812). He was called back temporarily into service in 1819 in order once again to look after Abul Hasan on another mission to England.

In June 1820 Morier married Harriet Fulke Greville and for a while they lived in a rented house, L'Espagnerie, near her father outside Boulogne. In 1822 Canning proposed that Morier should return to Persia as Minister. This was most welcome to Morier, but unfortunately for him some parts of his travel books had given offence in Persia and, learning of this proposal, an agent of the Shah in London discreetly made it clear that he would not be welcome, so the proposal had to be dropped.[12] (Meanwhile he had also begun to write the delightful book purporting to be written by a Persian, *The Adventures of Hajji Baba of Ispahan*, in which he made fun of the Persian character. This was published in 1824 (without his authorship at first being known), and was followed in 1828 by *The Adventures of Hajii Baba of Ispahan in England*. It was as well that he did not go to Persia as Minister, for these books also gave offence there, particularly to Abul Hasan on whom he only too clearly based one of the characters.)

Morier's mother, Clara, had been pleased by his choice of wife. She told her son David that she found Harriet to have an 'affectionate manner, without being either beautiful or pretty. She has in my opinion more than that, which is a very agreeable physiognomy, very animated, humorous black eyes and at the same time a soft expression in her manners which marks a sensitive heart'. Clara was particularly glad that she had 'no taste for vanities', for her father, whom Clara thought a very disagreeable miser, was providing only the minimum dowry. Morier had been comfortably off as a bachelor but found married life something of a financial strain, particularly with a young child. A son had been born at L'Espagnerie in March 1821, but had lived barely two weeks. Another, Greville, had been born on 10 September 1822 (and later became a Foreign Office clerk). Morier was by now, therefore, very keen to be re-employed in the diplomatic service. His family was well known to Canning, whose offer of Mexico may have been his way of making up for the disappointment over Persia. Possibly his brother John Philip had something to do with it. He had been one of the three commissioners appointed in April 1812 to go to Spanish America in an attempt to mediate between Spain and her revolted colonies, and was at that time British minister at Dresden. James wrote to his brother David that 'the whole thing is extremely flattering to me, in every way'; but he was not enthusiastic, adding that he could not have refused the appointment without shutting himself off from a diplomatic career for ever. His acceptance was perhaps a financial necessity.[13]

Ward had been instructed to 'give [Morier] all the assistance & information in [his] power' and found him full of anxieties over his lack of Spanish[14] and the likely living conditions for his wife and child. He told Sir John that he did

> not envy Morier his Commission .... He goes out to act the part of a cautious observer, wrapping himself up in perfect neutrality. This would have done very well at first, but after the line which

> H has taken, he will find it a most difficult and disagreeable task. *Backing out* is never a pleasant operation. All this Morier feels; but the prospect of the Mission ultimately is a temptation.[15]

Ward did everything he could to help Morier. He let him have all the things he had ordered for himself and Emily – even her special litter and dressing table. He spent three whole days with him and was begged to accompany him to Mexico, a request Ward felt unable to refuse even though it was 'the very worst season for going out'. He went to Planta to offer his services to Morier, but Planta revealed that they had thought in the Foreign Office that he would object to being sent to Mexico at that time, on account of Emily, and believed they were doing him a favour in allowing him to remain in England. This upset Ward: 'I did not like the thing being put in this way, as if my marriage rendered me less fit for active employment than before, or less willing to expose myself to any risks that my profession might require.' He put this to Planta, referring to Morier's lack of Spanish and saying that he and Emily could be ready to set out within a week. This offer, however, was declined and he was told that the Foreign Office did 'not consider [Morier's] ignorance of Spanish as any disadvantage, as it will enable him to hold back at pleasure and not be hurried into the expression of sentiments which they do not wish to encourage until things are settled'.[16] (At that time the Foreign Office were disposed in any case to consider a knowledge of French, then the international language of diplomacy, as sufficient for most postings.)

Morier thus embarked for Mexico not only without the support of Ward, but in the end without even the comfort of having his wife and child with him. He decided, probably on Ward's advice, that they should stay behind as Harriet was not very robust, and they would have been arriving at Vera Cruz at the time of year of the 'black vomit' from which Europeans frequently died unless they could travel on to the higher altitudes within a few hours of landing. (But it seems he did not return to Ward the special litter and dressing table originally intended for Emily's use). He and his party boarded HMS *Diamond*, the 46-gun frigate of the Leda class commanded by Lord Napier in which Hervey later returned, at Spithead at 1.20 p.m. on 3 August. At the last moment he was joined by a secretary/interpreter sent by his brother David, then consul general in Paris, who had once employed him as his own secretary. They sailed immediately, but because of contrary winds it was the evening of the 12th before they could really get started from Plymouth. Even then the winds remained unfavourable until the 19th, and it was 1 September before they were able to anchor at Funchal, no doubt cheered, however, by having fallen in with a Swedish vessel bound for Finland from whom they were able to purchase some wine on 25 August.[17] They remained at Funchal for three days and reached Antigua on 27 September, where they stayed another six days. From there Morier wrote to his mother that 'a public man ought never to marry. It is requiring too much of him to live away from those who form the "bone of his bone & flesh of his flesh." I do my best to submit to what I cannot help .... I no longer feel that relish which I formerly did in exploring new country so my public duty is my predominant feeling and when that is accomplished I shall be very ready to return home.' They finally anchored at Sacrificios on the afternoon of 23 October, 81 days after leaving Spithead. This was the start of a difficult few months for a man feeling very much his isolation from all that he was used to, and particularly from those he loved.

9

SIX UNEASY MONTHS FOR MORIER – OCTOBER 1824 TO MARCH 1825

Canning had given Morier his formal instructions in a despatch dated 20 July 1824 delivered to him in London.[1] They amounted in essence to ordering him to follow closely those given to Hervey: 'I have only to direct you to conform yourself strictly to those instructions; to be diligent and particular in your reports, & to be careful to avoid committing your Govt beyond the limits which those instructions prescribe.' Having studied these, Morier had asked what he should do if Iturbide should arrive in Mexico (he was known to be planning a return). He foresaw three possible developments: Iturbide's proclamation as emperor and the dissolution of the existing government; a partial declaration in his favour vigorously resisted by the government with the outcome doubtful; the creation of two opposing parties, one occupying Vera Cruz, the other the capital. Canning's advice was robust. Morier was to be only an observer and should have contact only with whatever government was *de facto* in power. But if there should be a struggle between parties with an outcome 'so doubtful as to suspend the functions of government', he was to suspend communication, 'stating to either Party, or to both, the grounds on which you feel it necessary to do so'.[2] But Morier had also asked what he was to do if he had to leave the country as a result of such development. Canning could not 'permit himself to imagine [a case] in which your personal safety would be endangered; and while I leave it to your discretion to act according to any circumstances which cannot here be foreseen, I must recommend to you not to resort to the expedient of leaving the country'. But if he felt it necessary to do so, he should go to Jamaica and await further instructions, unless Spain had managed to gain full control of the country again, in which case he was to return home.

Although Morier and his party reached Sacrificios on 23 October, because of a 'norte' they could not go ashore until the 27th 'under a salute of 13 guns which was returned by the shore with 15'.[3] Even then the passage from the ship in a small boat, and the landing, was a hazardous affair, according to Morier's description in a letter to his wife, with the surf breaking over the mole to such an extent that they had to make several attempts to get alongside. Once landed, however, they were 'received with every proper attention'[4] by the military governor of Vera Cruz and found that active hostilities between the town and the castle had ceased. They set off next day for Jalapa, which they reached on the 30th after two uncomfortable nights in very cramped quarters in what passed for inns. (At the first they had to request the removal from the only 'room' of a man dying of fever over whom a priest was bending to hear his confession '& by way of making a pleasure of a trial was indulging himself in a cegar [*sic*] at the same time'.) While at Jalapa, Morier received word that Hervey expected to be back in Mexico City about the 12th or 13th; but for some now unknown reason Morier was 'unavoidably detained'[5] and did not reach the capital until 1 December, deliberately spending three days at Puebla on the way in order to rectify Hervey's failure to listen to the views of the Bishop there.[6] While at Jalapa, Morier, with the help of Mackenzie (whom he described to his brother as 'a very highly educated man and a great addition to our society') met a great variety of people and wrote a total of 12 despatches, many of which were lengthy reports on the political situation as it was explained to him. He was careful, however, to make clear that he himself was not yet in a position to give his own views. He was not going to fall into the error made by Hervey.

It was only on arrival at Jalapa that Morier learned that he need no longer worry about Iturbide, who had returned but had been executed on 19 July, almost immediately after landing near Tampico in an ill-prepared attempt to regain popular support. The first news of this appears to have reached England on 16 September, when it was reported in *The Times*. Hervey did not report it until 28 July, in a despatch which reached the Foreign Office on 18 September,[7] the day after Michelena gave them a copy of *The Mexican Gazette* in which it had been announced.[8] O'Gorman, however, had made an immediate attempt to profit financially from this event. On 31 July, in the absence of Hervey up country, he gave Cochrane, then in command of HMS *Forte*, an urgent letter for London with the news, but suggested to him that if he could ensure that a business contact of his got the news before it became public a profit could be made in the market, of which Cochrane could receive a one-sixth share.[9]

With this anxiety about Iturbide out of the way, Morier would have been looking for a reasonably easy few months of maintaining amicable relations with the Mexican government until, as he assumed and hoped, Canning would decide to recognize its independence and the serious business of heading a proper diplomatic mission could begin. It was not, however, as straightforward as that. On 3 December he was formally introduced by Hervey to Victoria (who had become President on 17 September). On that occasion he did no more than exchange formal diplomatic compliments, but they met 'casually' at a social occasion three days later and Morier was impressed by Victoria's friendly, modest informality, which was very different from what he had been led by some Mexicans to expect.[10] However, it soon became clear to Morier that Victoria was none too pleased at the news he brought him that Britain was expecting very soon to recognize the independence of Buenos Aires with a commercial treaty. This was not surprising. After all, it was now 18 months since Mackie had first arrived with overtures of British friendship, 12 since Hervey's mission had arrived and six since the Mexicans had returned that compliment by sending Michelena to London. Britain was taking a very long time to translate words into action, and it was difficult to see why Buenos Aires should benefit first. Morier found too that there was a noticeable frigidity in the way government ministers treated him. He discovered one reason for this: because he had not brought with him a formal letter from Canning to Victoria appointing him as Hervey's successor his status was in doubt. Apparently his explanation was accepted;[11] but the coolness remained, and this, combined with his lack of Spanish, made it difficult for him to deal with some of the diplomatic problems he encountered.

The first of these in fact arose before he had even reached the capital. On 8 November the Mexican armed forces had begun to occupy and fortify Sacrificios (in preparation for later action which led to the capture of the castle of Ulloa). They had closed the port of Vera Cruz, and virtually all civilians had left the town to escape the renewed bombardment then expected.[12] They had ordered all ships, including

British naval vessels, using the anchorage at Sacrificios to move to another one at Antón Lizardo, some 8 miles away. At the same time they had instituted a blockade in which there was to be no landing at Vera Cruz and no communication with the castle. Captain Thomas Forrest of HMS *Isis* had been sent there with orders from the admiral in Jamaica to sort out with General Le Maur the matter of the complaints from British merchant ships that the Spaniards were insisting on receiving harbour dues even though the ships were using the Sacrificios anchorage. Mackenzie sent on to Morier a despatch from Forrest to say that although he considered the Mexicans were in effect insulting the British flag, he would temporarily agree not to attempt to land at Vera Cruz or communicate with the castle; but he was refusing to change his anchorage for one he considered unsafe.[13]

Morier was put in an embarrassing position by learning at the same time that Captain C. Crole of HM Sloop *Surinam* had just taken on board the 'Spanish King's Lieutenant' at the castle to give him passage to Havana (where of course he could then arrange for reinforcements to be sent to the castle). This seemed a blatant breach of proper neutrality. Morier replied to Forrest from Puebla that the actions of *Surinam* made it very difficult for him to convince the Mexicans that the British were genuinely neutral, so it was essential that their blockade and the request to leave Sacrificios should be observed. He felt sure the Mexicans had no intention of insulting the British flag, and he pointed out that protests about the harbour dues had already been made to Le Maur by Captain George Harris of HMS *Hussar* and Mackenzie. He was convinced that once the admiral at Jamaica was apprised of the situation he 'would not press the execution of the orders under which you inform me you are at present acting'.[14] Forrest replied on 4 December that he had done as Morier wanted.

Not long after reaching the capital Morier was again embarrassed by the navy, this time by Lord Napier, who had visited Le Maur at the castle despite having been told of the Mexican blockade. Napier's explanation to Morier was that he had visited the castle primarily 'out of mere curiosity', but also 'to take charge of a small quantity of specie for General Le Maur'. What he did not reveal to Morier was that he had been aided and abetted in this by Hervey, who had warned him that such a visit might lead to protests, but had told him that if he was determined to go ahead he 'had better … take me with you as I have already told Barragán [the military governor at Vera Cruz] … that I mean to go, to which [he] did not object, and I moreover really wish to see Le Maur'.[15] Hervey, however, thought better of this later that day, having mentioned the proposed visit to other Mexican military, who had begged him not to go. But he had not mentioned Napier's proposed visit, so made no further attempt to dissuade him, saying simply 'I suppose that they do not like to *see* the boat of a British man-of-war communicate with the Castle.'[16] The Admiralty later used this correspondence to justify Napier's action when the Foreign Office complained.[17]

Hervey acted somewhat irresponsibly, but this was as nothing compared to Napier's haughty reply to the protest from the military commander at Vera Cruz:

> I consider myself commanding HBM ships *here in a state of most perfect neutrality* on which state I shall feel it my duty as it is my determination to support, until official notice has been received that HBM's Government have acknowledged that blockade, to the prejudice of our more ancient allies of Spain .... As in my present state of neutrality I have already communicated with … all the authorities of the Mexican Republic, so it is my determination to avail myself of the same privilege with respect to the Castle – and in so doing I flatter myself I have too much respect for my own character as an officer, and for the honor of the British Flag ever to enter into any of those clandestine practices which the jealousy and suspicion of your Government has thus led you to suspect.[18]

One can understand Napier's view of neutrality, but the arrogance of his communication was extreme. It is to the credit of Mexico that it was officially treated with dignity. Alamán's note to Morier was unpolemical; but it was clear that Napier's view was not accepted. The Secretary for War and Marine had written to the military commander that

> the point which has given rise to this correspondence cannot be argued on the grounds of the principles of neutrality, or of the relations existing between the English and Spanish Governments, but of those principles which are acknowledged by all civilized nations; that those ships which remain in an amicable manner in harbours ought to be subject to the regulations which are imposed on them there, as they are at full liberty not to touch

> at them when for any reason those regulations are not agreeable .... [Napier] has violated the very perfect neutrality which he has designed to observe between this nation and Spain, although the latter is more ancient, since the laws of nations are not observed in the ratio of their respective antiquity.[19]

A not unreasonable view. But there was a very vicious anti-British article in the Jalapa press, and Morier had to try to defuse this potential petard. In reporting to London he wrote:

> Foreseeing that to enter upon a discussion of points of neutrality and blockade with this Government would only entail a correspondence which, under the present circumstances, would be more likely to irritate than convince, in our answer to Mr Alamán we have in the first place restricted ourselves to making friendly professions on the part of His Majesty's Government towards this nation. When we consider that the attention of this nation is turned towards the capture of the Castle of Ulloa as the one object of their present hopes and expectations, we need not be surprised at the irritation which they manifest upon seeing their plans frustrated by any supposed unfriendly interventions on our part.[20]

He enclosed the press article as an example of 'the sort of feeling that we have to contend with: a feeling proceeding from ignorance of international law and from too exalted an opinion of Mexico as a nation .... If our object be to conciliate, the mischief produced by any want of concert between HM diplomatic servants and the Navy is incalculable.'

Morier's reply to Alamán, signed jointly with O'Gorman, acknowledged the Mexican complaint 'with great regret', but pointed out

> that the commanders of HBM's ships of war are subject only to the orders of the Admiralty in England, and to those of their superior officers. They sail under instructions furnished to them by those authorities and consequently do not hold themselves amenable to the orders of HBM's diplomatic agents. Representations are made to them by those agents upon points

> relating to the interests of their nation, but the responsibility of attending to them, or not, rests with them.

They said, however, that every effort would be made 'to prevent … the recurrence of events which under existing circumstances cannot fail being productive of mutual embarrassment to our respective Governments'.[21]

Having to apologize for the actions of the navy the moment he arrived was bad enough; but Morier also found himself having to come to the defence of George O'Gorman, the brother of the consul general, who was the representative in Mexico of the London merchant house of B.A. Goldsmidt. That firm had negotiated with the Mexican agent in London, Migoni, to make a loan to Mexico of £3.2 million. The first instalment of £200,000 had been transmitted via George O'Gorman in the form of promissory notes to be delivered on the ratification of the contract in Mexico. The denominations of these notes were such that the Mexican authorities had difficulty in finding traders prepared to take them up, so they asked to be allowed to draw the loan directly in amounts acceptable to those prepared to buy the notes. O'Gorman said that this could only be done through him, and he stated publicly that any taken up other than through him would not be honoured. The Mexicans persisted in their request, so O'Gorman himself bought them up and dealt directly with individuals, charging 2 per cent commission.

These actions were closely followed by the passing by congress in secret session on 24 December 1824 of a decree giving the president power to expel any foreigner, and shortly after this an order was signed for O'Gorman's seizure and expulsion. Word had reached Morier that the decree had been passed specifically for this purpose, and he and the consul general, although saying nothing directly to the Mexicans about this, addressed a note jointly to the acting Foreign Minister, Juan Guzmán, to register their concern at the sweeping nature of the decree.[22] They drew attention to the undertakings Alamán had given Hervey in July about the protection of British subjects, when he had written: 'The actual laws protect the persons of all individuals residing within the territory of the republic.' Guzmán replied 'to your friendly and polite letter' by explaining that the decree 'should be understood as comprehending those foreigners who attempt or conspire in any mode against the independence or the system of government adopted by the Mexican nation' and that the decree was not expected ever to be applied to British subjects, given 'the experience of the excellent conduct of the individuals of your nation resident in these United States who have never given the slightest cause for complaint'. It would be applied 'merely to foreigners travelling through the country, and not to those who are naturalised, established or connected by commercial or other affairs with the nation'.[23] But the Mexicans took the hint and immediately destroyed the order relating to George O'Gorman. George, however, was not yet in the clear. He was next arrested on a criminal charge that 'by his conduct, his language and his declarations in the public papers he has materially impaired [the Mexican] credit, having turned the same to his advantage'. Morier was then told by the Minister of Finance, Esteva, that it was the intention to give George his passport after the trial and tell him to leave the country. Morier was very anxious to avoid getting officially involved in all this; but it appeared that George was going to be tried behind closed doors, without the evidence against him being properly and openly presented. Morier did feel that George was being hard done by as he had only been following instructions from his principals in London. Fortunately George told Morier that he would be prepared to leave the country if he could do so without a stain on his character.[24] In these circumstances, Victoria gave instructions that the charges be dropped, and what might have been a serious dispute between Mexico and Britain was avoided.

Next on Morier's list of problems was a difficulty over diplomatic privilege. Michelena, who had set off for England already somewhat irritated by the way Captain Murray had treated him, had had a brush with customs, on his arrival, over the import of his possessions. Later he also objected to postal charges levied on his official mail. On 27 December Morier received a note from Guzmán about these matters in which it was pointed out that no postage was charged on 'the letters of the English Cabinet … and those which come by sea should only pay the inland postage … [and] … that the baggage of Mr Hervey and yours should pass through the Mexican territory free from all search'. Guzmán asked for reciprocal treatment for Michelena.[25] Morier sent an apologetic reply suggesting that there might have been a misunderstanding:

> Perhaps landing at some distance from London, as I am told [Michelena] did, and anxious, as he doubtless might be, to reach the place of his destination, surrounded by the novelties of a new

> country and new regulations – [shades there of Morier's own experience of the reactions of Abul Hasan on reaching England] – and arriving at once without the Government being apprised of his approach, it will I hope be allowed that some mistake on the part of the authorities at the sea port, proceeding from ignorance of Mr Michelena's diplomatic character, may have unintentionally taken place .... It is the custom for diplomatic agents ... on their landing in England, to address a letter to the Under Secretary of State for Foreign Affairs, stating their arrival, enclosing a list of their baggage and requesting that an order may be granted that it should pass free. An order from the Treasury is usually forwarded within 24 hours after such an application, and every article is scrupulously delivered at the residence.[26]

Guzmán's reply was friendly, saying the president had been pleased by the tone of Morier's letter and felt 'the sincerest satisfaction in as much as the just complaints of this Government have been attended to and some trifling particulars properly arranged by which, although of small account, as well as by others of greater importance, our alliance and friendship ought to be maintained and consolidated'.[27]

Through all these little contretemps the Mexicans acted with formal courtesy; nevertheless it was obvious that they were losing no opportunity of showing their displeasure at the slow progress in obtaining British recognition of their independence. Morier appreciated this, but it did not make his position any easier, as he explained in the despatch in which in February he attempted his first analysis of the situation in Mexico. He reported that

> instead of that cordiality which existed between His Majesty's Commission upon its first arrival, and this Government, a decided change of tone and manner on the part of the Government has taken place towards us. Excepting the interchange of first visits between the different members of the Administration and myself, I have not received any single mark of attention from any one of them, still less from the President. Indeed, instead of attentions, it would be easy to sum up a list of vexations and discourtesies which indicate any thing but a conciliatory spirit.

Morier felt that 'distrust and jealousy of foreigners' was rife at all levels. But he was not too despondent: 'Considering in what state of ignorance, seclusion from foreign intercourse and religious despotism this country has been kept for centuries, every allowance ought to be made for the degraded state of the public mind, and much rational expectation entertained for its future amelioration.' And he gave very positive answers to the four questions that had been put to Hervey in his original instructions, and which were now his. On the all important question about the consistency and confidence of the people in their government, he pointed out that it was now 21 months since Iturbide's abdication and twelve since the promulgation of the new constitution, and 'every month may be said to produce a change for the better'. He thought it possible that by the time his report was received the question of recognition might have been decided. But in case this were not so, he concluded with a definite recommendation:

> I humbly trust that it will not be esteemed presumption in me if I venture to give an opinion that should that recognition be much longer delayed, the situation of His Majesty's Commission in this country will be attended with considerable embarrassment. I beg leave to repeat that the pleasure diffused throughout the nation upon the first arrival of His Majesty's Commissioners and Consuls seems to have been replaced by feelings of distrust – a distrust likely to increase, for should the present administration not be changed for men of more enlightened views, and should it continue in its present temper towards us, it is to be apprehended that we may have to struggle against circumstances which might compromise the dignity of the British nation, and which might lead to a state of things when it would be no longer possible to act with the forbearance which we have hitherto adopted as the rule of our conduct.[28]

Poor Morier! If he had accepted this posting to Mexico in the hope of then becoming the head of a full diplomatic mission, he must by now have become very discouraged. His separation from his wife and child must have seemed a price which was not likely to prove worth having paid. Had he had the support of Ward, with his good personal relationship with Victoria and his fluent Spanish, his sense of isolation might have been less. But the real trouble was the apparent lack of progress towards British recognition; and some of Michelena's reporting from London cannot have helped. Possibly his complaints about his treatment by customs on arrival had not in themselves been taken too seriously in Mexico; but undoubtedly Victoria and others will have reacted badly to his report of being refused recognition as a *diplomatic* representative and therefore a place in the diplomatic corps in London. He was not alone in this position: the Colombian agent, Hurtado, had also been refused full diplomatic status, as Michelena discovered very soon. But Michelena believed that Mexico would be treated differently, reporting in his first despatch home that 'as regards independence, public opinion here is in favour of early recognition & the Government seem to be of like mind'.[29] And at his first interview with Canning, on 3 July, when he handed over his credentials, he was received 'with the greatest courtesy and friendliness' and they had a long discussion about the situation in Mexico.[30] At his next meeting, however, on 9 July, Canning, answering an enquiry from Michelena, regretted that he would not be able to grant exequaturs to Mexican consuls because Britain could not yet recognize Mexican independence;[31] and by 25 July, when it was clear that he himself was not going to be allowed a place in the London diplomatic corps, Michelena wrote with angry bitterness that he was being treated like an Indian: 'The Mexican Government receives less attention in England than the King of Sandwich[32] and the Mexican nation suffers a slight from my appointment and its place at Court is on a level with the Comanche.'[33] Moreover, it was explained to him that Britain was not prepared to recognize Mexico so long as there was some hope that Spain might do so first. It seems, however, that Michelena was not at that stage given any explanation of the steps Canning was taking to try to persuade Spain to do so, and as a result his reporting home was full of suspicions of Britain's real intentions. He even suggested that they should be smoked out by his formally requesting exequaturs for consuls and then the Mexican government's withdrawing those granted to British consuls in Mexico when Canning refused the request. Added to his conviction that he personally had been insulted, and his difficulties in persuading banking houses to extend more credit to Mexico (partly because of the uncertainties over whether Iturbide was going to make a successful come-back),[34] it was perhaps not surprising that he was presenting a picture which many in Mexico would have taken to be good reason for coolness towards Morier, even though by the time his reports were received they had already had some explanation from Hervey of what was going on (chapter 6).[35]

This coolness, however, lasted longer than it need have because of the irregularity and slowness of communications. (Michelena himself had asked Canning whether a monthly mail service between the two countries could not be set up, but had got nowhere.) Meetings which Michelena had with Planta and Canning in October and November[36] had persuaded him that Britain was in fact acting in Mexico's best interests, not merely her own. Canning had explained that he intended to recognize Mexican independence, but that he must give Spain one last chance to respond to his urgings that she do so first. British recognition would have to be *de facto* first, but he would make an official statement which could be published to show the Mexican public that he was serious. These reports from Michelena, however, did not reach Alamán until the end of February 1825. When they did, Alamán's attitude to Morier changed completely and he offered to call on him for the first time ever. Morier decided to reciprocate this sudden cordiality by insisting on himself calling on Alamán instead, without, of course, then knowing what was behind the approach. He found Alamán 'to be greatly pleased with the tone and tenor of the language held by Michelena, and expressed himself convinced that the interest which His Majesty's Government had at first taken in the affairs of Mexico was unabated'. Alamán acquiesced in the 'propriety of the steps proposed to be taken' in a last effort to persuade the Spaniards, although doubting 'of any changes taking place in the conduct of Spain towards her former colonies'. However, he agreed that

> as long as there was a hope it ought not to be abandoned and acquiesced in opinion that the recognition of Mexican independence by Spain ought to be the paramount object of the policy of [Mexico]. At the same time he expressed himself delighted that England would consider this appeal to Spain as the last.

Next day Morier received a visit from Victoria himself, 'the first that he had ever paid me'. He was 'most conciliatory and friendly', the communications from Michelena having 'revived his hopes of a speedy recognition of [Mexico] as an independent State'. He did express some surprise that he had received no replies to three letters he had addressed to Canning, and Morier excused this by explaining that when he had left England it was not known that he had been elected president.[37]

Morier was naturally pleased at this change of attitude, but he decided to check whether it was truly representative of the feelings of the ruling party. He therefore arranged, through a third party, to obtain the views of the Minister of Finance, Esteva, who he thought would be likely to be a reliable indicator of this. He was told that the government was 'perfectly satisfied of the sincerity of the British Cabinet, particularly since it had given their ultimatum to Spain on the subject of American independence' but that the public 'from their ignorance of the nature of political relations' were concerned at the delay in granting recognition. If this could now be given 'the Mexican Government would be ready, as well as justified by public opinion, to afford every facility to British subjects, who would be admitted to the full participation, with the natives, of all the advantages to be derived from the country. The benefits would then be mutual, and Mexico, under the powerful protection of Great Britain, might defy the rest of the world.' Esteva apparently also felt, like the President, that once Mexico was known to be recognized by Britain she would be assumed to be under British protection and could therefore immediately reduce her defence expenditure by half. 'On the whole' Morier concluded 'I am happy to be able to state that there is a much more friendly feeling towards us than existed a month ago.'[38]

This was all very encouraging for Morier, but even more so was the information received on 10 March, in a letter dated 4 January from Michelena to Alamán, that Britain had announced recognition of Mexican independence. The text of this letter was published next day. Michelena had written: 'El Ser Supremo que dirige la suerte de las naciones ha visto el mérito y sacrificios de la nuestra, los apreció y decidió en nuestro favor la gran causa. Todo está acabado: la Inglaterra reconoce nuestra independencia.' ('The Supreme Head of all things which directs the fate of nations has seen the merits and the sacrifices made by ours, has appreciated them, and has decided the great cause in our favor. Everything is complete: England recognizes our independence', as Morier's staff rendered it in English).[39] And on top of this, Morier received newspapers from England reporting that Ward had sailed for Mexico with the text of a draft treaty to be proposed to the Mexicans.

In reality, Canning had simply announced that he was not going to wait any longer for Spain to acknowledge the independence of their former colonies before negotiating formal commercial treaties with them, thus giving *de facto* recognition.[40] But this did not stop the

Mexicans treating it as *de jure* recognition. On 14 March the president went in state to the cathedral 'to render thanks to the Almighty for so great a blessing', after a motion had been proposed and carried in the Senate 'that the recognition of independence by England be celebrated with extraordinary rejoicing'. This had met with some opposition on the grounds that similar earlier recognition by Colombia and the USA had been celebrated only in 'an ordinary manner' and that 'it would be improper to make any difference as to England, although they acknowledged the importance of the recognition by that country'. But the proposers had won the day, arguing that:

> The recognition of independence by England brought with it advantages, with respect to Europe, which the recognitions of Colombia and North America did not present; and besides the last nations were by nature formed to be their brothers in the cause of independence, and therefore they ought not to be offended if Mexico celebrated with more parade and ceremony the recognition of its independence by a nation belonging to that part of the world which had for three hundred years oppressed America: and that as the recognition by England was less natural so it ought to occasion greater joy.[41]

Morier, although without any official news from the Foreign Office, could not help feeling elated, and he optimistically believed that a treaty would be concluded within a month. In the event, however, things did not go nearly as well as he expected.

10

A TREATY IS NEGOTIATED – MARCH TO APRIL 1825

After Morier's departure for Mexico in August 1824 Ward had been left for several months in uncertainty about his future, and in growing anxiety over his finances. He had not been allowed to go on drawing his allowance as a commissioner for long and was soon reduced to pay 'en disponibilité' of only £75 a quarter – so a summons to the Foreign Office on 22 December raised his hopes. As usual he put up at Blake's Hotel from where he was able to write to his father-in-law next day with some good news:

> I have been most unexpectedly put under orders again, and that for immediate service: I know not whether you were all as sincere in the preference which you once seemed to give to S America over Europe as dear Em herself is; but if you were, your wishes are likely to be gratified: I return to Mexico; with what instructions, as they have been communicated to me under seal of secrecy, I dare not tell you: you may form some conjecture, however, as to their nature from the fact that I am happy to be the bearer of them .... I am only allowed a fortnight for preparations.

He explained also that Morier, 'after effecting what I am taking him out instructions to do' would be returning to England and

> I am to remain there alone. This is just what I have so long desired .... I have always had a feeling that S Am. was to be my line, & had I been appointed to some European court I should not have rested until I got back to it. The country in which I am

> most likely to work is the one I should prefer as a residence, and blessed as I am with a wife whose spirit is in this to the full as adventurous as my own, I can pursue my plans without any of the drawbacks which married men usually complain of, & with all the comforts which married men alone can enjoy.

Emily was now in the early stages of pregnancy and he added:

> On Emily's account I am most thankful that Gt has taken a resolution now. A month or two more would have made a great difference to her. As it is, tho' she will not certainly be as well able to enjoy the new scenes to which she is to be introduced, as if she were in possession of all her Capheaton activity, I am under no apprehension with respect to the journey. I have ordered her another litter.[1]

This was a radical change from Ward's earlier delight at his posting to Spain, when he thought that this would be more suitable for Emily. Probably what he said then was not really what he felt, and in the following months Emily herself must have shown a strong wish to go to Mexico. She had a spirit of hardy adventure in her blood. Two of her Swinburne great-great-great aunts had become known as the 'Capheaton Gallopers' from their exploits in carrying despatches on horseback over the border with Scotland during the Jacobite rising in 1715, when the then Catholic family supported the rebels.[2] And she and her siblings had been brought up accustomed to a free-ranging outdoor life, both her grandfather and her father (who both abandoned the Catholic Church for the Church of England around 1780) making them go barefoot in all kinds of weather. And once in Mexico she and her husband were intrepid travellers in rough conditions.

Although Ward had been bound to secrecy, his father had already heard about his posting and its purpose from Canning himself and felt free to tell Sir John that his son was to join Morier in negotiating a commercial treaty, and would become Chargé d'affaires, which would mean £3 a day additional salary '& what is still better the sole representation of perhaps the most important interests going. This is far better than any thing Europe could promise to so young a diplomat'. But he had regrets: 'Both seem in spirits about it, & I should be more so if Em had not become a little witch during her abode here,

& endeared herself so much that I shall feel the loss more than I like to say.'[3]

Ward was called again to the Foreign Office on 29 December, when he learned that there was now no time to go back to the country, but only to send for Emily at once.[4] During the next week there were hectic preparations to be made, and he had a personal meeting with Canning on 2 January, which he described to Sir John:

> Nothing can be kinder than the manner in which C has treated me throughout. I had a long private conversation with him … at Gloucester Lodge, when he talked over the whole treaty with me, and altered two whole articles in consequence of some representations which I made to him concerning them. We shall now have no difficulty in carrying them, which I do not think we could have done as they stood before. On parting he desired me to correspond with him privately, which will enable me to give him a great deal of information on points hardly weighty enough for a despatch, and as I am now aware of his thirst for news, you may depend upon my making a proper use of this privilege .... [I will have] allowances sufficient to enable us to do the honors of England as they ought to be done in a new country. The nominal salary is £1,700 per annum, with the house, which is a princely one; but as they give me attachés and all the paraphernalia of a Mission, & wish me to give great dinners, balls, etc, C has told me to send home by Morier an estimate of what I think the additional expense is likely to prove, & this I am to charge in my extries, & to draw upon Govt for the amount quarterly.[5]

However, because of his stretched finances he had written to Planta asking for an immediate extra allowance of £100–150, explaining that he had spent

> not only my salary, but all that remained of my former outfit [allowance] and have been forced to raise money by insurance in order to enable me to support the sort of appearance in Mexico which my situation after Morier's departure … will require. I have lost considerably by my horses which … I am forced to sell for what I can.[6]

This was the first small sign, possibly noted by Planta (see chapter 12), that Ward, for all his qualities, might have inflated ideas about how he should conduct himself when Chargé d'affaires. He was naturally ambitious to make a success of this sudden elevation to responsibilities he had not dared to expect so soon, and perhaps his head had been just a little turned by the personal attention paid to him by Canning. But it was his tendency to expect the cloth to fit the coat he thought he should wear which got him into trouble later.

Ward and Emily left London on 8 January 1825 for Plymouth to join HMS *Egeria*, a much smaller vessel than the one in which he had travelled with Hervey, only a 26-gun 6th rate frigate. They were accompanied by a Mr Ball, sent by the Foreign Office as a clerk-secretary to the Commission (at a salary of £200 a year plus an outfit allowance of £200) who remained in that position throughout much of Ward's time in Mexico.[7] They had to spend a few days in Plymouth waiting for all arrangements for sailing to be completed, some at least of which seem to have been for the benefit of Captain Samuel Roberts CB. In her last letter home before sailing on the 14th Emily wrote: 'There is a great country ball here tonight [the 12th], a popular amusement with all the sailors, which it is supposed is too great a temptation for [Captain Roberts] to resist, even if the Egeria should be ready.'[8] The voyage, at least as far as Barbados which they reached on 16 February, seems to have been agreeable enough apart from Emily's sea-sickness, which confined her to their after cabin. Ward wrote from Barbados of 'the most obliging Captain, the most lovely weather, a breeze which has never deserted us, yet never freshened so much as to prove disagreeable', and of averaging 6 knots a day all the way.[9] In later recollection, however, he painted a less idyllic picture. They were also travelling with members of the mission to Colombia (who were landed at Cartagena on 25 February). In his book Ward says:

> Our party was an uncomfortably large one, considering the size of the vessel .... It was only by dint of great good humour and kindness on the part of Captain Roberts, and a spirit of mutual accommodation amongst the other members of the party, that we were able to stow ourselves away at all, and when we got to warmer latitudes we suffered not a little from the effect of being so crowded.[10]

He also refers to bad weather at the start of the voyage, and describes an alarming experience as they approached Mexico, when they nearly ran aground on an uncharted shoal. The leadsman, who had been instructed to take soundings every 15 minutes

> suddenly obtained soundings in eight fathoms; the next cast of the lead gave seven fathoms; the third six; and although all hands were turned to put the ship about, if she had not obeyed the helm instantly we should have none of us, in all probability, ever seen land again. There was a good deal of sea running, and the Egeria was an old vessel, so if she had struck she must have gone to pieces.[11]

What Emily felt about these experiences is not recorded, but it cannot have been very agreeable for her in her first pregnancy. They got a warm welcome at Vera Cruz, however, the news of the reason for Ward's return having preceded them. There was no artillery duel in progress between the town and the castle so they could be landed at the mole, where they were received by the military governor's aides in full uniform and 'the salutes fired by the ships were answered separately by all the Mexican batteries both on shore and on Sacrificios, as well as by their schooners, so that for half an hour the firing never ceased'. They found the road to Jalapa animated 'which proves that in spite of the commercial restrictions of which everyone is complaining, it is impossible to fetter entirely the trade of such a country as this'. The shops were full of English goods and the people were dressing in the European style. 'Many are and must be jealous of Victoria, but his probity and patriotism are so well known that he has secured to himself many warm friends and I have hitherto found everywhere a strong feeling in his favor.' So wrote Ward to Canning.[12] They took ten days over the journey to the capital, having to travel carefully in view of Emily's condition, and reached it on Friday 25 March. For Emily, not only was there then the challenge of accustoming herself to life at high altitude (Mexico City lies at 7350 feet above sea level) with no mistress of the house to greet her and help her settle in; she was immediately left to cope with all this on her own while her husband and Morier got down to work at once. Morier had had no confirmation of the newspaper reports of Ward's departure from England until 17 March, when a courier had arrived with a personal message from him announcing his presence in Vera Cruz and giving the gist of the instructions he was carrying. So anxious was Morier to give the Mexicans no cause to complain of further delay that he insisted on spending the whole day after Ward's arrival going through with him the draft treaty (a copy of which was sent to Alamán immediately) and Canning's instructions; and on Sunday the 27th they began negotiations at the British residence.[13]

Morier and Ward could have been forgiven for expecting these would be simple. It is true that they had some misgivings over Canning's wish to have enshrined in the treaty recognition of the right of Protestants to practise their own religion. But Victoria had been demonstrating such anxiety to have an alliance with Britain, and expressing such readiness to grant her all the privileges she wanted, that surely Canning's offering should be seized upon with alacrity and gratitude. However, like many after them, they had overlooked the Mexicans' entirely reasonable belief in the dignity of social intercourse and their expectation that it would be applied equally to political intercourse. There may be differences in the relative power of two nations, and certainly the less fortunate must expect to work her passage to some extent. But this does not mean that dignity should not be mutually respected. Morier and Ward soon found that the Mexicans were not prepared to look upon Canning's draft treaty as something they should be grateful to accept as it stood. Relatively poor and defenceless they might be; but they had their pride.

International negotiations tend to start off with much discussion of matters which seem to the lay observer quite irrelevant to the substance of what has to be agreed. Like boxers in the ring the two parties circle round each other, making occasional jabs designed to test out the opponent's reflexes and tactics before the serious business begins. The first meeting with the Mexican negotiators, Alamán and José Ignacio Esteva (Minister of Finance) was no exception. The Mexicans began by raising a point which they saw as affecting their dignity. They objected to the wording in the British Full Powers which referred to Morier and Ward as being authorized to deal with the 'persons exercising the powers and authority of government' in Mexico. They asked why it did not refer to the president, who was the supreme head of state corresponding to the King of England. Morier explained that as in Mexico the president would change every four years, with Congress having the continuing power of decision, it could create difficulties to refer only to the president. The Mexicans accepted this argument, but insisted that the president should be mentioned in the preamble instead of the 'Executive Government of Mexico', a point conceded by Morier.

The Mexicans then queried the British use of the term 'State' of Mexico rather than 'Republic'. This had been anticipated by Canning. One of his anxieties was to avoid wording which might make it look as though Britain had recognized Mexico's independence *because* she was a republic: he felt that this might discourage other European powers with strong monarchical traditions from following suit. Canning had discussed this point with Ward and in his written instructions he had made clear that the negotiations were not to be allowed to founder on it alone. But he had suggested that the Mexicans might be persuaded to drop any insistence on being described specifically as a republic if this argument were put to them, and if it were also pointed out that the USA had never thought it necessary to be designated a republic in diplomatic documents. The Mexicans accepted this, but drew attention to the confusion that could arise if Mexico were to be described as the 'State of Mexico' when this meant the province of Mexico in which the capital was situated, not the whole country. So Morier agreed to refer to the 'United States of Mexico'.

Both sides having thus shown some cautious flexibility, the Mexicans then went into the attack, raising a matter of much greater difficulty, to which they attached such importance that an early end to negotiations at once seemed a real danger. This was the omission in the British draft of any specific reference to Mexican independence. Canning had not covered this in his written instructions, and Morier and Ward had to exercise ingenuity and diplomacy to get round it. The Mexicans laid stress 'upon the feelings of jealousy and distrust which the want of [a reference to independence] must excite amongst the members of an infant Congress, none of whom were much versed in the politics of Europe and who, from that very circumstance, would be inclined to see a mystery where none, perhaps, was intended.' They also hinted at valuable commercial privileges if a separate article could be agreed which specifically recognized independence. Despite the absence of any instructions on this point, Morier and Ward said that the British government had indeed anticipated it 'but they had naturally imagined that in a treaty, every line of which contained proofs of the liberal spirit which animated them, no doubts could be entertained respecting their intentions towards Mexico'. There could be no doubt but that Britain had fully made up her mind on the issue of the contest between Spain and her former American colonies; but the

Mexicans must realize that the other nations in Europe were far from giving up ideas of helping Spain to recover her colonies and 'the greatest precaution was necessary in order to prevent the latent spark from breaking out into a flame which might prove equally destructive of the New and the Old World'. This was why Britain felt it necessary to omit any specific reference to recognizing Mexican independence. 'No treaty could be signed with a nation not considered as having established its independence, nor could a diplomatic intercourse be founded upon any other basis: the facts therefore of the signature of the treaty and the appointment of Chargés d'Affaires ... were conclusive.' Far from wanting special commercial privileges, Britain wanted to show the world that she was not influenced by such motives. 'England knew that it might have been in her power to sell her friendship on any terms she pleased, in lieu of which she made an unconditional and disinterested offer of it, stipulating only for a competition on *equal terms* with any other Power.'

The Mexicans were not moved by such arguments. They were astonished that 'the most powerful nation' in Europe dared not 'acknowledge us as being in possession of that independent existence on which alone a treaty of any sort can be founded .... [The want of] a few additional words ... would give rise to a thousand suspicions [in Congress] which would destroy that influence to which Great Britain might otherwise so justly lay claim'. Morier and Ward felt they had to take some notice of the Mexican fears, but they wished to agree other points before giving way, so they suggested leaving this one until the next meeting while they went on to discuss matters of greater substance. They were then astonished to discover that the Mexicans wanted to be free to give special trading privileges to any country that would explicitly recognize their independence, including Spain, which would run counter to the principle of 'the most favoured nation' on which Canning was insisting, that is to say the principle that each party should be treated by the other in all respects no less favourably than any other country with which either would have treaty relations. They knew that Canning had been prepared to agree to Spain's receiving special privileges in exchange for recognition of Mexico's independence, but they considered that as Spain had rejected all Britain's mediation attempts they could not now 'neglect the interests of [Britain's] own subjects in order to promote those of a country to whom she certainly was under no obligation'.

Morier and Ward then tried to put this too aside for another day, only to find the Mexicans switching their offensive to another front. They said they could discuss nothing so long as the draft included the proposed article on religious toleration. This was indeed awkward, for Canning had made clear that unless the Mexicans were prepared to be more tolerant there could be no treaty. As described in chapter 6, Hervey had earlier won from the Mexicans a concession over rights of burial of those who were not Roman Catholics; but Canning was determined to extend this to full freedon for British subjects to worship openly as Protestants. He had been made aware by Ward that this would not be easy and he was prepared if necessary to be flexible over wording. If the Mexicans could not publicly commit themselves to the right of British subjects to worship as they wanted in their own homes or build their own churches, there must at least be wording allowing them 'to celebrate Divine Service with proper decorum', and a secret article making clear that the Mexican authorities accepted that they should be allowed to build their own churches 'so soon as the efforts of the Government shall have succeeded in obviating the difficulties now apprehended to such a measure'. But something about this was 'indispensable to the treaty'.[14]

Ward had obviously realized that feelings could run high against Protestants; but he had also, correctly, understood that Mexico's political leaders wished to get away from the old Inquisition atmosphere and demonstrate a new liberality in matters of conscience. What he apparently was not aware of was the provision in the constitution which absolutely forbade the practice of any other religion than the 'Catholic, Apostolic and Roman'. He and Canning could be forgiven for not having seen the specific reference to this in the depatch reporting the adoption of the constitution which Morier had sent from Jalapa on 2 November 1824 since this was not received in the Foreign Office until 20 January 1825.[15] But Hervey had also drawn attention to it in his despatch dated 18 July 1824 and this had been received on 18 September of that year.[16] As the Foreign Office docket is marked 'Copy for The King' it is inconceivable that it was not seen by Canning then, and very remiss on someone's part if it had not been shown to Ward when he was being briefed for his return to Mexico. It was quite clear from this that it was not in the power of the Mexican government to allow the practice of the Protestant religion in any form. And Alamán and Esteva now made it very clear to Morier and Ward that while they personally, and the president, were sympathetic to the British wishes

> such was the state of public feeling upon this subject that it was as much as their own individual existence was worth to propose it to Congress .... Whatever might be the *private* feelings of the members of the Adminstration, & of that body, yet *publicly* they would be obliged to vote against it ... that if they did not do so unanimously the consequences to themselves individually, to all strangers, and to the whole future of the Government might be of the most fatal kind .... They lamented the present feelings of bigotry and fanaticism which pervaded the great mass of the nation, but they were to be laid to the deplorable effect of three centuries of darkness and religious despotism.

All they were prepared to concede in the treaty was wording guaranteeing that British subjects would 'not be disturbed, prevented or annoyed on account of their religion'.

Morier and Ward were unprepared for such an unqualified rejection of the proposals and they were in a quandary. Were they to disobey instructions, or should they break off all further negotiations? In either case the responsibility was heavy. It was now clear that for the Mexicans there were two absolutely vital matters, specific British recognition of their independence and the exclusion of an article by which they would concede the right of Protestants to practise their religion. But Morier and Ward could not, as present day diplomats can, get further instructions more or less instantaneously. At best this would take four or five months. Could they risk such delay, with the possibility that the Mexicans in the meantime would lose patience? There must have been long hours of anxious discussion between them that evening before they decided that they should depart from their instructions and make concessions to the Mexicans. But they were not going to give in without a struggle.

On his way back to England Ward had renewed his personal contact with Victoria in Vera Cruz and their friendship had been warmly reinforced. On his return a year later he had immediately sent a personal letter to Victoria in the capital expressing his pleasure at being back. Morier had approved of this, realizing that the cultivation of this friendship could be of value. And Victoria's reply to Ward had been very warm:

> My dear Sir and esteemed friend
>
> Your happy return to a country which you have thought deserving of so much consideration and kind offices was always to me an object of the greatest interest, even had you not arrived charged with instructions which must (without doubt) conduce to the felicity and prosperity of our respective countries .... It is most agreeable to me that Mr Morier and yourself should be the Commissioners appointed to conclude a treaty of commerce with us, and the result will prove to you more strongly if possible that my opinions and wishes are the same as those which I had the honor of expressing to you in Vera Cruz .... I am also most anxious that your lady should enjoy in her journey to the Capital all accommodation possible and the strictest orders have been given to this effect.[17]

In light of that Morier decided at this difficult moment that Ward should seek a private audience with the president. This took place early next morning, the 28th.

Ward found Victoria 'not only mortified, but deeply afflicted by the failure of the negotiations' and he must have felt very sure of the president's regard for him, for he spoke almost as a parent to an erring son. He stressed 'the blow which the credit of the Mexican Government would receive if a treaty which it had been at such pains to announce in the most solemn manner ... should be broken off'. He challenged Victoria to say whether he was satisfied with the good faith of Britain and, if he was, to say why therefore he was prepared to risk the complete breakdown of negotiations on the matter of an article about independence. Victoria could not understand the refusal to have a specific mention of independence in the treaty when, according to Michelena, Canning had told the diplomatic corps in London 'in the strongest and most unequivocal manner' of this recognition: 'Mr Canning's very words had been transmitted to him by Mr Michelena.' Ward begged to question this: 'Without wishing to accuse Mr Michelena of having been too precipitate in his communications' there was no doubt that he had not been present at the interviews between Canning and the accredited foreign representatives. Canning, he knew, had simply told them that Britain was about to enter into treaties of friendship and commerce with Mexico and Colombia, and they were left to draw from this the natural inference that Britain conceived these states 'to have established their independence on so solid a basis that she did not risk seeing her own dignity compromised by entering into treaties with them, the stipulations of which nothing but the firm establishment of their independence could enable them to fulfil'.

Victoria was persuaded by Ward's arguments to give way over the need for a separate article; but he stressed the need for unanimous ratification by Congress, who would be looking out for issues such as this. Could not something be said in the preamble, such as 'the provinces of America which now form the independent Republic of Mexico'? Ward explained the objection to the word 'Republic' but agreed to see what could be done. He then turned to the issue of religious toleration, explaining that he had not understood that the constitution tied the president's hands and had assured Canning that some concession on this would willingly be made. Victoria was sympathetic but said that to give preference to British subjects would be disastrous and might arouse popular fury which could not be controlled. He would, however, be prepared to consider any formula which avoided this danger. Ward then suggested a sentence 'Perfect liberty of conscience shall be granted to [British subjects] provided they respect the laws and customs of the country.' Victoria objected to this on the ground that from time immemorial 'liberty of conscience' had been the term used by priests in Mexico to express a total want of all religion or morality whatsoever: 'Moreover, the Inquisition, now happily abolished, was the only tribunal that ever pretended to take cognisance of affairs of conscience. Why therefore introduce a term which might give umbrage without the possibility of conferring any substantial right? .... The more that could be *done* and the less *said* the better.' Ward explained that it was essential to have something in the treaty 'by which, in case of any disturbance originating in … fanaticism … the representative of Great Britain might have the right to *demand* the most energetic interference on the part of the Mexican Government' and that without such an article a treaty could not be signed. With this Victoria gave way, agreeing, moreover, that there should be an additional article ensuring that the many important points remaining to be decided would be reconsidered after 'the shortest possible period'. (Ward failed to get Victoria to agree to a definite time of five years.)

Ward had done well and it was clear when he and Morier met Alamán and Esteva next day that they were under instructions to be as accommodating as possible. Nevertheless, it was still not easy going.

They reverted, for example, to the need for a provision allowing them to grant special privileges to Spain and indeed to any other European power which recognized their independence – and, surprisingly, to the other former Spanish colonies. When they told Morier that such mutual privileges were already in their treaty with Colombia, he felt bound to agree to their inclusion in the treaty with Britain; but he still objected to these being extended to Spain, on the ground that if Spain now recognized Mexican independence they would be doing no more than Britain was doing. The Mexicans argued that Spanish recognition would be different, because it would not be recognition of a fact so much as a cession of a right. And they reminded Morier that it had been the British who had urged them to make such a concession. Moreover, there was an article in the Colombian treaty with the USA which allowed this.

Eventually, after three more days of discussion, it proved possible to agree a full text, mainly because Morier and Ward made considerable concessions (many of which Canning later refused to endorse). The formula finally agreed for religion was that British subjects in Mexico would

> enjoy in their houses, persons and properties the protection of the Government; and, continuing in possession of what they now enjoy, they shall not be disturbed, molested or annoyed in any manner on account of their religion, provided they respect that of the nation in which they reside, as well as the constitution, laws and customs of the country.

Their burial rights were also confirmed, and it was understood that in effect this meant that British subjects could practise their religion within the privacy of their own homes without being persecuted, while it avoided an overt declaration to this effect, which would have been contrary to the constitution.

As regards trading privileges, Morier and Ward agreed to these being extended to the other former colonies, and to Spain if she recognized Mexican independence but only for a strictly limited period. They also agreed that the Mexicans, for a limited period, could grant better terms for imports into and exports from their ports when carried in Mexican ships than they would grant to British ships, thus departing from the principle of strict reciprocity to which Canning attached importance. There was also a completely new article, not envisaged by Canning, giving the protection of the British flag to Mexican persons and goods carried in British naval ships and, to the extent that Britain gave this to other nations, in merchant ships as well. This had been requested by the Mexicans to provide some protection in case of war with Spain in which Britain remained neutral (and was another concession which Canning later refused to sanction).

Morier and Ward tried to get exemption for British subjects from military service and 'forced loans'. They were successful over the first, but had to yield over the second. The Mexicans argued that if circumstances should arise, for instance in case of foreign invasion, when the government might find it necessary to raise additional funds from all inhabitants, it would not be fair if the 'wealthy' British merchants were exempt. It was finally agreed that the text would make clear that in no circumstances could British subjects be compelled to pay any tax greater than one payable by native Mexicans.

Finally, the Mexicans wanted an article recognizing their blockade of Ulloa. Morier considered that this was quite unsuitable for a treaty designed to establish principles governing the relations between the two countries. But he wished to show that he understood the importance of this for the Mexicans. He did so by showing them the despatch he had sent to London after the Napier business, and this persuaded the Mexicans of British sincerity. Morier went further, however, making a solemn and public declaration:

> During the negotiation of this treaty we have been repeatedly urged by the Mexican Plenipotentiaries to make the strict observance of the blockade of St John of Ulloa the subject of a separate article, to which we have been forced to refuse our assent, not being duly authorised by our instructions to enter upon this subject. But we have no hesitation in stating, and we do hereby state it to be our opinion that the greatest regard ought to be paid by such Captains and Commanders of His Majesty's Navy as may enter the port of Vera Cruz to the regulations established by the Mexican Government upon this subject, and that any Captain who shall in any way infringe these regulations will incur the heaviest responsibility. We further take this opportunity of pointing out to Captains and Commanders of His Majesty's Navy the necessity of perfect concert between them and His Majesty's diplomatic servants in Mexico, as the consequences of any difference of opinion between them upon a

> point in which all Mexicans take so deep an interest cannot but prove highly detrimental to His Majesty's service, as well as to the character and influence of Great Britain.[18]

There cannot often, if ever, have been such a thinly disguised public rebuke to the British navy pronounced by a British diplomat.

Morier and Ward felt they had done well, and the agreed text was signed on 6 April (see Appendix I). They realized that they would have to convince Canning that it was right to have departed in so many ways from their instructions; and one of their justifications would be that they had wanted to avoid difficulties over Mexican ratification. They assumed, after yielding to so many of the Mexican arguments in which precisely this point had been made, that this would be little more than a formality; and Morier, with much relief, made his preparations for an early departure for London with the Mexican instrument of ratification, while Ward looked forward to being left for the first time in charge of a diplomatic mission – and in the glow of a thoroughly satisfactory understanding with the Mexicans. Emily looked forward to her first confinement taking place in a house she could almost call her own, with her husband relaxed and less hard worked. As they were all to discover during the next two years, however, in Mexico it is the unexpected rather than the expected which happens.

11

RELUCTANT MEXICAN RATIFICATION OF THE TREATY – APRIL TO MAY 1825

Morier and Ward, having believed that Mexican ratification of the treaty was a formality, had to wait almost six weeks for Congress to approve it. Twice during this time they had to exercise brinkmanship of a high order, for both the Chamber of Deputies and the Senate got it into their heads that Mexico was being cheated by a nation bent on obtaining exclusive privileges and denying full recognition of her hard won independence. This was not the fault of Victoria, but the result of the make up of an infant elected body, many of the members of which had had little real education and few of whom had had any opportunity to gain an understanding of the world outside their own frontiers. They had thrown out the Spaniards by their own unaided efforts and then had had to deliver themselves from a despotic, self-imposed emperor. It was perhaps understandable that they were suspicious of the motives of these emissaries of an imperial power and reluctant to accept without deep questioning what they proposed. What was less understandable was the failure of either Victoria or the British commissioners to anticipate this reaction.

To Morier and Ward, the way their treaty was received in Congress was a great disappointment, and they were hard put to it to explain it to Canning, especially as at the time they did not realize that there was also a deliberate attempt being made by some of Victoria's closest colleagues to sabotage the new treaty completely. They asked Canning to understand 'the difficulties with which any negotiations here must be attended until time has softened down that extraordinary compound of ignorance, suspicion and fanaticism which now forms the most striking feature of the national character'. There had been wild rumours circulating, they explained, that Britain was demanding such things as the cession of all Mexican territory north of Tampico, the right to garrison Vera Cruz with 20,000 troops and, greatly garbled, religious freedom. In this atmosphere, the committee of twelve deputies instructed to report on the treaty, 'individuals, most of whom were entirely ignorant of the forms of diplomatic intercourse and consequently apprehensive of being overreached in the simplest stipulations', were 'inclined to discover mystery in the most ordinary expression'.[1]

The main stumbling block for the deputies was the reference to the 'most favoured nation'. This principle was a central plank of Canning's foreign policy. Although Britain at that time really did rule the waves and could have sold her protection of infant nations such as Mexico for all kinds of exclusive trading advantages, this was no part of Canning's philosophy. All he wanted was the same conditions for all so that Britain's merchants could win on merit alone. But the Mexican deputies, unable to believe in such apparent philanthropy, were convinced that the most-favoured-nation clause meant that Mexico would be losing for ever the power to give any privileges to any other country. Alamán (who, with Esteva, was described by Morier and Ward as being 'indefatigable' in efforts to clear up misunderstandings) advised Morier not to try to intervene in this directly, as this 'would inevitably produce a contrary effect'; so the two commissioners could only sit anxiously in the wings for some ten days. Then, on 17 April, they were told that all was well – except that the President himself now wanted changes.

The text agreed by Morier and Ward allowed Mexico, if she wished, to give certain trading advantages to Spain which need not be extended to Britain so long as they were granted to Spain alone. It was understood that the Mexicans still hoped to use this departure from the most-favoured-nation principle to persuade Spain to recognize their independence. Victoria now suddenly decided that he would rather not have this specific reference to Spain and, moreover, that he wanted the phrase 'most favoured nation' to read 'any other nation whatsoever'. Alamán professed not to know the reason for this, but he urged Morier and Ward to accept. Because they thought it must indicate a hostility towards Spain, they were prepared to agree.

Next day Morier received from Alamán, in confidence, a copy of the report the committee were about to present to Congress. This contained a long and turgid explanation of why the committee had eventually decided to accept the absence of an article specifically recognizing independence, even though this did not satisfy public expectation, and also an equally long discourse on the most-favoured-nation issue which showed that they still completely misunderstood this term. They still thought it meant that *Britain* would be more favoured than any other nation. This document greatly upset Morier and Ward, who thought that 'instead of doing justice to the liberal policy of His Majesty's Government' it appeared 'to hold up England as an object of jealousy and suspicion, to cry down the services which she had already rendered this country, to excite doubts and fears with respect to her future conduct'. And they found that it contained contradictions and a 'great deficiency of talent'. They conveyed their dismay to Alamán, who 'expressed as strongly as we could desire his sentiments with respect to the injustice and ingratitude of the Committee' and agreed that steps must be taken to counteract the effect it might have on Congress. He allowed Morier and Ward to take a copy so that they could prepare a reply, but 'requested us to draw up two protocols of imaginary conferences in which he and Esteva might be supposed to have communicated to us the principal arguments of the Committee, and thus enable him, if questioned upon the subject, to account to the Congress for our having answered them without having been in possession of the report itself, which he ought not to have entrusted us with'. Morier and Ward agreed to this, but not without expressing themselves forcibly:

> If we could for a moment suppose that we should find in the Congress the same illiberal feelings towards England which had been displayed by the Committee, we would never so far lose sight of what was due to the character of our country as to stoop to solicit their friendship. If, as he assured us, the report of the Committee were nothing more than the last effort of a few infatuated men who wished at any price to avert a blow which they thought would prove fatal to their own petty interests, we would gladly do all in our power to prevent the public from falling into the snare. But if the Congress allowed itself to be led astray by their arguments, and gave its sanction to this report, we should consider it inconsistent with out duty to hold any further

communication with an Assembly capable of such gross injustice, and should leave Mexico without waiting, or even applying for any further instructions.

Alamán assured them that this was no more than he had expected, and urged them to express themselves equally robustly in their written reply to him and give it as much publicity as possible. So Morier and Ward did so:

> It is neither the wish, nor would it be worthy of the character of Great Britain to force her friendship upon any of the American States. If they choose to accept it upon such terms as may appear likely to promote the interests of both nations, well and good; if they do not, it is not England that will be the loser by a temporary suspension of intercourse .... It is in Mexico's interest to see merchants from every part of the world flock to their markets and endeavour to undersell each other to them. The Committee appears to have mistaken, by some extraordinary mental delusion, a free competition for an absolute monopoly, words which we trust Congress will know how to appreciate in a very different manner. England neither demands nor wishes to be considered as *the favored nation*. All that she requires is to be put upon equal terms with every other, and she trusts to her own resources and industry to give her the only advantages in the Mexican market which she wishes to possess.

There was a passage in the committee report which asked rhetorically what England had done to deserve the privileges which Mexico would be conferring in the proposed treaty. Morier and Ward responded vigorously to this, pointing out that Britain alone had prevented the powers of the Holy Alliance from intervening on Spain's behalf. And how, they asked, could Mexico develop without the help of British industry and capital? By dealing with Mexico as an independent state, Britain was risking war with the whole continent of Europe. Yet all she was asking was that she should have equal privileges with those that had not done as much. And they said that if the treaty were not ratified, or if one of its fundamental articles were rejected, Morier would return to England and Ward (who might be compelled by family circumstances to remain in Mexico for a while) would hold no official communication with the government, nor await fresh instructions. The

Consul General would also leave. They were both convinced that Britain would never conclude a treaty except on the terms now proposed, and that, consequently, 'there must be a cessation of all communication until the Congress of Mexico be inclined to approve of them'. They deeply regretted having to make this threat but unless 'we meet in the Congress a more liberal and amicable spirit than we have found in the Committee, we should conceive it to be a positive dereliction of duty not to carry it into execution'.

It was daring of Morier and Ward to go public with such a threat, for if their bluff had been called they might have found themselves in deep water at home, given the very great anxiety of the commercial community to have a treaty.[2] But the publicity given to this outburst had the desired effect – except in one respect. The committee, perhaps somewhat riled by the language used (the reference to 'mental delusion' cannot have helped) made 'a most insidious proposal … at a time when they probably began to be sensible of their own weakness'. They proposed that the treaty should be accepted, but with a terminal date. This news was given to Ward in person by the President on the 21st. Ward naturally rejected the idea out of hand, while nevertheless expressing pleasure that at least Congress seemed to be taking some notice of public opinion. Victoria replied 'that he most sincerely hoped this might be the case, as he felt that the honor of the Mexican Government was as deeply interested in carrying the treaty through as that of Great Britain'. And he then explained that the real problem was the question of preferences for Spain. There was one faction in favour and one totally against, and as the one thought the treaty gave too little in this respect while the other thought it gave too much, unless some change was introduced all would be against it. He thought the only way of getting a vote in favour of ratification was to conciliate with one or other of these two factions, either by allowing Spain to make her own terms with Mexico without restriction, or by having in the treaty a clause that no privileges should ever be granted to her. For his part he gave his 'vote for the last measure, for though as President I may have been persuaded into consenting to the clause in favor of Spain … as an individual I shall always oppose any concession in favor of that infamous country or her odious government'. Ward made clear that either alternative was quite unacceptable; and he and Morier then let Alamán know that a special courier had been sent to Vera Cruz to hold up the departure of the Jamaica mail, so that if necessary they could send a special despatch to England reporting their own imminent departure and the reason for it, and that *Egeria* had been warned to stand by for them.

Alamán and Esteva called on Morier and Ward that evening to make a last appeal for something with which they could soften Congress. Morier and Ward stood firm. Esteva then suggested that because Congress attached weight to keeping in line with Colombia (with which country Britain was negotiating a similar treaty at the same time), perhaps there could be agreement to a time limit for the Mexican treaty with Britain if one were accepted in Britain's treaty with Colombia. Morier and Ward 'gave a most reluctant consent' to this, but only on the understanding that it was presented to Congress as a last resort. They 'considered it as childish in the extreme .... But still, as the Mexican Plenipotentiaries represented they were treating with children, unacquainted with business ... rather than break off the treaty absolutely they might venture to humour them ... if it were impossible to avoid it'. (The treaty with Colombia had in fact been signed in Bogotá three days before this, on the 18th, without any time limit. Possibly the Mexicans had had some design to try to get them to include one.) Next day, however, Morier and Ward thought better of this and wrote to Alamán to suggest that as Congress might now understand the proper significance of the most-favoured-nation principle, there was no need for a link with the Colombian treaty, which indeed would be undignified for Mexico. 'Word it how we may, the article proposed must still wear a character of puerility which cannot fail to throw a shade of ridicule upon all parties concerned ... we ... trust that you will not commit us by proposing an alternative to which it will not be in our power to consent.'

The debate on the committee's report began in the Chamber of Deputies on Friday 22 April and was then interrupted until Monday the 25th. The next day the preamble and first four articles were approved by 44 votes to 12. Morier had already asked Alamán to warn Congress that if he did not get back to England with the Mexican ratification by early June there would be no hope of British ratification before Parliament rose for the summer recess during the last week of that month. But the pro-Spanish faction fought all the way, even though the majority in favour of the treaty never dropped below 40, and final approval of the whole was not obtained until the 29th. Morier and Ward felt that an article in the paper *El Sol* on the 25th, written unattributably by Alamán, had helped considerably. In this the writer, purporting not to know in detail what the treaty contained,

1. Guadalupe Victoria, first President of Mexico. Engraving reproduced in Alaman's *Historia de Mejico desde 1808*, volume 5, published in 1952.

2. George Canning. Portrait by Thomas Lawrence. (By permission of the National Portrait Gallery, London.)

JAMES MORIER

3. James Justinian Morier, *c* 1832. Engraving by Alfred Croquis appearing as the frontispiece for *Hajji Baba of Ispahan in England* in the 1942 edition (first published in 1833).

4. Henry George Ward, Britain's first chargé d'affaires, aged about 43. Engraving by W.H. Mote from a painting by James Holmes, *c* 1838. (By kind permission of Philippa Richards.)

5. Emily Ward (née Swinburne) aged about 18. Portrait by William Mulready RA, *c* 1816. (By kind permission of John Browne-Swinburne.)

6. Chapultepec, Mexico, from the lake, 1826. From the sketchbook of Emily Ward. (By kind permission of Philippa Richards.)

7. Church of Our Lady of Guadalupe, Mexico, 1826. From the sketchbook of Emily Ward. (By kind permission of Philippa Richards.)

8. HMS *Phaeton*, 1822. From a watercolour by Schetky. (By kind permission of the National Maritime Museum, London.)

declared that it was

> already ascertained that England has required no exclusive privileges … that every thing has been concluded upon the basis of perfect reciprocity … if one nation is to be preferred above another is there any one which deserves it better than England? She in fact is the first among those of Europe which has done us the justice to declare that we ought to be admitted in the rank of Nations … her resources have supplied the deficiencies of our finances …. But she asks nothing – she desires nothing but to have our markets opened to her upon equal terms with other nations …. England without Mexico will always be the first nation in the world, whereas Mexico without England can be nothing …. To what would be reduced the friendship which we think of gaining from other nations if they knew that we had lost that of England [by rejecting the treaty]?

And he gave a clear and simple explanation of the term 'most favoured nation' which was worrying deputies.[3]

When Morier and Ward reported to Canning that the Chamber of Deputies had at last agreed to the treaty, they thought their troubles were over and seem to have been torn between a desire not to give a bad impression of Mexico and a natural wish to show what they had had to overcome. They wrote: 'As things have terminated favourably we could wish, Sir, for the credit of Mexico to throw a veil over the events of the last three weeks; but we feel we cannot, consistently with our duty, refrain from laying before you all the circumstances of the case.' But they ended on a very optimistic note, believing that the passage through the Senate was no more than a formality. Indeed they had been assured that they had 'overcome the only difficulties which we could possibly have to encounter' because of the difference 'between the manner in which the treaty was about to be received in the Senate, and the frivolous pretences under which its progress through the Chamber of Deputies had been delayed'. Alamán had told them that 'the party which had hitherto opposed us was much too discouraged by its late defeat to venture upon a fresh attack, and only wished to seek in obscurity a refuge from public resentment'. In this Alamán was wrong, and Morier and Ward had to eat their words. Or at least they chose to, for in their final report after the Senate had eventually approved the treaty they wrote: 'We will not attempt to modify the terms [of their earlier despatch although] it might indeed be in our power in doing so to acquire credit for a penetration which, we acknowledge, we did not possess .... But it is our wish [to give] a clear perception of the impossibility of drawing any inference in this country from appearances or even facts which in any other would be conclusive.' And, considering that absolutely everyone who counted had assured them that approval by the Senate was only a formality, they can surely be forgiven for again getting it wrong.

In fact, it all began very well. On 3 May the Senate foreign affairs committee was instructed to examine the text and report without delay. They began on the 6th, a Friday, when discussion was stood over until the Monday. Alamán and Esteva were so sure that all was now safely gathered in that they urged Morier to set off for Vera Cruz at once, saying that they would send the Mexican instrument of ratification after him by special courier. They had even had the instrument, complete with seal, prepared, ready for Victoria's signature. Morier handed over to Ward on the Sunday and left next day. By Wednesday, however, Alamán had to confess to Ward that things were not going as expected: 13 out of the 30 members had signed a motion demanding an article specifically recognizing independence. He had in fact realized some time before that this would be the case, but, with a disarming explanation characteristic of so many Mexicans, who do not like to give offence with unwelcome news, he said that he 'had wished to conceal or at least palliate what was passing … but he was now convinced that secrecy was impossible'. In reply to a suggestion from Ward, he said he thought it would be wrong to recall Morier 'as it would give an importance to our adversaries which he would be very unwilling to allow them'. Ward then wondered if the opposition might be able to spin things out until the time when the present session of Congress would end and so achieve the same result as if the Senate had refused to ratify. Alamán thought this would only be possible if they introduced a proposition which required Morier to return for further consultation with them, and he did not think the Senate would agree to this. Ward, however, was taking no risks. He wrote to Alamán inviting him to make known to the Senate that he would rather take upon himself 'the whole responsibility of breaking off the treaty … than countenance a delay by which, under pretence of holding communication with Mr Morier at Jalapa, time would be gained and the session, perhaps, brought to a close without any definitive resolution being adopted'. He made clear that if that should happen, he himself would remain in Mexico pending the receipt of further instructions from London, because 'the proposal [for an article on independence made in the Senate] is not couched in that illiberal spirit which characterised the report of the Committee'. However, he expressed the view that the British government would choose 'to break off all connexion with Mexico until she is disposed to do more justice to the liberal policy of Great Britain'. The Senate gave way, and the Mexican ratification was signed on 19 May.

In the joint despatch reporting the final ratification, Morier and Ward were at pains to explain that the opposition to the treaty was not a true reflection of the feelings of the nation or of the opinions of the government. They gave credit to Alamán and Esteva, and indeed to every member of the government, for their efforts to get it ratified. They drew particular attention to the report of the Senate committee which had said:

> There was never perhaps a treaty concluded which, in all the great principles, as well as in the minor stipulations, bore so marked a character of liberality and good faith .... England, already the asylum of liberty in Europe, is destined to become the champion of that of the nations of America, against the designs of the other governments of the Old World; and America, in her turn, may perhaps become some day the prop and support of England.

Perhaps this had stuck in the gullets of some of those senators who were not to approve the treaty on the nod. If so, who can blame them? It must have looked like unseemly toadying for a proud and newly independent nation, and may well have upset some who were not particularly opposed to the treaty. But, as emerged much later, Michelena had apparently been doing his best from London to sabotage Mexican ratification. In a private letter to Canning a year later Ward wrote:

> Would you believe, Sir, that the difficulties which we experienced last year in carrying our treaty through the Chambers originated almost entirely with *Mr Michelena himself*? Irritated, probably, at your not reposing in him a confidence to which he was not entitled, but which he wished to persuade people that he possessed, he wrote from London not to *one*, but

> to *several* deputies and senators exhorting them to be upon their guard and not to allow themselves to be deceived by the artifices of the most treacherous cabinet in all Europe! Everything, he assured them, would be liberality and candour in appearance in the articles proposed, but they would soon find to their cost that the simplest terms in English diplomacy admitted of a double interpretation.[4]

Whether Alamán and Esteva had really worked as hard as they made out to secure ratification was later brought into doubt; but at this time it gave Morier and Ward real pleasure to hand over to them the sum of 5000 pesos as 'the customary present from His Britannic Majesty to the Mexican Chancery' in celebration of the final approval of the treaty by Congress. They did, however, have a nagging fear that Canning might raise objections to the text finally approved by the Mexicans because they had been compelled to depart from the strict letter of their instructions in one or two places. Their main worry was over the concession they had made to the Mexicans in the matter of religious freedom. In their despatch reporting the signature of the treaty, they had defended this departure from their instructions by reference to the risk, had the rights requested even been mentioned publicly, to the lives and property of British subjects, explaining that it 'would probably lead to anarchy, to the entire destruction of social order and to all the horrors of religious warfare'. They had felt that to go on pressing for what Canning wanted would have run counter to the 'broad principle of liberality and generosity' with which Britain had been acting and might 'retard the consolidation of that liberty (however defective in its essence) for which this country had been so long contending and which England was so desirous she should secure'. They felt that at least they had secured 'the option of ratification, an advantage by which, however we might personally expose ourselves to censure in order to attain it, we trusted that the dignity of Great Britain would be preserved'.[5]

That was their joint explanation, but Ward insisted on taking much of the responsibility for what they had done. In a separate and personal despatch to Canning, he wrote that he had 'unfortunately been the means of misleading His Majesty's Government with respect to a point which was considered of such importance that it was made … a condition indispensable to the conclusion of the treaty' and made clear that he did not wish 'to shelter myself in any way under Mr Morier's superior experience or rank'. He suggested that Morier, because he knew that Canning had personally briefed him, might have 'attached more weight to my opinion than he would, probably, have done under other circumstances'. Having thus magnanimously tried to absolve Morier from any blame, Ward then, however, stressed that they had 'concurred throughout both in the view which we have taken of the line to be adopted … and in our resolution to expose ourselves cheerfully to any responsibility rather than allow the friendship of Great Britain to be rejected by a State which is too little known as yet to be entitled to treat with her upon a footing of equality'. He said that 'nothing could have induced us to act as we have done but the determination, at every personal risk, to consult what we conceived to be the best interests of our country .... [I do not] repent of the share which I have taken in this'.[6]

Politicians at home, and indeed the public too, do not always agree with the opinions of Foreign Office officials over where the dignity of Great Britain lies, and such high minded reasons for departing from instructions will not necessarily persuade them otherwise. In this case, it would be difficult to argue now that Morier and Ward were wrong. Had ratification gone smoothly, one could perhaps legitimately wonder whether the Mexicans might not have exaggerated the dangers of having an article which openly allowed the private practice of a religion other than the 'Catholic, Apostolic and Roman'. But, in view of the difficulties which in fact arose, it was as well that the additional problem of religion had been quietly put aside. Canning, however, did not feel inclined to agree with them, and he declined to submit the treaty for ratification by Parliament. But it was not the concessions made over religion which was the main stumbling block in his view. In departing from the original draft in other respects they had offended against important principles governing British treaty relations. As a result, it was almost two years more before a treaty was finally agreed and ratified by both governments. The satisfaction and relief felt by Morier and Ward on 19 May 1825 turned out to be misplaced, unaware as they then were of the many tribulations to come.

12

THE PROBLEMS FACED BY HENRY GEORGE WARD – MAY TO DECEMBER 1825

With Mexican ratification of the treaty now secured, Ward at last became Chargé d'affaires, changed from fledgling to fully grown professional diplomat. But he had already been showing his mettle. In his family correspondence and in his relations with Canning there was evidence of growing self-confidence. He had considerable natural charm which, allied with an intelligent and industrious application to the job in hand, obviously appealed to Canning and Morier. He had an infectious enthusiasm which they rightly did not mistake for presumptuousness, for there was still a genuine modesty behind it. On the other hand, his success in cultivating Victoria's friendship and trust, and the realization that his opinions were carrying considerable weight with his superiors, had the effect of making him less aware than he should have been of the dangers of assuming, and acting with, more independent authority than his masters in London meant him to have. In face-to-face dealings his personality would have helped to avoid this. At a distance, in correspondence, he did not have this protection, and he ran this danger particularly with Planta, through whose hands all but his most personal correspondence with Canning passed and who in fact drafted almost everything signed by Canning to be sent to Mexico. (Amendments to those drafts by Canning were rare.) Planta was by then an old hand and a stickler for form. Born in 1787 at the British Museum, where his father was Keeper of Manuscripts (and later Principal Librarian), he had become a Clerk in the Foreign Office at the age of 15. By the age of 20 he was Canning's précis writer and he went with Castlereagh to the Congress of Vienna and other such international meetings. He was already Permanent Under Secretary when Canning succeeded Castlereagh in 1822 and it is probable that he did not altogether share Canning's enthusiasm for Spanish America. It was not long after Ward became Chargé d'affaires in Mexico that Planta began to feel that they had in him a young man who was possibly too big for his boots; and it is more than probable that it was his influence that turned Canning against him less than two years later.[1]

At this time, however, Ward was showing political sensitivity and an appropriate degree of diffidence in his reporting. Canning obviously felt that if anyone could advance his policies towards Mexico, Ward could; and Morier must have realized that without Ward, with his background in Spain and fluency in the language, he would never have succeeded in steering the negotiations and the ratification to such a satisfactory conclusion. It was Ward who saw more clearly than Morier how it was necessary to deal with the Mexicans (even if he did not see it with complete clarity). Possibly Morier may have felt slightly piqued that it was Ward, his junior, who received the personal briefing from Canning and who, indeed, had even managed to persuade him to shift his position on some issues. Another in Morier's place might have taken umbrage and might have swung rank, refusing to listen to the younger man; but he did not, and the course of the negotiations and the very drafting of the reports on them bear much evidence of Ward's influence. Indeed, Morier put his signature in Vera Cruz to a final despatch sent to him from the capital by Ward, who must have drafted much of it after Morier had left for the coast.

Morier, of course, had not embarked on the Mexican mission with any great enthusiasm; and by the time Ward had arrived with the draft treaty he had probably become disillusioned about reaping any personal advantage from it. Mexican society at that time can have been little to his liking and he would have been glad to let Ward, on his return, make the running, especially as he found the place bad for his health. Writing to his brother not long after his arrival he had said: 'I have scarcely been well since I have been here, and the swellings in my legs, gout or rheumatism whatever it may be, have returned with undoubted vigour ... one is subject ever & anon to dysenteries that leave one in a sad state of langour.' And Francis Baring (of the banking family), who was in Mexico at the time, had observed that 'the whole household at S' Cosme (Morier's) is sick by turns – rheumatism & intermittent fever are the most common & are dangerous to persons of weak habit'.[2] Morier was glad to get back to England and probably no longer interested in the prospect of returning to be Britain's first Minister Plenipotentiary in Mexico. He must have felt, at least, that he was leaving things in excellent hands, an opinion which Ward himself undoubtedly held. But Ward soon discovered that the change from fledgling to fully grown diplomat meant that he was cast, alone, into a not wholly friendly environment.

Ward had felt the strain of the long drawn out ratification processes and the anxieties over the birth of his first child. A daughter, Frances, was born on 19 April 1825. Emily showed great spirit in going through this experience uncomplainingly even though her husband could not give her his undivided support. Ward himself felt this keenly. He wrote to his father-in-law after the ratification was finally obtained: 'I have had an immense deal to do, but this, as I like to work, is exactly what I wished. The only thing which I have regretted has been my being continually kept away from dear Em .... I need not tell you how well she has borne what she knew was an unavoidable evil. From today I hope to be more at liberty.' And he was delighted with the child: 'The only fault I have to find with the little wretch which she has brought into the world is that the Ward nose has beat the Swinburne quite out of the field, which, as the creature happens to be a girl, I think might have been dispensed with. In all other respects it is a very fine lamens and squalls quite as melodiously (tho' not I must say quite so often) as a lamens of its dimensions usually does.' But he admitted to being 'completely tired & overworked'. However, he had the great consolation of being 'now installed in all the honors of my chargé d'affaireship. I wish you could see our splendid establishment here – Si, Señor! Splendid! – for I do not know a more delightful home anywhere, and the furniture which we brought out with us has enabled us to fit up a suite of rooms beautifully'.[3]

It was indeed a splendid home. But the government property in it, which Ward took over on 8 May, originally purchased by Hervey and added to by Morier, was an odd assortment. For example, the inventory included only 12 silver teaspoons, but 60 knives and forks. There were 16 champagne glasses, but 252 wine glasses. There were a piano and two carriages, one English and one Mexican, with seven carriage mules to go with them, plus five load carrying mules and five horses; but the harnesses were deficient. There was a double-barrelled shotgun, but no mention of cartridges. However, as though in compensation, there were seven boxes of cigars. And, no doubt very welcome to Emily, there were three cows and a calf.[4] Modern diplomatic inventories can be tiresomely illogical, but not usually to that extent.

Ward presented Canning's letter appointing him Chargé d'affaires to Alamán on the 21 May.[5] On Tuesday the 31st he was presented in that capacity to President Victoria. This was a formal occasion at which both he and Victoria made the usual polite speeches; but the formality simply concealed the warmth of personal regard they each felt for the other, warmth that continued to be of the utmost value to Ward. At first, however, Ward felt that it would be a breach of correct diplomatic etiquette to attempt to take full advantage of this. He felt bound to conduct his official relations through the Foreign Minister. Alamán, however, now turned out to be not quite the whole-hearted friend of Britain he had seemed during the negotiations, and Ward was soon confronted by some tricky problems. The first of these came up within a few days of the ratification of the treaty by the Senate, when a version of its text appeared in a pamphlet on sale on the streets. Morier had impressed on Alamán the need for complete secrecy until the British government had seen and agreed it, so Ward naturally turned to him for an explanation of this breach of confidence. Alamán told him an extraordinary story. The text had been sold to the printers by two 'léperos' (ruffianly scoundrels) who had given their names and claimed to be the writers of the pamphlet. They had been paid for it. When arrested it became obvious that they must have obtained the text from someone in the Congress, but they refused to reveal a name. The only punishment which the law could inflict was a short imprisonment, and it was assumed that they thought this was worth the money they had received. Alamán assured Ward that the few copies of the treaty which it had been necessary to provide for members of Congress had always been collected at the end of every day; but it had been impossible to control them while actually in the possession of deputies and senators. Ward accepted Alamán's assurance that he deeply regretted what had happened and told him that he was sure Canning

> would acquit him of having had a share in a publication from which the Mexican Government could derive no possible advantage, while it must naturally tend to produce the most unpleasant impression in England where a sort of publicity would be given to the treaty before His Majesty's Government

> had had time to consider whether it should be honored with His Majesty's ratification or not.[6]

The possibility that Alamán himself had been party to this breach of confidence did not occur to Ward. It may be unfair to suggest now that he was; but he was certainly behind the next problem that Ward had to deal with. This was a Mexican attempt to make political capital out of Britain's treaty with Colombia, a copy of which was received in Mexico about the middle of June. The text was published in the press, with an anonymous article referring to it as 'perhaps the most complete justification of all that we have said respecting our treaty with Britain', and saying that although the two texts were almost identical, there was the important difference that the Colombian treaty did not contain 'the articles essentially favourable to Mexico, or at least the advantageous stipulations of those articles exist only in a less degree'. After giving some examples of this, it ended: 'In short, this treaty with Colombia is a most complete triumph for the Mexican negotiators who have secured to their country advantages which Colombia under similar circumstances was unable to obtain.'

As Alamán was known to be closely associated with the newspaper concerned, it was generally assumed that he was the author of this commentary; and he did not attempt to deny this when tackled by Ward. But he tried to justify his action by reference to the need 'to raise the character of the Government in the eyes of the people'. Ward accepted this explanation; but he was nevertheless highly irritated, particularly at Alamán's having made a special point, in the commentary, of the 'success' of the Mexicans in forcing the British to climb down over religious freedom. Ward pointed out that in accepting the text of their treaty as proposed, the Colombians had made sure of British ratification, whereas there was now no such assurance in the case of the Mexican treaty: moreover, if the Mexicans were now going to crow over their 'victory', what store could he set by their assurances that they would do everything in their power to work for more religious toleration? Alamán does not seem to have responded to this; and to make matters worse, a society had been formed, to which even Victoria himself and other ministers were open subscribers, for promoting new religious processions 'to counteract the effect of an influx of heretics'. No wonder Ward expressed the fear to Canning that the Mexicans were losing sight 'of the tacit engagement which they entered into with us, and to be taking steps rather to encourage than diminish that spirit of fanaticism which His Majesty's Government may still consider as a bar to any cordial or immediate union between the two countries'.[7]

Ward was someone who found it difficult to believe that people he was doing business with were not as straight as he. Although irritated by Alamán's actions, he still did not see in them any ulterior motive suggesting that he might be a 'false friend'. But, alas, this was the truth, and Ward was forced to believe it might be so when he discovered that he was behind the attempt to get an entirely unsuitable man appointed to London as Chargé d'affaires to replace Michelena. When Ward had been sent back to Mexico in January 1825, Canning had instructed him and Morier to take an early opportunity of making clear to Victoria that Michelena would not be acceptable to His Majesty's Government as Mexico's plenipotentiary once the treaty was ratified. Canning's explanation had been not unreasonable:

> I beg to be understood as not finding any fault with [Michelena's] conduct during the arduous time that he has passed here, nor making any complaint against him. Quite otherwise. But M. Michelena is a Spaniard[8]; he is connected by ties of familiarity with many of the individuals most obnoxious to the Spanish Government; and his presence here, in an acknowledged public character while the war (however nominal) between Spain and Mexico continues, or while civil commotion continues to agitate Spain, would not fail to expose His Majesty's Government to endless remonstrances and representations from the Court of Spain, and to create lasting difficulties for the friendly reception of the Mexican Envoy among the corps of foreign Ministers in London.
>
> The independence of Mexico once established, it is to its interest to forget and to put out of sight as much as possible its former connexion with Spain, not to keep alive the memory of it by petty and avoidable causes of irritation. For this purpose, above all things, the Mexican Minister in London should be a *Mexican*, not a Spaniard.[9]

This request from Canning was not mentioned to Alamán until the end of the negotiations in April. They were assured that it would be met. What was not revealed then, however, was that Victoria already had his own reasons for wanting Michelena out of London. As Ward discovered some time later, Victoria had never trusted him, and it was only because he was anxious to get Michelena out of the country at that time that he had been persuaded to ratify the appointment to London.[10] Indeed, it seems that moves may already have been afoot to recall Michelena before Morier and Ward mentioned Canning's wishes. In November 1824 Michelena had written bitterly to Alamán (whom he nevertheless addressed as 'dear friend') to complain of the lack of confidence in him and threatening to 'look for another country where I might be accepted as a good citizen and where I could from time to time speak my mind without fear of being disowned'.[11] A reference in this letter to something having been said about him in a Madrid newspaper suggests that he might have been speaking out of turn about Britain's attitude to Spanish recognition. But there were also personality clashes and intrigue at work. From the start Michelena and Migoni were at loggerheads.[12] There was also, apparently, a coolness for a time between Michelena and Wavell, who believed he was behind some intriguing against him in Mexico. Wavell became concerned when he learned that Michelena was doing business with the group of British speculators with whom Sir William Adams was involved. Very possibly because of his failure (largely brought about by Migoni's tactics) to organize loans and purchases for his government from which he would have been able to take the 2 per cent commission he had been authorized to receive, Michelena was selling his own mining interests to them. Lady Adams, however, in letters in May and June 1825 to Wavell (who was acting in Mexico as her husband's agent), was insistent that Wavell was 'entirely mistaken' about Michelena's character. 'He certainly is not a bright man' she wrote, 'but as good & affectionate a man & I and Dr Mackie believe him to be as honourable man as breathes [*sic*].' She said that Michelena actually hated the banking group with which Migoni was dealing and through whom, she said, Migoni (and the Colombian representative, Hurtado) had 'made *immense fortunes*. You ought to cultivate Michelena's friendship … we have taken all his mines & of course *he will do anything for us*'.[13]

Michelena was evidently a frequent and intimate visitor to the Adams's home, and Lady Adams described him as 'the only envoy from the New States here who has kept himself wholly out of parties and intrigues here & who has taken no one step to serve his own private interests and in consequence of this & his quiet retired conduct he is held in higher estimation by Mr Canning & at the Foreign Office than any of them. I believe him to be *very sincerely* our friend.'[14]

Certainly this endorses the opinion expressed by Canning to Morier and Ward; and Michelena himself had expressed his belief to Alamán in October 1824 that 'Mexico's best interests lie with England.'[15] Yet he could apparently try to sabotage the treaty. But he seems to have been somewhat mercurial in his attitudes and inclined to express views to the Foreign Office not necessarily in line with those of his masters at home. In March 1825, for example, he addressed a memorandum to Planta expressing impatience over Britain's insistence on trying to persuade a reluctant Spain to accept mediation between her and Mexico.[16] He was then intending to return to Mexico very soon (his departure was postponed) and he wanted to know before he left whether Spain had made up her mind. 'It would derogate from the dignity of the Mexican nation' he wrote 'to make her subservient to the vacillating and irresolute policy' of Madrid. He said he had been authorized by his government to discuss the details with His Majesty's Government and if Spain had accepted, he wanted to get on with it. If she had not, he thought the books should be closed once and for all. He thought this would in fact be best, and he wanted to know whether Britain would support a Mexican move to absorb Cuba. He may have gone beyond his instructions in putting this forward so openly, because although he personally was a keen supporter of a movement in favour of invading Cuba to liberate it from the Spaniards and make it part of Mexico, Victoria was being careful to keep his distance from such ventures. Ward thought he was probably content to put no obstacles in the path of such a movement because if it succeeded he could gain credit; but he wanted to be able to disclaim responsibility should it fail.[17]

In fact the 'very angry feelings' with which Ward said Michelena returned to Mexico[18] were directed more at Victoria than against Britain, although they did tend to have a spill-over effect on Ward's attempts to defend British interests. Michelena was bitter at Victoria's decision, as soon as he returned, to send him as the Mexican representative to the conference of the Spanish-American states being arranged to take place in Panama, and Ward reported that his behaviour convinced 'all impartial observers that he is ready to sacrifice every thing to his ambitious views and would rather throw the whole country into confusion than remain in it without being admitted to a share in the Government'.[19] If he really did harbour bitterness in his heart against Britain, it had evaporated by July 1826, when he wrote a friendly letter to Planta from Panama giving him some information about the proceedings. He also referred to his removal from London. He was well aware that Canning had asked for him to be replaced; and he had apparently received some garbled reports of the reason (perhaps deliberately garbled by those who wanted to make mischief). He told Planta that they had given him 'pain because of the value and consideration in which I hold Mr Canning, whose opinion is not indifferent to me', a view which he said he had conveyed to Rocafuerte who must have let it be known at the Foreign Office; but apparently he had received some explanation with which he had been satisfied, and he assured Planta that 'the thing is now past and of no moment … let there be nothing more said about it'.[20]

It is impossible now to be certain about the real cause of Michelena's removal,[21] but it does seem that when Alamán had been approached about it in April 1825 he had accepted Canning's request without quibble. He had suggested, however, that it might be difficult, given that Canning was still only prepared to accept a Chargé d'affaires, to find someone suitable 'to accept the employment without a rank being attached to it such as his services at home might give him a fair claim to'. But he had been assured by Morier that the right man could count on being accepted as Minister Plenipotentiary as soon as both governments agreed to progress to this ranking; so Victoria had chosen, as successor to Michelena, General Manuel Mier y Terán, whom Morier had reported to Canning as being 'one of the most distinguished of the revolutionary generals, and one whom we both consider as highly calculated to give you satisfaction'.[22] Unfortunately this appointment had come up against opposition in the Senate, and indeed from Alamán himself. Ward now, after Morier had left for England, discovered that Alamán was trying to get Francisco Fagoaga appointed. Considering Fagoaga to be quite unsuitable, because of his close connections with Spain, his pro-French views and his proprietorship of mines, he tackled Alamán. He explained that Fagoaga 'possessed almost every one of the qualifications which [Canning was] desirous not to find in the representative of Mexico … his intimacy with all the Spanish émigrés now in England rendered him just as liable as M. Michelena to be involved in intrigues which could not but render him particularly obnoxious to the Court of Madrid. What acquaintances he has in England, where he has resided some time, are almost all members of the opposition.' Moreover, Fagoaga had 'given proofs of a decided preference for France' and had been a prominent opponent of the treaty with Britain. Ward explained to Canning that he had not expected 'that these representations would be particularly agreeable to M. Alamán, as from the nature of his own earlier political connections and the fact of his combining at present in his own person the situation of Minister of State and director of a mining company, there were some parts of my remonstrances which, however anxious I might be to avoid any thing like a personal allusion, would apply equally well to M. Fagoaga and to himself'.[23] But, unaware of Alamán's personal involvement in the choice, Ward was nevertheless surprised by the warmth of his reaction and even more so when he implied that Victoria himself had urged Fagoaga to accept the appointment. And Ward later reported that Michelena had been an active opponent not only of Mier y Terán, but of having anyone sent too quickly to replace him. According to Victoria, this was because he did not want anyone investigating his activities in London before his accounts had been approved by Congress, for there were two items, each of $50,000, for 'secret service money' which required explanation.[24]

It was shortly after this that Ward's eyes were fully opened to what he could only regard as Alamán's duplicity. He discovered that Alamán had not reported his protest over Fagoaga to Victoria; but he himself had mentioned both it, and his earlier remonstrance over the publication of the treaty, to Wavell from whom (indirectly) Victoria learned of them. Victoria immediately sent his confidential secretary to let Ward know that Alamán (contrary to what Ward had earlier been told) had not been authorized to publish the treaty with Britain, or to make the observations on it which had appeared in the press. At this meeting Ward discovered that Alamán had actually told Victoria that he (Ward) approved of Fagoaga going to London. As a result of this conversation the confidential secretary was sent three days later to tell Ward that Victoria had made sure that the treaty would not be officially published; and on Sunday 10 July Victoria himself called upon Ward, apologizing that ill health had prevented his doing so earlier, for what turned out to be a two-hour frank discussion.

During this tête-à-tête, Victoria assured Ward 'that he never had changed and never should change his political creed … [he] regarded England as the natural ally and protectress of Mexico, *the* nation *par excellence* with which she ought most intimately to connect herself'. He expressed great regret for the way Alamán was behaving, especially as he had a high regard for his abilities. But there seemed to be no way 'of inducing him to play a fair, honorable and manly game'. He told Ward that he should no longer use Alamán for his communications with the Mexican government but should come straight to him, Victoria. And he urged Ward to be active in countering the opposition to Britain's policies which people like Alamán and the French were encouraging, emphasizing that 'in a country like Mexico it would be folly to rely upon the goodness of [Britain's] cause or the purity of [her] intentions as affording any security against the intrigues of [her] enemies. The errors of public opinion must be corrected before they take root. The antidote must accompany the poison': the English papers must defend British interests as energetically as the French attacked them: he would ensure that his secretary arranged to insert in the Mexican papers 'anything or everything' that Ward wanted.

It was this frankness on the part of Victoria that finally convinced Ward (apparently never thinking that Victoria might have his own political reasons for wanting to discredit Alamán). He explained to Canning that he had been slow to realize what was happening because he could not believe in such duplicity, even though he had been told by many members of Congress that they felt that Alamán had not been energetic enough in trying to persuade that body to be more reasonable over ratification of the treaty: they were convinced that had he 'taken at once the high tone which the importance of the question warranted, there would have been little or no opposition'. Ward had been unable to

> credit the assurances which I received that an intimate connection with England was neither [Alamán's] object nor his wish, and that having, as he thought, secured his own personal interests as a Director of the Anglo Mexican Mining Company, by obtaining from England a recognition of the independence, his next object would be to associate himself anew with the Bourbonist Party, of which he was formerly considered the leader, and to second all their exertions to prevent Great Britain from acquiring the influence here to which her generous policy so fully entitles her.

As against this, he retained absolute confidence in Victoria, whose talents he thought had been greatly under-rated: 'Of the sincerity of his friendship for England I have always been convinced, and every thing that I have seen of him since my return here induces me to believe not only that he thoroughly understands his countrymen, but will manage them as well as any man whom they could possibly have placed at the head of the Government.'[25]

How much of the criticism of Alamán voiced to Ward was simply a manifestation of internal political rivalries, and how much represented the truth, is hard to say. There had been no sign of any unwillingness on Alamán's part to show support for Ward, a month earlier, when a Papal Bull had been received, in which the Pope exhorted all clergy to lead their flocks back to the path of the commandment 'of that Lord whose most precious gift is the alliance amongst Princes, who places Kings upon their thrones and connects by indissoluble ties the welfare of His Holy Church with the preservation of their rights and authority'. The clergy were to convince their parishioners of the qualities of King Ferdinand and the merits of those Spaniards residing in Europe 'who have sacrificed all in the defence of religion and legitimate powers'. This was hardly the stuff to appeal to Mexican revolutionaries and, when it first reached Mexico, Victoria had been all for reacting strongly to what he regarded as open aggression. Others, however, had wanted to avoid an open dispute with the Church, so the matter was handed to a junta to consider. This junta, after being addressed by Ramos Arispe, the acting head of the Ministry of Justice and Ecclesiastical Affairs, had taken the decision to publish the Bull, but with accompanying observations.

Ward, learning of this, had swiftly intervened to try to ensure that the Mexicans did not again trot out the arguments that Alamán had used in his infamous article about the treaty with Colombia. He was delighted to discover that Arispe regretted what Alamán had then said and 'tho' a churchman, desired nothing so much as to see his country rival Colombia in liberality and tolerance'. Alamán too 'entered more readily than I expected into my ideas and promised that I should have no reason to complain again upon this subject'. All this had encouraged Ward to tell Canning:

> There is something very manly and open in the line which the Mexican Government has taken upon the present occasion, and I am happy to add it appears as yet to have met with universal approbation.
>
> There is little that savours of bigotry or superstition in the notes which have accompanied the publication of the Bull. They contain no affectation of humility, no eager expression of a wish

> to be reconciled with the See of Rome, but on the contrary they enter boldly into the question of the Pope's spiritual and temporal sovereignty, declare the two to be incompatible, and even hint, very distinctly, that any further attempt to exercise authority in the affairs of this world will not only prove unsuccessful, but may be attended with the loss of his spiritual jurisdiction likewise.

He had also reported his belief that there was 'a spirit of enquiry abroad which must sooner or later produce beneficial effects', and he had taken the opportunity to warn again that any attempt by British representatives in Mexico to hasten the process 'would be attended with the most unfavorable consequences'. He was convinced, basing himself on what Wavell (now working for British mining interests) had told him, that the parochial clergy, at least in areas where there were British mines, were well aware of the importance of such companies to the local economy and were prepared to be very tolerant: 'In every nook and corner too where a vein of silver exists (to use the words of General Wavell)' he wrote 'the arrival of some one of His Majesty's subjects is looked forward to with eager expectation and he is received as a sort of Messiah who is to disseminate blessings of all kinds.'[26]

The question of religious tolerance continued, however, to bedevil relations. In August an anonymous pamphlet appeared entitled 'The English will be massacred or the Government must protect them', in which the government was attacked for not doing its duty to protect foreigners. Alamán was concerned that this could produce a most unfortunate impression when reported in England, and he addressed a note to Ward asking him 'to do the Mexican government the justice to correct, by detailed and accurate accounts' this unfavourable impression of the facts. Ward chose to take this as a reflection on the standard of his reports to London and protested to Victoria, who assured him that this had not been intended. But he too expressed his anxieties and his fears that the pamphlet might 'be turned to account by the enemies of Mexico in Europe'. Ward therefore addressed a formal note to Alamán about 'the assurances' on religious toleration given privately during the treaty negotiations, emphasizing that in reporting to London he had sometimes had the 'painful duty' to mention the legacy of prejudices left by the Spaniards which were 'heightened by the existence of a spirit of intolerance in religious affairs ... by which the interests of His Majesty's subjects cannot but be materially affected'. He added, however, that he had been able to

> place in the opposite scale the constant assurances which I have received of the enlightened views of the Mexican Government, of their desire to promote the best interests of their country by introducing that system of toleration without which the liberality of their political code would be a mockery, and of their determination to afford the most prompt and decisive protection to foreigners should that spirit of fanaticism which it was the object of Spain during three centuries to inculcate give rise to any disturbance and render the interposition of the Supreme Government necessary. For my part, I have no scruple in assuring Your Excellency of my conviction that this protection would be as promptly granted as it would be demanded by me.

This alarmed Alamán, who tried to get Ward to withdraw the note, assuring him that the government 'was most highly gratified by the eulogium which [Ward] had bestowed on their conduct, but the President was apprehensive that it might be turned against them in the Congress should it fall into the hands of any of their enemies'. He particularly wanted the removal of any mention of the government's enlightened views. This Ward refused to do, saying he had 'given the Government credit for nothing which it had not pledged itself to perform, and that as verbal assurances were all that had been given to His Majesty's Commissioners during the negotiations, it became more peculiarly my duty to see that those assurances were most strictly adhered to'. Alamán then asked that at least Ward should alter the reference to a 'system' of toleration, which suggested something unconstitutional 'and might even furnish matter for an impeachment against the whole Government'. Ward had anticipated this, but had deliberately left himself with a point to give away. He offered to refer instead to a 'spirit' of toleration. Alamán was equally dissatisfied with this, but Ward insisted, saying

> that this single word was sufficient to remove every thing that could be construed into an unconstitutional engagement; and that should Ministers be attacked upon the subject, if they did their duty and wished to promote the real interests of their country, they would boldly maintain that this spirit of toleration

> was indeed indispensable if Mexico wished to preserve a good understanding with foreign powers, as without it neither the lives nor property of strangers residing here could be said to be safe .... By pursuing this straightforward manly course, they would deserve the thanks and secure the cooperation of all the leading men of Congress.[27]

Ward showed courage and political flair in thus pressing home his advantage. But he was constantly having to react to anti-British sentiment fuelled by reports now reaching Mexico that Britain might not after all be going to ratify the treaty. He was therefore naturally anxious to avoid any action which might introduce a needless irritant into his relations with the government and encourage this anti-British feeling further. Nevertheless, he did not hesitate to intervene when the Mexicans tried to prevent Francis Baring buying some land.

Francis was the grandson of the younger of the two Baring brothers who had founded the merchant bank of that name. At that time his father, Alexander (later 1st Baron Ashburton), had sent him to Mexico to report on the opportunities for business and he had conceived the idea of buying from the creditors of the Marqués de San Miguel de Aguayo, as an investment for the firm, an estate of some 9 million acres at Parras, between Monterrey and Torreón in northern Mexico. (His father was horrified when he learned of this and his other ideas for investment in Mexico – with justification: twenty years later they had to write off some £170,000 in losses arising from them.) Francis had been assured by the local speculators with whom he was involved (among whom was Staples who had been removed from his consular post by Canning the year before) that his proposed purchase was quite legal. But there were those who did not approve of such foreign 'exploitation' and a proposal was put in Congress to annul the sale by a decree making it impossible for foreigners to become landed proprietors in Mexico. Francis appealed for help to Ward, who heard that Victoria himself was behind this and was determined that if Congress would not stop the sale to Baring the government would. Ward went first to Alamán, whom he found very reasonable over the matter. He then tackled Victoria, who denied expressing the views attributed to him: he said that he merely felt that if foreigners were to be allowed to purchase land there must be some regulatory controls. Ward for once did not believe Victoria, and made clear to him that if he allowed a retrospective law to be passed adversely affecting a British subject he could expect trouble. He was particularly concerned about the apparent intention to make adherence to the Roman Catholic faith a pre-requisite for land ownership and warned Victoria against using religion as a criterion for controlling such purchases. Victoria assured him there was no question of this, but again Ward was sceptical. He wrote to Canning:[28]

> I entertain great suspicions with regard to the President's sincerity. Not that I conceive him to be in any way a bigoted man, but I do not think he has nerve enough to oppose the prejudices of the people, or to set an example of liberality at the risk of endangering that popularity which it is his study to court.[29]

And in an earlier letter to Planta he had said 'I cannot conceal from you my opinion that there is no injustice and no illiberality of which these people are not capable. I have witnessed more petty intrigue and a more decided want of principle here during the last four months than I did during the four years which I passed in Spain – and that is a bold assertion!'[30]

This rather abrupt change in Ward's opinion of Victoria may have been induced by ill-health. He was suffering at that time from what may have been a form of hepatitis and should have been resting. Emily, writing to her father on 17 August, revealed that he was 'exceedingly unwell' and had had to go 'to the Palace when he was not fit to go out, & as soon as he returned lay down, and could not do any thing all day, but took 100 drops of laudanum, & 24 grains of calomel'. He had been suffering from 'inflammation of the liver when this violent attack came on'.[31] But there was no let up in the pressure of work. On 15 August he had been shown by Alamán alarming secret intelligence reports from Jamaica that seemed to indicate that a large French fleet was secretly engaged in landing perhaps as many as 10,000 troops in Cuba. To the Mexicans this was a clearly hostile act which meant either that the French were preparing to invade their country, or that they were making it possible for the Spaniards to do so by providing garrison troops for Cuba and possibly a naval force to support a Spanish invasion. Alamán told Ward that they were putting their army on a war footing and were considering closing all ports to all French shipping and expelling all Frenchmen from the country. Although the evidence shown to him did not entirely hang together, Ward decided that he had to accept the potential seriousness of the situation and to give the

Mexicans such assurances as he could of British support, even though he had no instructions covering such an eventuality. But he feared that such extreme measures on the part of the Mexicans might simply serve to precipitate a crisis which could be avoided. He made it clear that he could not commit His Majesty's Government to any specific action, and that he doubted if anything short of direct hostilities by France would be regarded as a violation of neutrality calling for British intervention. Nevertheless, he did tell Alamán that he thought that if hostilities did break out, Britain 'would see itself eventually compromised.'[32] However, while accepting the need to put the army on a war footing, he urged Alamán not to take the other overt actions which they were contemplating, but rather to ask both the British and the Americans to mediate.

Alamán, however, was apparently trying to make political capital out of the threat. Without authorization he published the intelligence, even suggesting that the French were acting to forestall an American attempt to take over Cuba. Ward immediately suspected Alamán of playing some kind of double game, even possibly of colluding with the French, a suspicion reinforced when he discovered that he had sold all his shares in his own mining company except the minimum necessary to remain qualified as a director. Next day Ward was summoned to see Victoria, who was clearly annoyed at Alamán's actions and apologized for them. Nevertheless, he too was taking the situation seriously and begged Ward to say something publicly so that silence from Britain would not be misinterpreted. All Ward felt he could do was to promise to forward a formal request for British mediation. Even then Alamán continued to try to make mischief by submitting drafts of the request which were quite unsuitable, despite Victoria's ready acceptance of the need for very careful language, and it was only at the third attempt that Ward decided that he could send to Canning a document which he felt did not put Britain in an impossible position. In this, the Mexicans called attention to the fact that the British government had 'declared in the most solemn manner that it will not permit any third power to interfere in the question which is now pending between Spain and the independent states of America'. Calling the French actions 'an interference which, however it be glossed over, is still indefensible', it expressed the hope that 'motives of friendship will induce [the British government] to demand those explanations from [France] which the circumstances of the case may seem to require .... The explanation, when received, will serve as a rule for the conduct of this Government, with the exception of such measures of precaution with regard to France as circumstances and a proper regard for the honor and political existence of this country may render necessary'.

It was worrying enough for Ward to find himself having to take on the responsibility of responding to a request which could involve his country in war. To have to do so when he was far from well made it worse, and it was a worried man who wrote to Canning: 'If I have in any respect deviated from the line which you would have directed me to take had the circumstances been foreseen under which I have been compelled to act, I can only plead the total want of instructions as a plea for indulgence. In the absence of these, I have endeavoured to shape my course by those principles which His Majesty's Ministers have constantly laid down as the rules of their conduct. To remain silent was impossible on an occasion when every eye was turned to Britain.'[33] But he was still able to demonstrate considerable diplomatic skill in his choice of language when replying to Alamán. He agreed that the

> facts certainly furnish strong presumptive evidence in favor of the conclusions which Your Excellency draws from them; but at the same time Your Excellency must be aware that in the peculiar position of Great Britain, no appearances, however suspicious, could justify His Majesty's Agent here in giving an opinion with regard to the light in which an event, which may possibly never take place, would be regarded by His Majesty's Government.

There could be many reasons for the French actions, he continued,

> all calculated to render it extremely difficult for His Majesty's Government to regard it as an interference … as long as it be not accompanied by some overt act of hostility. Should such an event occur it would be a matter of deep regret to Great Britain to see her pacific views frustrated. The declaration of His Majesty's Ministers are before the world, and I have no hesitation in assuring Your Excellency that they will be acted up to.

He did express his personal view 'that under whatever circumstances the occupation of Cuba be effected … Great Britain cannot remain an indifferent spectator of such an event'. But he hoped that Mexico would remain calm 'until time be allowed for the amicable representations of Great Britain at the Court of France to produce the desired effect .... Mediation, even when carried to excess, is still reconcileable with a determination to repel unjust aggression, but a single hasty step (however natural in the first moment of irritation) might be construed into an act of hostility and this would weaken the arguments of the friends of Mexico while it furnished her enemies with a plausible cause for complaint.'[34]

And he was able later to report that his representations had

> certainly produced a good effect. All idea of the violent measures which were at first in contemplation has been dropped and yet the good faith of England has not been called in question. I have acquired too a sort of right to interfere should circumstances require it, and should certainly avail myself of it in order to keep these people from getting into a scrape should the news of the occupation of the Havanna be confirmed, and the irritation which is now beginning to subside be renewed.[35]

Once again, however, the slowness of communications between Mexico and England meant that Ward suffered needless anxiety. There had in fact been an earlier incident, in June, when he had also had to report a local scare over French actions, although he had not himself at the time thought it very important. At that time it had appeared that the French had simply provided a naval escort for some Spanish troops being taken to Cuba, and Ward had suggested to the Mexicans that this was not a direct threat to their security. Canning had heard about this in May, long before Ward's report of it reached him, and had learned from the French that the governor of Martinique had acted in accordance with discretion given him to send troops to Cuba at Spanish request 'to assist in the repression of internal disturbance ... but not to aid in repelling external aggression'.[36] And in response to his subsequent firm warning to the French that 'no plea whatsoever could justify ... the introduction of a French military force into the Spanish Islands',[37] Canning had received an assurance that 'no French troops would be sent to the Island of Cuba' and that the governor had received orders which would ensure that no French ships of war were again used to convey or escort Spanish troops to the area.[38] Canning had not, however, reported any of this to Ward at the time, so that his reply to Ward's despatch about the incident reached the latter only after he had had to decide for himself how to react to the August scare. This was a pity, for in it Canning instructed Ward to make absolutely clear to Victoria that his declaration to Polignac in October 1823 meant that

> in the event of any other Powers taking an active part in [the contest between Spain and her former colonies] His Majesty reserved to himself the discretion of considering what course the interests of His People might call upon His Majesty to adopt in a war which would then assume a general instead of a civil character .... It never was intended by the British Government that this declaration should be held out to the American provinces, or understood by them, as a treaty of defensive alliance, and yet such would be the character of an engagement which pledged this country generally and indefinitely to defend the new states of America against all attacks from Europe.

However, if the present war between Spain and those provinces should become extended, it could not be expected that

> England could long avoid being drawn into its vortex. But, while every consideration, alike of interest and of humanity, will induce the British Government to continue to employ every effort to avoid a calamity so grievous to mankind as such a war would be, it must not be conceived that this country either has contracted, or is disposed to contract, any engagement, express or implicit, such as would make its taking part in any war, which its efforts may not be successful in preventing, a matter of positive obligation.[39]

Had Ward had this in August, he would have known what to say to the Mexicans and would have been in a happier frame of mind.

Equally, Canning had heard about the August incident before Ward's report reached him, and had been able to discover that the French troops had in fact been landed in San Domingo, not Cuba, and that the French fleet had simply paid a visit to Cuba after this. 'Why the French fleet should have taken a course so likely to create jealousy and alarm in Europe and in both Americas' Canning was unable to explain when replying in October to Ward; but he had been satisfied that the French 'had no serious design in contemplation'[40] and he considered it 'fortunate that no rash step was taken on the part of the Mexican Government to turn this idle evolution of the French fleet into a ground for quarrel with the French Government'. He was able to assure Ward that he approved 'the general course of [his] language & behaviour under the very difficult and embarrassing circumstances in which you were placed by the unexpected intelligence which threw the Mexican Government into so much consternation. The advice tendered by you to the Mexican Government was perfectly judicious.'[41]

With all these problems to deal with, Ward was finding it no sinecure to be Chargé d'affaires. But in fact they were as nothing compared with what he had to put up with from the American minister, who was determined to prevent Britain getting in first with a treaty ahead of the United States. Ward showed courage and dash in dealing with this; but his lack of previous experience not only showed in his failure fully to appreciate all the ins and outs of Mexican politics, it also led him into a course of action which ultimately caused Canning to dismiss him.

13

UNITED STATES MEDDLING – MAY TO DECEMBER 1825

Just as Ward had been slow to discover that Alamán was not to be trusted, so he was as regards Joel R. Poinsett, the American minister. The United States had formally recognized Mexican independence in May 1822 and a Mexican minister plenipotentiary had arrived in Washington in December of that year. But, although Poinsett had been sent on a mission to Mexico, similar to Hervey's, in October 1822 which led to the establishment of American consular posts, no diplomatic representative was appointed there until May 1825 when Poinsett himself was chosen. It must have been galling for him (after whom the Poinsettia flower was named) to find that he was officially presented to Victoria as Minister Plenipotentiary only the day after Ward was presented as British Chargé d'affaires. But he gave no outward sign of this at the time. Ward was invited to attend the ceremony and heard him, in his formal speech, refer to the 'justice which was now done to [Mexico] by the *first* nation of the Old World, and the nation which had *first* sown the seeds of liberty in the New'[1] (a passage which must have been an impromptu insertion, for it does not appear in the text in the State Department archives[2]). Ward felt this augured well for a close cooperation between them, and a month later he was reporting to Canning that 'Mr Poinsett is a man of great abilities and is, I really believe, inclined both to think and speak of England with much more liberality than his countrymen in general.' But already there were signs that politically they were likely to be in different camps. He found that Poinsett was 'naturally anxious to form here an American party, and in order to do so, I observe that he cultivates the acquaintance of all those who were our opponents in the debates upon the treaty. Whether he hopes by their assistance to carry through his own treaty, I know not; but unless they possess infinitely more talent than the late discussions would dispose me to give them credit for, he will be much deceived in his expectations.'[3] Poinsett was indeed from the very first conscious, as he put it in an early report home, 'that the British have made good use of their time and opportunities'; but he believed that the Americans had 'a very respectable party in both houses of Congress and a vast majority of the people are in favor of the strictest union with the United States. They regard the British with mistrust.'[4] He was being over sanguine in referring to the vast majority, and in fact he had the greatest difficulty in negotiating a treaty, as Ward anticipated. But there were undoubtedly people of influence who mistrusted Britain, and Poinsett set out to turn this to his advantage and endeavour to bring Mexico under the American thumb.[5] He was much helped in this when rumours began to reach Mexico that the British government was not going to ratify the text taken home by Morier.

Ward was not slow to recognize that Poinsett was working hard to influence Mexican opinion in favour of the United States. In this, however, he saw no more than a diplomat carrying out his duty to do his best for his own country. He was not prepared to emulate Poinsett in his involvement with freemasonry[6] when competing for influence, but he did push out the boat in expensive entertaining of those he considered to be important (thus unwittingly taking the first step towards his own downfall). At first he thought he could hold the field in this way, but gradually he became aware that Poinsett was actively intriguing, and in August he gained a surprising (to him) and disturbing insight into what Poinsett was really after.

Ward had learned in July that Colombia had refused to ratify the treaty they had negotiated with Mexico. In this, each country extended to the other certain privileges for shipping. But Colombia had not, in her treaty with Britain, obtained the right, as Mexico had in hers, to give such special concessions to other former Spanish colonies which need not be extended to Britain under the most-favoured-nation principle. When it had come to ratification, Colombia had not been prepared to extend shipping privileges to Mexico which she would then be obliged to grant to Britain as well; but in their negotiations with Morier and Ward, the Mexicans had won this exception from the most-favoured-nation principle on the ground that they had already agreed exclusive mutual shipping privileges with Colombia. Now that Colombia was going back on this, Ward felt that the Mexicans should voluntarily release Britain from the concession they had extracted from her, and he put this formally to Alamán, suggesting that, while he might be justified in entering a formal protest and reserving his government's right to cancel this clause in the treaty, he had 'too high an opinion of the liberality and amicable sentiments of Mexico towards Great Britain to think it necessary to take so decisive a step'. He and Morier had only agreed to its inclusion because they had believed that Mexico had committed herself and he asked 'Is it, therefore, or is it not, worthy of Mexico to insist upon retaining this clause …? Is it not rather her interest to seize this opportunity of giving a brilliant proof of the delicacy of her honor in engagements of so solemn a nature?'[7]

In justifying to Canning this soft approach 'without sacrificing the chance of using the harder later if need be' he explained that Victoria, in one of their now weekly private meetings, had assured him that the Executive would consent to the change, provided Ward's note was worded in such a way 'as to render it palatable to the Congress, whose suspicions … it was as easy to arouse as it was difficult to allay'. Poinsett, however, when he learned of this British move, saw in it a serious impediment to American aims, and he urged Ward to be tough and arrange for the immediate unilateral annulment of the clause. His reasons caused Ward much concern. Poinsett thought it right in principle that Britain should have agreed to such a clause because 'she was a European Power and could have no right or pretence to interfere in the family arrangements of the American States; but it would be absurd to suppose that the President of the United States would ever sign a treaty by which he would be excluded from a *federation of which he ought to be the head*'. In Poinsett's view, the USA would not be able to insist on having the same trading privileges in Mexico as the other former Spanish colonies unless Britain had them too, therefore Britain should insist on the present clause being annulled. Ward was not prepared to accept this. He made clear to Poinsett that 'the British Government conceived the United States to be exactly in the same position as any of the European Powers with regard to the New States of America, and was not in any way inclined to admit the existence of a general American Federation, and still less their claim to be head of it by virtue of which they might, in the event of a rupture with England, attempt to close the ports of the whole American continent upon her vessels'.

When Victoria was told by Ward of this brush with Poinsett, he commented that 'if the United States were not inclined to treat upon the same terms *exactly* as Great Britain, Mexico would wait patiently until they were so; that he was as little disposed as [Britain] to acknowledge them as the chiefs of the American Federation, and thought that nothing could be more just than that they should be considered with regard to the former Spanish colonies (which certainly did form one great family) in the same light as any of the Powers of Europe'. He said he would not take any steps to alter the wording of the treaty with Britain unless formally asked to do so by His Majesty's Government: meanwhile Ward's note would be regarded simply as establishing his right to make a formal request later. Victoria told Ward that he could 'depend, however, on no preference being given either in this or in anything else to the United States while he remained at the head of the Government, as he was too well aware of their intriguing policy to become the dupe of their professions'.[8]

Ward was pleased by Victoria's robust attitude and even more so when Esteva told him that the negotiations for a treaty with the USA had been suspended while Poinsett sought further instructions. Esteva had had a lecture from Poinsett on the same lines as that delivered to Ward and had made plain that

> Mexico had no reason whatsoever to consider the United States as her natural ally or to attach more importance to her friendship than that of England … and he was authorised by the President to propose that, as the treaty with Great Britain had served as the basis for that with the United States in all other articles, it should in this; consequently the treaty should be signed *with* the exception, and that a clause should be added stipulating that the question having been already referred to His Britannic Majesty's Government, the United States would abide by whatever arrangements might be definitively agreed upon between Great Britain and Mexico.

Not surprisingly, Poinsett had refused to hear of this.

Ward now realized that Poinsett's efforts were 'being directed to undermine the influence of Great Britain, to decry the advantages which the South American States have derived from her friendship and to convince the Mexicans that it is their policy to ally themselves with their brethren of the North to the exclusion of every European Power'. He wrote privately to Canning about this, expressing the hope that the line he had been taking would be approved. In the absence of guidance he had used his 'knowledge of those principles which you have always laid down both in and out of parliament as the rules by which the conduct of England would be determined'. He was a little worried lest in trying to prevent a treaty with the USA which he saw as possibly harmful to Britain he had gone too far; but he explained that in giving Victoria a memorandum on the subject 'signed merely with my initials [I] could commit no one but myself' and he was 'willing to run this risk in order to gain my point'.[9] He referred to his increasing intimacy with Victoria who 'visits me once if not twice a week and invites me to come whenever I please to the Palace. In his confidential Secretary too, M. Tornel (a clever man), we have a staunch friend. Some personal views are, of course, at the bottom of all this cordiality; but if it be an advantage to have an influence here, we are certainly much indebted to Mr Poinsett who, by his ill judged personalities, has thrown the President entirely into the hands of Great Britain.'[10]

Ward, nevertheless, was by no means sure that he could count on Victoria to be as robust in deeds as he was in words, and he wrote privately to Canning about the way Poinsett was making use of freemasonry in order to 'facilitate intrigues of all kinds on the part of the United States against every European Power, but more particularly against Great Britain'. He was in fact doubtful whether Poinsett would succeed in this outside Mexico City because 'such is the detestation in which the people have been taught to hold the name of Freemasons in the interior that he must be a bold man who first attempts to introduce it into any of the States'. He said that Victoria was trying to counteract this by placing 'several of his most confidential friends in different Lodges; amongst others M. Esteva who, however erroneous his finance system may be, is certainly a sincere friend to England and as jealous as I could desire of the United States'. He had suggested that Ward himself should join one of the lodges for the same purpose, but he had declined to do so because he was 'aware of the light in which all secret societies are regarded in Europe, and of the inferences which would be drawn from the fact of any public agent of His Majesty being known to belong to one'. Also he wanted 'to make the contrast between [Poinsett's] conduct and mine as strong as possible'.

Ward wanted Canning to know 'that nothing had been further from his wishes', on Poinsett's first arrival, than to find himself in contest with him. Indeed, he had used his intimacy with the president 'to surmount General Victoria's dislike to [Poinsett] which, not being aware at first of what was going on, I was at a loss to account for'. But on realizing that Poinsett, as he thought, was bent on establishing 'an influence in favor of the United States to the exclusion of every European Power' he lost all 'scruples with regard to the means to be taken in order to counteract the execution of this project'. He was seriously concerned, however, that Poinsett had gained sufficient influence to be able to command a majority, even against the wish of the government. He was persuading members of Congress that Victoria's election as president had been obtained by intrigue, that he was a weak and ambitious man, and that 'the friends of the Constitution must be on their guard against his designs, as it is evidently his object to centralise and perhaps afterwards to become an humble imitator of Iturbide'. What really worried Ward was the possibility that Poinsett was right, and he ended this letter to Canning with a passage in cypher about Victoria:

> He certainly possesses very respectable abilities, and great influence in the country, but I am by no means sure that the Minister of the United States is far from wrong in attributing to him ambitious views. Nothing certainly can be more unwarrantable than such an assertion in the mouth of a foreign Minister without having anything but suspicions to allege in support of it; but I must confess that my own ideas upon the subject coincide with those of Mr Poinsett .... I never saw a man more wedded to power or more unwilling to allude to the tenure by which he holds it as only a temporary one. His vanity is certainly egregious, and it is by paying due attention to it that I prepared the way for my present intimacy with him. I do not think, however, that he has any intention of imitating Iturbide.[11]

In fact, however, Victoria remained loyal to his friendship for Britain, despite the very real danger which then developed that Poinsett would win the day. Michelena on his return from London joined with Poinsett's masonic 'junta' which was gaining a worrying degree of influence both in Congress and with ministers. Ward attributed Poinsett's success to 'personal interest, which is all powerful in a country where venality prevails to a most scandalous extent', reporting that he had been 'entrusted with full powers by various capitalists of the United States, England & France for different projects' and was making 'a judicious distribution of the advantages to be derived from' them. He had also, according to Ward, thought up a scheme for reducing Mexico's debt by lowering the rate of interest on credits and his cronies could profit by buying them up before this was generally known. In the light of the reports that Britain was not going to ratify her treaty with Mexico he suspended his own negotiations and set about trying to persuade deputies that any changes which Britain might be about to propose would be 'not only tantamount to a release from all their engagements, but an affront which they ought to resent by entering at once into a most intimate connection with [the USA]'.

Victoria was extremely worried at the growth of Poinsett's influence, agreeing with Ward that he might well be able to secure a majority in Congress for anything he wanted. He feared that if the British treaty had to be brought before Congress again it would be thrown out. He wanted some constitutional excuse for refusing to lay it before Congress 'until explanations were received from England'. He suggested that Ward should notify Alamán that he was sending someone immediately to England to explain the situation and that he was convinced that this would lead to immediate British ratification of the treaty. Victoria thought that armed with this he could gain time and defy Congress to vote for the annulment of the treaty with Britain. Furthermore, 'if [Ward's] protest against the clause in favor of the South American States were withdrawn at the same time, Mr Poinsett's exertions would be paralysed and his party would fall to pieces before he could turn it to any account'. He recognized that Ward would be taking on a very heavy responsibility if he were to do what he wanted; but he felt sure that Ward would not allow 'personal apprehensions' to deter him from 'taking a step which [he] conceived the interest of England to require'. He knew that Ward could not in fact guarantee that Britain would in the end ratify the treaty, nevertheless he still urged him to do what he asked.

Ward decided to take the gamble and presented a confidential note on the lines requested, which was to be kept confidential as long as possible, but let it be known that he was despatching a member of his staff to England. He explained to Canning that he had fallen in with Victoria's request to avoid any appearance of acting in response to any definite news of British refusal to ratify that might arrive. He realized that 'as a Mexican [Victoria] must naturally be anxious to preserve unchanged a treaty by which Mexico has acquired advantages which have not been conceded to any of the sister States', and that Victoria 'hoped that if the objections of His Majesty's Government to the treaty did not turn upon any of the more important articles, the uncertainty of the result might induce [Canning] to waive them for the present, and perhaps even to give them up altogether'. On the other hand, he feared that to refuse Victoria's request 'might indispose him, at a time when we should stand most in need of his assistance, and even induce him to throw his personal influence into the opposite scale'. He was convinced that Victoria's friendship for Britain was sincere, although he was 'equally convinced that unless roused to action by what he conceived to be a case of absolute necessity, he would not risk his idol, popularity, in order to serve her ... he will feel that he must either give up his favorite idea of an alliance with England or make every possible effort in her favor. Nothing but this conviction would induce him to place himself even for a moment in opposition to the very strong party which certainly is formed in both Chambers against us, and I was too well convinced both of this fact and of the necessity of his assistance if the treaty were to be again referred to Congress, to think it too dearly purchased at any rate.'[12]

Ward was again taking a considerable risk with his own career by acting in this way; but so convinced was he that he was acting wisely, that he still sent this despatch even when events made it unnecessary for him to implement this plan. He had sent Ball to Vera Cruz on 10 October, but three days later some letters were received from England with news up to 18 August. These did not include any official information for Ward from the Foreign Office, but the Mexicans had news from Rocafuerte (who had been acting as their Chargé d'affaires in London since Michelena's departure) which made clear that British objections to the treaty were fundamental. In the circumstances, Victoria agreed that 'palliatives' were no longer sufficient, Ward's note was withdrawn and a special courier was sent to Vera Cruz to stop Ball sailing for England. But Ward was still prepared to risk his career in an attempt to stop Canning taking a step which he thought might mean the loss of all hope for a treaty. In adding to this despatch after these developments, he promised to do his best with any instructions that eventually reached him, if by then he had not been recalled, but he felt compelled to sound the alarm. He explained that the name of England was no longer 'sufficient to set intrigue at defiance and to bear down all opposition in a country which is indebted to her for its political existence'. He considered that it was no longer possible, now that diplomatic recognition had been accorded, to use strong language to Mexico:

> Even were England to … resolve upon breaking off all connection with Mexico should her demands not be complied with, she could not deprive this country of the advantages which it has already derived from the fact of having been admitted to treat as an independent State. The Mexicans know this. They are aware, likewise, of the immense interests which England has already invested here [and the progress of the Mexican economy and defence capability] .... With all the vanity of a proud and ignorant people, they dwell upon the advantages which they possess and forget the source from which they derived them: they see their army improving in appearance and discipline, but forget that England has clothed and armed them; and at this very moment, when they are elated in the extreme at the success of their little fleet in repulsing the Spanish squadron destined to convey reinforcements to the Castle, not a Mexican seems to remember that in this fleet ships and officers and men are almost all English .... Gratitude for former service is not to be looked for here.

Ward considered that even those favourable to Britain among the ministers would turn their coats if the treaty were not ratified, while 'I can reckon [on the president] up to a point but no further': if he has to risk his popularity 'he will rather go with the stream'. And he expressed alarm at the possibility that major changes were going to be demanded in the treaty:

> I cannot conceal from you my opinion that a temporary suspension of all intercourse with Mexico may be the consequence of the changes about to be proposed.
>
> At all events, the attempt to introduce them could not be made under more unfavorable circumstances; and so convinced am I of this, that I would still most willingly take upon myself any responsibility, however great, if the state of the case were such as to admit of delay.

For one so comparatively young, Ward was showing a daring disregard for the possibility that he might find himself disowned and recalled; but it is clear that he felt very strongly that Britain was on the verge of losing out to the United States, and he was prepared to risk his own career for what he considered something far more important. This was partly a conviction held from the start, but partly a consequence of developments in Mexican internal affairs and his belief that Poinsett was behind them. Alamán resigned in September. The reasons were connected with internal politics;[13] but one of the effects of the resignation was to worsen still further the strain which had been developing between Ward and Poinsett. Neither fully understood why Alamán had resigned, and each thought the other had had a hand in it. Ward thought Poinsett was behind the (unsuccessful) attempt to have Michelena made Foreign Minister instead of Alamán, and that Alamán would now be free to intrigue with Poinsett against British interests. Poinsett believed that Ward had used 'his influence direct and indirect with the President to obtain [Alamán's] dismissal' and that Alamán, becoming aware of this, had resigned before he could be dismissed.[14] He was sufficiently concerned over what he thought Ward might be reporting to write both to the American minister in London and to Washington. He claimed it was all the fault of Esteva who, pretending after Alamán's resignation to be pro-American, had also 'told the grossest falsehoods of me to Mr Ward .... The state of society here is scarcely to be credited. I hardly know a man however high his rank or office whose work can be relied upon, and many of the leading members of both houses will receive a bribe to advocate a private claim with as little scruple as if you would have received a fee to argue a cause before the supreme court: from such men I would have kept aloof had I been permitted to have done so, but they sought me out and I found it necessary to form a party out of such elements as the country afforded or to leave the English masters of the field.' Of Ward himself he wrote that he had 'despatched a messenger to Mr Canning with the most exaggerated accounts of my influence. I only wish one half of what he believes were true, his want of tact and overwrought exertions may contribute to establish that influence he so much dreads.'[15]

Even now it is impossible to be sure of what was really happening then, and who was against whom. What we do know is that Ward and Poinsett patched up their latent quarrel after a fashion. Poinsett probably put his finger on it when he referred to Ward's 'overwrought exertions', and Ward may have come to realize that he might have been over-reacting to what was undoubtedly a tense period of political intrigue, difficult for one so inexperienced to understand fully. Poinsett reported that Ward had made 'a sort of amend honorable [*sic*] through a mutual friend, Mr Francis Baring' and called on him. Ward himself did not refer to this when reporting that meeting to Canning. He simply said that Poinsett had been very disturbed to learn of Ball's departure for England, assuming it was 'connected with the differences of opinion which existed between [them]'. Poinsett, according to Ward, explained that he had not himself created the masonic 'junta' but had 'been almost forced into it'. He had not made use of it for political purposes, although he did not deny that he thought it useful for acquiring influence. He had never tried to persuade the Mexicans against alliance with Europe, but 'as a good American' he had 'naturally endeavoured to inspire them with feelings of a still more amicable nature towards his own country'. This did not persuade Ward to change his personal view of Poinsett, but he told him that he accepted this explanation that his hostility to England and Europe was not personal, and that he only wanted fair commercial competition. While assuring Poinsett of his continued personal friendship, he emphasized that the 'junta' was dangerous to the interests of Britain. But Poinsett maintained his view that the existence of the clause in the British treaty allowing special trading privileges between the Spanish-American countries meant that they would become separate from the rest of the continent, which was something to which he would never consent. He was very disturbed to learn that Ward had withdrawn his note objecting to this clause.[16]

As regards Alamán, Ward was relieved at being freed from the constant anxiety of dealing with a Foreign Minister he could no longer trust; but he told Canning that he regretted Alamán's departure because he was 'certainly better qualified, both by nature and education, for the place which he held than any other person', even though 'his good qualities were obscured by such a want of frankness, or rather such duplicity in all his communications, that it was really impossible to place any reliance upon any thing which he said .... With regard to his systematic insincerity there can be no doubt.'[17] But it cannot have taken him long to realize that Alamán was not, as he had thought, playing the American game: he was in fact the last man to want to help the Americans to get a controlling influence in Mexico. Ward, indeed, must have become quite friendly with him again. They were both witnesses at O'Gorman's wedding in 1826; Alamán attended the baptism of Ward's child; and even after he left Mexico, Ward remained in touch with him, for instance writing to him in September 1828 to keep him informed of the attitude towards Mexico in British financial circles.[18]

Alamán's eventual successor as Foreign Minister was Sebastian Camacho. Ward believed he had one particular advantage in that he was a personal friend of Victoria and Esteva; but he thought he had no other qualification.[19] He never succeeded in striking up with him the rapport he had for so long had with Alamán. But his troubles were now becoming considerably lightened. He believed that Poinsett had overplayed his hand and that his masonic 'junta' could not survive beyond the end of the year. '[Michelena] and his friends' he reported 'are highly enraged at having been stigmatised … as Bourbonists. The holders of credits are alarmed at the idea of their whole property being at the mercy of a secret association: and the clergy are equally irritated at seeing a heretic venture to introduce in so very open a manner an institution which has hitherto been regarded as little less than sacriligious.' But he warned Canning 'to expect a most tedious, unsatisfactory negotiation; indeed so strong are my sentiments upon this subject, that my hopes of the result not being unfavorable are founded upon that feeling in favor of England which certainly does exist out of the Capital, and which would lead the Provinces to witness with great reluctance the departure of His Majesty's Commissioners, which would I presume be the consequence of the rejection of the present proposals'.[20] And Ward had not been idle. He had discovered that some of the 'junta' were beginning to hold private views at variance with Poinsett's and he managed to let this be known, with telling results. By the end of October he was able to report that Poinsett had

> played a desperate game and has failed in it entirely. In the provinces … a strong feeling in favour of England prevails, public opinion has pronounced itself so very decidedly against the United States, and so general an outcry has been raised against the 'junta' in the capital, that those who were its warmest supporters in the commencement have been the first to disavow all connection with it .... Finding themselves obliged to sacrifice their party or their speculations, most of the gentlemen have broken off all connection with the first in order to pursue the latter under what they conceive to be more favorable auspices.[21]

This led Ward to feel that after all there was a good chance that the Mexicans would agree to changes in the treaty, although a development in November seemed to make it less likely that there would be any further concessions over religion. Victoria received an indirect response to the earlier criticism of the Papal Bull, in the form of a personal letter from the Pope referring to him as 'hijo mio predilecto' (my favourite son), congratulating Mexico on its adherence to the Roman Catholic faith and promising that there would be no political interference from the Vatican. But Ward felt that this 'would tend to enhance the character of the Government in the eyes of the people and therefore might in fact make it easier for them to accept [other] changes to the treaty'.[22] And he retained this confidence even when faced with what seemed a last desperate attempt by Poinsett to poison the atmosphere. On 19 November a vitriolic pamphlet was published referring to 'English tyranny and selfishness' and Britain's 'rejection' of the treaty agreed to by the Mexicans. Ward was convinced Poinsett was behind this because there was 'a striking resemblance between the language which he is in the habit of holding here and many passages in the pamphlet'. He thought Michelena too was probably involved. The pamphlet referred to 'the Mexican Legation [in London] being openly affronted' and to Canning as having 'informed Mr Michelena that he could not receive him publicly as our Envoy, a communication which was neither more nor less than a polite way of turning him out of London and insulting by doing so the whole nation whose representative he was'. Ward's continuing confidence rested on Victoria's quick reaction to this in having the author arrested and expelled, and a strong refutation printed in the newspapers.[23] But from the Mexican point of view, the really important event in November was the final surrender of the castle of San Juan de Ulloa on the 21st, news which was naturally received in the capital with great rejoicing. And this, Ward felt, might increase his difficulties. He wrote to Canning:

> I have more than once told you that inordinate vanity is the President's greatest fault and I own I am not without apprehension that the good fortune which has hitherto attended him will turn his head … the attainment of his wishes [over Ulloa] will only make him more sensible to anything like a slight (which he has always been keenly alive to) and there are but too many persons about him whose object it is to inspire him with an idea that England is inclined to carry things with a high hand …. You must I am sure wish that whatever arrangements you may think necessary should be effected in the most amicable manner.

> It will be time enough to hold strong language when the Mexicans refuse to comply with your demands, in which case it wd be a real satisfaction to give them a severe lesson.[24]

That last sentence is revealing. Ward never lost his affectionate respect for a nation he was convinced had an important part to play in the development of Britain's position in the New World; but he found the Mexicans difficult to deal with and the altitude of Mexico City a strain on patience and health. In one of his letters to Sir John Swinburne, written at intervals over the period of 12 days ending on 30 September, he had begun with some rather bitter comments on Mexico, which he considered was

> certainly advancing in the career of civilization, but not as fast as her admirers & proneurs in England seem to imagine. There is a most lamentable want of talent & probity in those who are at the head of affairs .... I assure you that to preach the necessity of honesty, liberality & fair dealing here is no sinecure … [but they] … have some good men, whose exertions give me hopes that they will improve by degrees; & really, when one considers the last legacy of fanaticism & prejudice betrothed upon them by Spain, and the existence of a strong Spanish party here still, whose interest it is to give these amiable qualities every possible encouragement, one cannot wonder that so much remains to be done.

Emily too had been ill, and he said this had 'contributed to retard her recovery from the effects of her confinement, and she continues so wretchedly thin that I do not know what to do with her'. He doubted whether they would be able to stand remaining in Mexico. But he thanked God for the child, 'such a round plump little animal you never yet saw: very good natured too, and really not at all the bore that I thought it would be, for I had a great horror of its howling'. And he believed Emily would hardly have got on without it. 'It is a complete doll for her, & what with dressing, washing & carrying it about, she fills up a number of leisure hours with it which otherwise, as I am a good deal engaged, might hang heavily upon her hands.

Their social life, however, the Wards found tiresome:

> No Englishwoman ever will or can get on much with these people. She may have as many acquaintances as she pleases, but nothing more: the manners, mode of life and ideas are all too different. Our dinner & evening parties go off well & are allowed to be better than any thing that has been seen yet in Mexico, but they do not bring us a bit nearer to the natives, who never give any thing in return & are hardly to be seen anywhere out of their own houses except in the theatre .... The residents here [by which Ward meant the British merchants] are a terrible set; however, by dint of doing penance occasionally at a great dinner, and listening with patience to a great deal of vulgarity & stupidity, both Em and I stand high in their good graces. Some of the ladies would amuse you with their airs and graces ... but we are determined to affront none of them if we can help it during our reign.[25]

At much the same time he had written to Vaughan, now serving in Washington, that

> Mexico is of all others the place to make one appreciate the value of a wife, for as to society, there is less of it than at Madrid. Fortunately the constant occupation which my friend Mr Poinsett gives me makes up for the want of private amusement; and I can assure you that I have no sinecure of it.[26]

By now Ward was feeling he had had enough of Mexico and he took the opportunity to ask Canning to give him a break:

> If Mr Morier comes out ... in order to remain in possession of the Mission here as soon as the negotiation is satisfactorily concluded, I hope that you will not consider my most earnest request to be allowed to quit Mexico as either improper or unreasonable. My correspondence will have convinced you that I have been placed here in a very difficult situation, and the consequence is that in pursuing the line which I have thought it my duty to take it has been impossible for me not to make some enemies, a circumstance which, though of no sort of consequence to me at present, would render my position here unpleasant if I were to remain in a subordinate capacity. I trust, therefore, that you will not refuse to give me employment in

> some other part of the New or Old World in any situation in which you think I can be of use.[27]

He expressed himself more openly in a letter to Vaughan:

> The responsibility which I have been forced to incur is so great that it almost makes me anxious for Morier to return here ... in order to take his share of the credit, or blame, which under present circumstances may fall to the lot of any English agent in this country .... It is almost impossible to make our Govt understand the difficulties which one has to contend with.

He wrote gloomily of his prospects and the probability of being posted somewhere unpleasant, because

> I am not of consequence enough to have a choice as yet, but must go wherever by the sacrifice of some years of my life I can ensure promotion for the remainder. I have the advantage of being a married man ... and of having a wife who certainly possesses the talent of making a home comfortable, so that I do not much care what becomes of me, provided the place they send me to be but tolerably healthy.[28]

These outpourings were not surprising from one whose health and morale had been sapped by the combination of liver infection and a difficult diplomatic job at high altitude. To make matters worse, he had had a very unhappy experience which must have upset him considerably, although he had coped with it calmly. Morier had brought out to Mexico a young cousin of his, the Hon. Augustus Waldegrave, the son of Granville-George, 2nd Baron Radstock (whose mother was Morier's mother's sister). He had been helping by occasionally copying official correspondence and in April Morier had appointed him officially as a member of the staff of the mission at a salary of £200, pending Foreign Office approval to be paid out of his own (and subsequently Ward's) expense allowance.[29] This approval was obtained, but the letter giving it arrived only after Waldegrave's death on 26 October.[30] Ward had taken him, then aged 22, in a shooting party on an estate recently acquired by Francis Baring (Hacienda del Cristo near the church of Nuestra Señora de los Remedios) then in the outskirts a dozen or so miles north-west of the capital. On this expedition Waldegrave had been accidentally and fatally shot. The circumstances were reported officially to the Foreign Office by Ward in a despatch dated 30 October.[31]

The weather was very hot – 'we remained exposed to a burning sun from six o'clock in the morning till eleven, at which time breakfast was prepared'. No water was available and Baring 'drank a large glass of wine, fasting, which, heated as he was, produced an almost instantaneous effect. During the whole of breakfast both Mr Waldegrave and myself perceived that he was violently excited, and to all appearances unconscious of what he was saying; but conceiving that, from the small quantity of wine which had occasioned this temporary intoxication, it could not last long, we paid less attention to the circumstances than it deserved.' Baring seemed to become more normal, but they became exposed to the sun again, particularly Baring 'having insisted upon putting up his hat to be shot at with a rifle loaded with ball'. It became clear that Baring should not be trusted with a gun so it was taken from him and 'remained *unloaded* upon the ground near us'. A little later, when Ward and Baring were in conversation, Waldegrave came up carrying a gun which looked very like Baring's and asked whose it was. Baring claimed it and continued in conversation with Ward 'holding the gun in a loose, careless manner' with the muzzle 'not a foot from' Ward's body. Ward realized that Baring was 'playing with the cock' and called out a warning to him. Baring turned away from Ward, and while doing so 'his finger must inadvertently have touched the trigger, as the gun went off, and the whole charge, passing over my right arm, entered the left side of Waldegrave a little below the heart'. Ward immediately set off on horseback to Mexico City to summon medical help, but Waldegrave died before he was even out of sight.

Ward was convinced it was a pure accident, saying that Waldegrave and Baring had been close friends. He learned that Baring 'had a nervous affection in the hands' from childhood which caused his hands never to be still but also meant that he had had the triggers of his guns specially adjusted because he could not apply the normal pressure. Baring was so upset that he tried to commit suicide when he realized what he had done, and was only prevented from doing so by force. Ward, on his return to Mexico, 'aware of the dilatory proceedings of Mexican Tribunals in general' summoned 'all the English Residents established in Mexico' and made a deposition on oath before them. They all agreed 'after a most impartial investigation', which included taking evidence from other witnesses, that it had been an accident. Baring was allowed by the Mexican authorities to remain 'under nominal arrest' in Ward's house while the official enquiry was conducted (which eventually came to the same conclusion). The funeral was on the 28th and Ward conducted a service at his house, in the garden of which Waldegrave's body was interred.[32] It was attended by many distinguished Mexicans, and he had to 'limit the number of Mexicans admitted lest the ceremony should be construed into the public exercise of our religion'.

It was heartening for Ward to see such an open demonstration of religious tolerance; but what he really needed was official word from the Foreign Office about the treaty. He had heard that Canning wanted major changes; but he would rather find this true than go on in this continuing uncertainty. It was becoming increasingly difficult to defend the apparent indifference in Britain towards Mexico after all that he had been putting into his relations with the people and their leaders. Victoria he knew to be still determined to have a treaty with Britain before agreeing one with the United States if at all possible, and because of this he was confident that the president would be ready to be as accommodating as he could over changes wanted by Canning; but in the absence of any news at all, even Victoria was likely to weaken in this resolve and might not be able much longer to hold the line against those who favoured the USA rather than Britain. He could not believe that the delay in receiving instructions from London was due solely to the slowness of communications, which he had so often complained about without result. (It was taking 10 to 12 weeks for his official mail to reach him, compared with as little as six for private letters.) He had suggested to Planta that a direct packet should be established 'sufficiently armed to resist Cuban pirates' which could earn revenue by being used by merchants for the shipment of bullion to England.[33] He had complained about the Admiralty refusal to agree that in case of need he could order a naval vessel to sail direct to England with despatches from him.[34] But nothing had been done.

Ward's gloom deepened on 11 December. That day he received some private mail and English newspapers which had been despatched two months earlier. Among this was a package from Rocafuerte addressed to Victoria which he was asked to pass on. He immediately took this personally to Victoria, who asked him to wait while he opened and read the letters. These confirmed that Canning wanted changes to the treaty.[35] No full details were given, but it seemed that Canning was particularly concerned to restore the absolute reciprocity in shipping which had been given up in the April negotiations. Victoria was not pleased, but Ward could only explain that he still had no instructions and therefore could not discuss this. Victoria made clear that he was hurt at receiving no direct communication from Canning about the treaty. He once again stated that he wanted a treaty with England before any other country, but he did not disguise his opinion that England was treating Mexico rather slightingly. He emphasized that any further delay would make it very difficult for him to realize this wish: 'Many people would be inclined to look to the future rather than to the past and to prefer expectations to services already rendered.'[36] Ward could only rather lamely suggest that the delay might be due to Canning's illness, of which news had reached Mexico. But when he got home again and looked at the English newspapers, he realized that this was not the explanation.

14

RENEGOTIATION OF THE TREATY – DECEMBER 1825 TO JANUARY 1826

Ward returned home from his meeting on 11 December 1825 feeling depressed, even though he had parted from Victoria 'on most amiable terms', as he reported to Canning. But before writing his report of this meeting, he had time to read the English newspapers, and in these he found to his surprise that HM Cutter *Vigilant* had reportedly sailed on either 12 or 15 September with despatches for him. If the Foreign Office were sending a special fast ship, the despatches must be important, probably about the treaty. But why had they not yet reached him? A fast cutter, sailing direct, should not have needed more than about six weeks for the passage to Vera Cruz; but if the newspaper report was correct it had already taken twice that time and the ship was still not arrived. He feared the worst. There had been some violent storms in the Gulf of Mexico a few weeks earlier and he could only assume that *Vigilant* had foundered; but he immediately sent a note to Camacho to explain what seemed to have happened, giving it publicity in the hope of scotching rumours that Britain had lost interest in Mexico. And he quickly completed his despatch, sending it via New York as the quickest way to alert the Foreign office to what had happened. He urged Canning to send fresh instructions immediately, for 'amongst a people so prone to suspicion a thousand ridiculous causes will be assigned for the delay … and there are but too many here whose wish & interest it is to turn even the most absurd reports to account provided they can create a momentary prejudice against us'.[1]

This despatch was received in the Foreign Office on 6 February 1826, so he might have got something back from them by the end of

March or early April. But this became unnecessary. On 13 December, just after Ward had signed his despatch, a Foreign Office messenger, Charles Tylecote, turned up with the missing papers. *Vigilant* had indeed sailed from Plymouth – on 11 September – with him on board. All had gone reasonably well (except for some delaying contrary winds) until they were only some 70 miles out from Vera Cruz on 8 November. That night they had been battered by strong gales and lost their bowsprit. Despite this they had then got to within 20 miles of the coast when currents and winds carried them south-west; and on the 15th and 16th there were further gales which dismasted the ship. They eventually managed to get close into Coatzacoalcos, some 150 miles along the coast from Vera Cruz, but they were unable to get over the shoals into the shelter of the river. With difficulty, under jury rig, Lieutenant Sam Meredith RN, in command, succeeded in working back along the coast (despite further gales on 3 December) to make the protection of San Juan de Ulloa and put the messenger ashore on the evening of the 8th (the day before a total eclipse of the sun).[2] There he received generous practical and material help in effecting repairs from the Mexican frigate *Libertad* (which Michelena had bought in England and which still had a British crew).[3]

Tylecote was carrying two particularly important despatches dated 9 September. One contained the first authentic news that the treaty agreed in April was not to be ratified and instructed Ward to assure the Mexicans that 'nothing could be more disagreeable' for His Majesty's Government. But Canning suggested that 'there must have prevailed some strong misapprehension as to the motives and objects of this country … which led the Mexican Ministers and Congress to believe that we were prepared to abandon for the sake of this new connexion principles which we never have conceded in our intercourse with other States'. Canning then listed all the changes he wanted made to the treaty. In particular he objected to the unauthorized insertion of Article 8, giving the protection of the British flag to Mexican persons and goods on board British ships in time of war, which was 'wholly inadmissible' as running counter to all principles followed by His Majesty's Government: it was the 'one [article] which decided beyond doubt the impossibility of ratifying the treaty, and of which the total omission is indispensable', and he 'would rather leave our relations with Mexico altogether unascertained by any positive compact than consent to retain the substance of these stipulations to any extent, or under any modification whatsoever'. Canning also disliked the provisions allowing Mexico to depart from the most-favoured-nation principle in respect of the other former Spanish colonies and Spain (although prepared to see some concession to Spain for a limited time if this would induce her to recognize Mexican independence). And he objected to the concessions given Mexico which departed from the principle of full reciprocity in shipping matters. Other changes required were verbal rather than substantive, but nevertheless of potential difficulty. However, Ward was instructed not to reopen negotiations until he had been joined by Morier, who would be leaving in October. He was only to 'put the Mexican Ministers in possession of the nature and extent' of the objections to the existing text and the new proposals so as to give them time to consider them before Morier's arrival.[4]

In the other despatch Canning made clear that he thought the Mexicans were getting above themselves:

> Although it is hardly to be expected that the refusal of His Majesty's ratification of the treaty should not create an unpleasant impression upon the mind of the Mexican President and Ministers, yet it may perhaps have a salutary effect in sobering, to a certain degree, the somewhat extravagant estimate of the importance of Mexico to Great Britain which appears to pervade the whole mass of the Mexican nation, and which may in all probability have stimulated the unreasonable pretensions of their Plenipotentiaries.
>
> I am persuaded that the solidity and continuance of a good understanding between Great Britain and Mexico will depend upon a right estimate, on both sides, of its real value to each party.

But he added an assurance that whatever happened over the treaty there would be no going back on the appointment of Chargés d'affaires. However, the raising of this level of diplomatic representation could not be considered until a treaty had been ratified. Canning explained that it had been hoped to arrange this simultaneously with Mexico, Colombia and Buenos Aires; but as ratifications had already been exchanged with the last, and were about to be exchanged with Colombia, 'the Mexican Government must not take it amiss if it should happen that the appointments to those two

States shall have taken place previously to the return of the treaty which Mr Morier and you are authorised to conclude and sign. They are not to infer from that priority any partiality to those States over Mexico'.[5]

Ward realized that there might now be little time before Morier arrived in which to try to prepare Victoria and public opinion for the need to climb down over some of the points on which Mexico had extracted concessions during the earlier negotiations; so he arranged to see the president next day, the 14th. Esteva was present. Victoria's first question was to ask whether Canning wanted to reopen what had been agreed on religious toleration. On being assured that Canning had not mentioned this subject, Victoria expressed great relief. But both he and Esteva were guarded in their comments on everything else. There was some discussion of the objection to Article 8 and Ward was able to report to Canning that this would probably not turn out to be a problem; but he warned that there would be difficulty over the special privileges for the other former Spanish colonies, and he recommended that it would be wiser not to insist upon some of the relatively minor verbal changes.[6]

Ward arranged to meet Victoria and Esteva again on the 16th, but before he could do so another messenger arrived from Vera Cruz with the news that Morier was already there. He was an even more reluctant traveller this time, telling his brother before he left 'I gulp the bore of it as well as I can; but it sticks in my throat greatly'. But at least his journey had been pleasant and uneventful. Sailing from Plymouth in HMS *Pyramus* on 20 October, with only a two-day call at Funchal, they had reached Vera Cruz on 13 December,[7] from where he had immediately despatched this messenger with copies of some despatches from Canning dated 14 October. Ward was profoundly disturbed by some of the contents. On 10 October Canning had received Ward's despatch number 12 of 23 June in which he had reported Alamán's 'crowing' over the Mexican success in getting a better bargain in their treaty with Britain than had Colombia (see chapter 12). He had immediately responded angrily:

> There must be an end to all confidential discussion and of all inducement to concession and accommodation on the part of the Plenipotentiaries of Great Britain if every concession made by them is not only presumed as valid before the pleasure of their Government has been taken upon it, but to be held out to the Mexican people as a triumph of Mexican diplomacy. A faithful

> and unbending adherence to instructions will henceforth be the bounden duty of any British Plenipotentiary in Mexico .... The new treaty which you are to negotiate ... must be concluded and signed precisely according to the Project which you are instructed to bring forward, or not at all.

Moreover, while Canning had originally been ready to accept the compromise on religious toleration, being prepared to rely upon 'the gradual but sincere efforts of the leading men in Mexico for producing a more enlightened way of thinking among their countrymen', now he must 'insist upon an Article of a more liberal and tolerant character'. Morier and Ward were instructed to get Mexican consent to a text identical with that agreed to by Colombia 'or one as nearly as possible approaching to it ... or you will not sign the treaty'. The text agreed with Colombia read:

> The subjects of His Britannic Majesty ... shall enjoy the most perfect and entire security of conscience without being annoyed, prevented or disturbed on account of their religious beliefs. Neither shall they be annoyed, molested nor disturbed in the proper exercise of their religion, provided that this take place in private houses and with the decorum due to Divine Worship, and with due respect to the laws, usages and customs of the country.

Even now, however, Canning, unaware then of Alamán's resignation, left them with discretion as to the precise wording 'because, although there is plainly and confessedly much exaggeration, there may be some truth in the representations of the unpreparedness of the Mexican people for such a concession. I do not, therefore, bind you to words; but the Article must be substantially different from that which you before agreed to, and substantially equivalent to that agreed to by Colombia; although it may be varied in phrase to save Mr Alamán's honour.'[8] Despite this sensitivity towards Alamán's honour, however, Canning expressed himself vehemently. He felt that Alamán had an inflated idea of Mexico's position in the world:

> If the Mexican Government shall refuse to sign the treaty ... [it will be seen by the world that] nothing was witholden from Mexico which had been granted to Colombia, and that nothing

> was asked from Mexico to which Colombia had not previously agreed .... [Alamán cannot expect] that England should make extraordinary sacrifices to Mexico ... for the purpose of giving a triumph over both England and Colombia to Mr Alamán and Mexican diplomacy.[9]

Canning had also by then received Ward's despatches reporting Victoria's assurance that Alamán had been speaking out of turn and the reactions to the Papal Bull (see chapter 12) and in another despatch he instructed Ward to convey his pleasure at the president's attitude.[10] Ward realized from this that Canning had misunderstood the significance of what Victoria had been saying to him. And he was much concerned at the contents of a personal letter from Canning to Victoria, to be delivered by Morier. In this he referred to despatches received from Ward

> in which he describes to me in language which does credit to his feelings the satisfaction which he has derived from his recent intercourse with Your Excellency and particularly from the sentiments which Your Excellency has expressed with regard to religious toleration .... I ... assure Your Excellency of my participation in the satisfaction expressed by Mr Ward and ... declare to Your Excellency my conviction that in conceding the utmost which it is possible for you to concede in point of religious toleration in the treaty about to be negotiated, Your Excellency will most effectually exalt the character of your Government, conciliate the good will of His Majesty's subjects, and contribute to strengthen the ties which I trust are henceforth to unite Mexico with Great Britain.[11]

Although Canning obviously thought this would appeal to Victoria's vanity and make him ready to oblige, Ward felt it would have a disastrous effect. It seemed to him that Canning had totally failed to understand the constitutional position of the president and the danger to stability if he even attempted to get this changed. He therefore decided to say nothing on the subject at this stage to the Mexicans, in the hope of persuading Morier to get further instructions from Canning. He had his meeting with Victoria on the 16th as arranged and explained that it was now clear that Canning was not prepared to allow Morier any latitude in the forthcoming discussions. He had also received from Canning the information that the Colombian mission in London had now been raised to the rank of Minister and that the same would apply to Buenos Aires as soon as the necessary Letters of Credence were received. So he informed Victoria of this as well, albeit with the explanation that this was not meant to reflect on Mexico. Ward reported that he had 'seldom seen General Victoria so mortified'.[12] The president begged him to keep this news secret because of the effect it would produce on the public; and he told Ward of a letter he had received from London suggesting that Britain's refusal to ratify the treaty was the result of an agreement that Spain would first recognize the independence of Mexico – provided she remained a monarchy and accepted a member of the Spanish royal family on the throne. This was of course nonsense, and Ward told the president so, taking the opportunity to explain that even if there were no treaty with Britain this would not affect the existing diplomatic relations. But he had also received a copy of another personal letter from Canning to Victoria (written before the one about religion) and he decided to let Victoria know what was in it. After assuring Victoria that the non-ratification of the treaty by Britain 'could not be a greater disappointment to Your Excellency than it has to me', Canning had written:

> Trifling deviations from the course which was prescribed to His Majesty's Plenipotentiaries in the negotiation would have been willingly passed over by my Government for the sake of accomplishing a work which they had so much at heart. But these gentlemen having (although with the best intentions) departed from their instructions upon points essential and fundamental, points which the British Government could not have overlooked in a treaty with any Power in the world, and which therefore it is no affront or disparagement to Your Excellency's Government that we could not overlook in the treaty with Mexico.[13]
>
> The project which is now entrusted to Mr Morier and Mr Ward will I trust be received by Your Excellency with favour; and great will be my satisfaction in exchanging against that of Mexico His Majesty's ratification of a treaty founded on that project.
>
> No man, I entreaty Your Excellency to believe, can be more

> anxious than I am for the arrival of that auspicious moment when the relations of Great Britain with Mexico shall be established in an authentic form; and when I shall be enabled to recommend to my Sovereign the interchange of accredited Ministers between them. But no forms are wanting to confirm the high personal esteem with which I have in the mean time and ever the honour to be.[14]

This went down very well: Victoria said it removed all his doubts. But Ward did not want there to be any misunderstanding, so he also sent in a formal note[15] next day to confirm in writing the main points of Canning's instructions on the treaty. In this he also reproduced some of Canning's strictures about the misapprehensions in the Mexican minds. As he explained to Canning, he had spoken strongly in this lest 'too conciliatory language would only lead the Mexican Government to hope for concessions which it would not be in the power of His Majesty's Government to make'.[16]

Ward thus showed his readiness to do generally what he was told. Provided religion could be kept out of it, he was quite prepared to face a breakdown in the negotiations if this was caused by Mexican obstinacy. On religion, however, he felt that Canning was being unreasonable and that it would be foolish to allow the treaty to founder on that. He therefore once again put his future on the line in a despatch he finished late on the 16th reporting his latest meeting with Victoria. He explained that he had not told Victoria of the second personal letter. He said he was fully aware that 'I must expose myself to a charge of presumption by venturing to place my opinion in opposition to that of His Majesty's Ministers, but upon the present occasion it is my duty to do so, and nothing shall induce me to shrink from the task.' If Canning persisted in pressing for some concession over religion, it was

> likely to prove fatal to all my hopes of seeing your wishes upon other points complied with .... Your resolution appears to have been taken after receipt of despatches which I hoped to see produce a very different effect .... It was never my intention to give His Majesty's Government to understand that in … renewing confidentially to me the assurances of his sincere desire to second the views of His Majesty's Government with regard to the introduction of a more tolerant system, General

> Victoria either intended or could possibly intend to contract any new engagement or to pledge himself to anything to which he was not pledged already.

To do now as Canning wanted would only compel Victoria 'to disavow the pledge altogether and to entitle him to regard himself as relieved from all his former promises'.[17]

Ward followed this up with a private and personal letter to Canning, written at '6 in the morning [of the 17th] ... after sitting up all night in order to finish some despatches', in which he emphasized that it was 'not in General Victoria's power to make *any* concession in favour of the private or public exercise of our religion, both being equally prohibited by an express article of the Constitution'. He was concerned lest Victoria would conclude from Canning's letter that he, Ward, had misrepresented his position and that the consequence would be the loss 'for ever of the unreserved communication which I have hitherto enjoyed with Gen[l] Victoria, and with it, in a great measure, of the power of making myself of use both during the negotiations and afterwards'. Ward made clear, however, he would abide by Morier's decision on the line to be taken in the renewed negotiations. But he would 'at least have the satisfaction of thinking, if forced to pursue a course, the fatal consequences of which are inevitable, that I have done my utmost to avert the blow, and have not allowed any personal considerations to prevent me from stating, most unreservedly, my opinion'.[18]

This is a classic example of a diplomatic officer doing everything short of resigning rather than comply with instructions with which he profoundly disagrees. And Ward then made determined efforts to get Morier to agree with him. He sent his despatches under flying seal to the consul in Jalapa to be shown to Morier on his way from Vera Cruz, with a letter proposing that they should seek further instructions and should meet in Puebla to discuss the problem. Morier got this on the 18th and immediately wrote to Canning to say that while Ward's despatches made the outlook rather uncertain, so far as he was concerned 'nothing shall be wanting to the fulfilment of your instructions'.[19] He replied to Ward agreeing to a meeting in Puebla, but suggesting that he was making a lot of fuss about nothing: in his view the Mexican constitution did not specifically prohibit the *private* exercise of non-Catholic religions, which was all that Canning was asking for. On seeing what Morier had written to Canning, Ward wrote another despatch repeating his conviction that it would be hopeless to try to get the concession on religion.[20] On Morier's view on the constitutional position he argued that the possibility of regarding the prohibition applicable only to *public* worship had never hitherto been considered: as it was not in the power of the Executive to decide such a question, an appeal to Congress would be necessary and this would

> be opposed by the Clergy whose members are considerable both in the Senate and in the Chamber of Deputies, by those who … are conscientiously fanatics, and by the more enlightened deputies on constitutional grounds .... His Majesty's Plenipotentiaries have no means of opposing this formidable coalition .... There is not therefore in my own mind the least doubt as to the result of the discussion, and whatever prospect His Majesty's Commissioners might have had of terminating the negotiation successfully under other circumstances, from the moment that it was deemed necessary to insist upon religious concessions their task became a hopeless one.

To bring the religious question forward now would 'give Mexico the only vantage ground which she could possibly have in a discussion with England, and enable General Victoria to state to the world (as he must do in his own defence) that although a treaty with His Majesty's Government, next to the independence of his country, had been the great object of his political career, he has sacrificed it without hesitation to a feeling of religious respect for the infant institutions of the state'.

Ward set off on the 30th to meet Morier in Puebla. So anxious was he to get there without delay that he arranged to have four of his own horses stationed at suitable intervals along the road so that he could have fresh mounts to enable him to cover the whole distance of some 80 miles in one go, which he accomplished in eight and a quarter hours, doing the return journey three days later in just under eight hours.[21] But he found Morier determined to stick to his instructions and had to give way. On his return to the capital he sent Victoria a private letter[22] to explain that the question of religion was being reopened entirely because of Alamán's actions. He conveyed as *Canning*'s view (although it was in fact Morier's) that the Mexican government had it in their power to interpret the constitution as prohibiting only the *public* exercise of religions other than the Catholic, and that the firmness shown over the Papal Bull suggested that this interpretation could be adopted without difficulty. (He explained to Canning later that he had thought this would carry more weight if presented as his opinion.) Although he made clear that he did not personally share that view, he tried to persuade Victoria to accept Canning's point by suggesting that the enterprise was 'worthy of Your Excellency in every respect. But the greater the difficulty, the greater the praise, and if Your Excellency can succeed in enabling His Majesty's Government to carry their views upon this subject into execution, you will have the satisfaction not only of raising the character of your country in the eyes of the world, but of cementing by new ties that friendship which is, I hope, for many years to connect Mexico with Great Britain.' But this flattery did not work. When Ward called on him next day, 4 January 1826, to give him a full translation of Canning's instructions of 14 October and the personal letter about religion, Victoria expressed all his usual assurances of wanting to meet Canning's wishes – 'he would call Heaven to witness that the happiest day of his life would be that upon which he could see his country in a fit state to adopt all Mr Canning's views'; but he remained adamant that he could not move yet on religion. Time must be allowed. To attempt now to amend the constitution as regards religion would be fatal. He would not even be prepared to enter new negotiations upon the basis proposed.[23]

When Morier reached the capital, he and Ward saw Victoria together; but the latter was still adamant that he would not enter any negotiation so long as the religious question was to be reopened. He said that 'every member of his Government' and almost every member of Congress 'deplored the existence of the restrictions in their constitution' and if he had had any hand in forming it he would never have agreed to it. But there was unanimous agreement throughout the country 'upon the necessity of preserving that constitution, be it good, or be it bad, sacred and untouched until the time appointed for its revision .... To agitate the question of religion, the only one upon which they now were vulnerable by Spain, would throw the whole country into such a ferment that the most fatal consequences might be expected to ensue.' He spoke in 'the bitterest terms' of Alamán's conduct 'which he allowed had so justly roused' Canning's indignation; but he felt that once the actions taken against him were known in England (he referred to Alamán as having been dismissed), that indignation would evaporate. Could Morier and Ward not refer back for further instructions? Meanwhile he hoped the reason for delay could be kept secret from the Mexican public.

This development had of course been foreseen by Ward, but Morier had declined to allow it to affect his actions. He was now in a difficult position. Was he simply to give up, await further instructions from London (which at the very best would take some three to four months to reach them) and so risk leaving the field clear to the Americans? He was persuaded by Ward to compromise. They would ask Canning to reconsider the question if the Mexicans would first agree all the rest of the treaty exactly as he wanted it. The Mexicans agreed to this as a basis for opening the negotiations. Morier and Ward informed Canning of this, saying that Ward, 'who feels himself more particularly interested in the result of this negotiation', would return to England, taking with him a declaration signed by the Mexican plenipotentiaries confirming that all the rest was accepted provided the religious article could remain as agreed before. If Canning would then agree to this, the treaty would be signed upon Ward's return to Mexico and Morier would immediately take it to England.[24]

It is a measure of Ward's passionate determination to see a treaty successfully concluded that he was prepared to leave Emily (who was now two months into her second pregnancy) alone in Mexico while he made this dash across the Atlantic and back, involving an absence which would probably not have been less than four months. As it turned out, however, he was not called upon to perform this service because the negotiations unexpectedly broke down for another reason. It is nonetheless ironical that only a month after this despatch was sent off, and before it reached the Foreign Office, the point was being surrendered by Canning. Ward's December despatches having by then been received, Planta wrote to him: 'If in consequence of what you now represent to be the feeling in Mexico (however different it may be from what Mr Canning collected from your former reports) you and Mr Morier shall have determined to forbear either to press the article respecting religion upon the Mexican Government or to deliver Mr Canning's private letter upon the same subject to the President, Mr Canning will not disapprove of such determination.'[25] If only communications had been quicker in those days! But this was not received before the second attempt to agree a treaty began on Friday 20 January 1826.[26]

Surprisingly, the first rounds with Camacho and Esteva went well.

By the following Sunday the Mexicans had agreed to drop the provisions giving special advantages to the other former Spanish colonies and the article giving protection to Mexican persons and property in British ships in time of war which had so offended Canning's principles. There were a few arguments over some of the other changes required by Canning, but by the 25th even these were all settled – except for one. The Mexicans flatly refused to agree to the restoration of complete reciprocity in shipping matters. They explained that Congress had just introduced a proposal for allowing a reduction of 3 or 4 per cent in duties on goods exported from or imported at Mexican ports in Mexican ships. They felt this was the only way of providing some financial incentive for the creation of a Mexican merchant fleet. Morier and Ward said they could not depart from their instructions on this point, and the Mexicans said that in that case they could not sign a treaty. They asked that this, as well as the religious issue, be referred back to London. Morier and Ward refused and 'became perfectly of one mind that under the existing circumstances the negotiation as far as regarded ourselves ceased from this moment and it was agreed that the Mexican Plenipotentiaries should without delay state this fact to us by an official Note'.

Victoria, however, would have none of this. Sending a message to say that he regretted he was unable to call on Morier and Ward jointly, he asked that Ward should call on him that evening. (That Morier should have agreed to this is surprising; but he knew that Ward could not agree anything behind his back and he must have decided that there might be something to gain by letting him use his special personal relationship with Victoria to try to find a way out of an apparent impasse.) Victoria made clear to Ward that he was not prepared to consider the negotiations at an end. He thought 'that Mexico had a right to expect that His Majesty's Plenipotentiaries would allow her to make that reference to England which their own instructions did not admit of, and that they would not, by any decisive step upon their side, break off a treaty which might almost be said to be concluded'. He wanted to prove 'that the misconduct of one man was not to be regarded as a fair criterion of the feelings either of the Government or of the nation, and that [Mexico] was ready to make any sacrifice in order to secure the friendship of England not entirely inconsistent with what she conceived was to her own interests and safety'. He accepted the principle of reciprocity which Canning wanted, but he wanted time before it was applied. He would make clear in an official note to be delivered next day that he considered the negotiations still open and that he would send Camacho to England to continue them. In selecting his Minister for Foreign Affairs for this he was giving proof of the importance he attached to the mission and of his personal respect for Britain. 'Were England alone interested [in the question at issue] he would gladly comply with her demands and he was *ready to do so at the present moment* provided she would consent to accept of the reciprocity demanded by her as a *privilege* conferred upon her in return for having decided by her interference the struggle for independence in the New World.' But he had to make clear that there was a special reason else he would have to concede the same to France and other European powers; and if they conceded full reciprocity in shipping 'before Mexico possessed a single ship of her own, it would be impossible that she should ever possess one'. He made clear that he regarded a treaty with England as the basis of all future treaties and that 'until this treaty was satisfactorily arranged nothing should induce him to conclude one with the United States or with any other Power'.[27]

Morier agreed with Ward that this proposal should be accepted, although in the despatch reporting their actions, he insisted on telling Canning that 'as far as regards ourselves, and the instructions and Powers under which we have acted, we have declared the negotiations at an end', making clear that they did not regard themselves as acting as a channel for communicating Mexican wishes to Canning, and that they had told the Mexicans that they had accepted their proposal on the basis that the *only* issue to be raised by Camacho was that of shipping reciprocity. But he did agree to add that 'in justice to the President and his Ministers with whom we have negotiated, we must take the liberty of stating our conviction that they have acted towards us with perfect good faith'.

All this must have put a strain on Ward's relations with Morier, who remained reluctant to make even this departure from instructions which he felt left them no discretion.[28] Ward wrote personally to Canning to say that he had endeavoured 'most honestly … to assist Mr Morier in presenting [the religious article] in the most favourable light' but

> when I found that the President was even more decided in his opposition than I had apprehended, I laboured as earnestly to induce Mr Morier not to break off the treaty without another

> reference to yourself .... Upon every other point I have been to the full as inflexible as Mr Morier; but, feeling as I do that the members of the present Govt of Mexico are most sincere in their desire to meet your wishes, and that they have made all the amends in their power for the unprincipled conduct of an unprincipled man, I should be sorry to see them pay the penalty of his errors; and such would have been the case had negotiation been broken off, *in limine*, upon an article which, but for him, H M's Govt had determined to concede.[29]

However, Morier, in his personal letter to Canning, accepted responsibility:

> When I bring to mind the kind manner in which you were pleased to express yourself towards me on my departure for this Mission, I feel in great measure consoled for the unsatisfactory form which it has taken. I was soon satisfied on my arrival here that we could not expect any religious concessions for the present – but I own I was not prepared for a failure on any other point.
>
> I trust, however, that you may be induced to give Mr Camacho a favorable reception, because I am convinced that this Govt have been sincere in their endeavours to conciliate England, and that it is only the fear of their Congress which obliges them to act with great caution.

And he added that he could 'scarcely allow myself to say how difficult a people we have had to deal with'.[30]

It was now nearly the end of January 1826 and it was not unreasonable to suppose that Camacho would get to London before the end of April and there would be a treaty, agreed and ratified, well before the end of the year. Once again, however, fate was to decree otherwise.

15

A TREATY IS FINALLY AGREED – JANUARY 1826 TO JULY 1827

The second attempt to agree a treaty with Mexico came to an end on 25 January 1826. The decision by Morier and Ward next day that a third attempt should be made in London was a triumph for Ward over Morier, his senior. But Morier by now had lost such small interest as he had ever had in the fate of relations with what he considered to be difficult people. He had returned to Mexico at the end of 1825 with unambiguous instructions: unless the Mexicans accepted every last word of the text now to be presented to them there would be no treaty: Mexico, in Canning's view, was simply not important enough to Britain to be allowed to go on trying to persuade His Majesty's Government to make special concessions which offended against sacrosanct principles governing Britain's international policies. Morier, left to himself, would almost certainly have followed those instructions to the letter and would have left Mexico a second time with a public declaration that negotiations for a treaty had finally failed because of Mexican intransigence. Had he done so, who knows what the consequences might have been? Canning would not have regarded this as a reason for reducing relations to consular level. But might Victoria have felt so disillusioned that *he* would have decided to turn his back on Britain? Or might he have come under such political pressure that he had to make some gesture, however distasteful personally? One thing is as certain as anything now can be: he would not have climbed down over the treaty in the face of such action by Morier. It would have been political suicide to do so.

Fortunately, Ward saw further ahead than Morier and persuaded him to be flexible. This was despite all the personal irritations he so often felt over the Mexican refusal, as he saw it, to behave sensibly towards the one European power which was in a position to help them consolidate their independence from Spain. There may have been a small element of personal determination not to let Poinsett have the satisfaction of seeing him defeated after all; but his main motive was a genuine belief that Canning was wrong to be so intransigent, and that Britain's real, long-term interests went beyond a matter of principle in shipping reciprocity. He felt strongly, as apparently Canning did not, that in the long term Britain's interest lay in helping Mexico to remain independent, not simply from Spain but from commercial and political imperialism on the part of the United States, and that more than simple diplomatic recognition was needed to achieve this. As Ward saw it, they had in Mexico at that time a leader who understood that getting Britain's help in this way was also in his own country's interest; but he also saw clearly that politically Victoria was not in a strong enough position to give more weight to this longer-term interest than others gave to the immediate question of national dignity. And indeed Victoria himself, he was sure, was not ready to put that aside, even had he been strong enough to do so. Nevertheless, even Ward felt there were limits to how far Mexico could be allowed to go before Britain's own dignity was at risk.

Morier no doubt felt that, provided he could get home to his family with as little delay as possible, it mattered not how this was achieved. He had already decided that he did not want to be minister in Mexico. So he prepared to accompany Camacho. But almost immediately Camacho fell dangerously ill and once again the way was open for Poinsett and those Mexicans opposed to a treaty with Britain to make mischief. Had Victoria been able to name Camacho while announcing the proposed mission and the reason for it, perhaps Congress would have made no difficulties. As it was, however, there was a delay while he chose a substitute, and when he then proposed instead to send Gómez Pedraza, his Minister for War, the Senate refused to sanction it. Morier and Ward were convinced that this was Poinsett's doing, working on 'a spirit in the Senate at variance with the friendly disposition of the Government towards [Britain]'.[1] When tackled, Poinsett strenuously denied any anti-British prejudice but admitted that his advice had been sought on a constitutional question. And as the Mexican constitution was modelled closely on that of the United States, he had simply confirmed that in his view the Senate had the power to veto any diplomatic appointment abroad. He did, however, tell Morier that he believed the feeling in the Senate was such that they would never agree to any minister being despatched to Britain on a mission of the kind in question. National dignity was at issue, and to send a minister looked like undignified begging.

It was by now the middle of March and Camacho had recovered sufficiently for Victoria to confirm his original appointment for the mission to England. But Morier, fed up with this shilly-shallying, and believing there was a serious risk that Camacho too would be rejected by the Senate, decided that it would offend British dignity if he were any longer to 'wait an event which depends upon the decision of a body shewing itself so little inclined to second this particular act of their Government, and which seems to manifest so little alacrity in giving any facility towards strengthening the bonds of friendship between their country and Great Britain'. HMS *Pyramus* had been kept waiting at Vera Cruz long enough, and he set off from the capital on 18 March to take passage home in her alone,[2] leaving Ward with the responsibility of finding on his own a way of implementing the proposal to continue the negotiations in London. Ward, with his concurrence, sent with him a despatch explaining, as justification for departing from instructions, that they had hitherto put their faith 'in the sincerity and good intentions of the [Mexican] Government'. While still believing in Victoria's own feelings for Britain, they could no longer count on his ability to persuade Congress to feel the same way. They could not 'sustain properly the dignity of our country and the character of His Majesty's Government were we to allow any longer an opinion of General Victoria *personally* to influence our conduct in a question of such importance'.[3] Ward told Canning that if the appointment of Camacho were also to be rejected by the Senate, he would advise Victoria to leave it at that; and he would make clear that he would not be prepared to ask for a ship of the British navy to convey anyone else to England: 'The compliment to His Majesty's Government consisted in the mission of a *Minister*. It was under this impression that His Majesty's Commissioners consented to allow the negotiation to remain pending until your pleasure was known.' He was convinced that Poinsett, 'jealous of the proof of friendship and respect which the President wished to give His Majesty's Government, was exerting himself to create difficulties by exciting the passion and playing upon the vanity of a factious body'. He felt that a second refusal by the Senate would 'convert … the proposed compliment into a slight', so he proposed to make that body 'aware of the very serious consequences with which [their refusal] will be attended', and that it could lead to a refusal by His Majesty's Government to hold any communication at all with anyone they might eventually agree to send to London. He hoped he would not have to use such strong language, but if he did have to, and subsequently the Mexicans did send someone other than a minister, he hoped that person's reception in England would be such as to demonstrate clearly His Majesty's Government's resentment. 'I thought' he wrote 'that allowances should be made for a people in their infancy and hoped that they would be productive of a good effect. But when I see that concessions only lead to new demands, and that condescension on the part of England is repaid by an increase of obstinacy and infatuation here, I should conceive myself wanting in my duty were I not to recommend a very different course.'

Almost immediately Ward received information from some friends that Poinsett had indeed been trying to convince senators that to send a *minister* to Britain on such a mission was undignified and, moreover, would lead to an even worse indignity should the mission fail. He therefore confronted Victoria personally in order to try 'by using very strong language' to rouse him to take some positive action. But he found him dejected and unwilling to stand up to the Senate. He made absolutely clear to Victoria that Britain would find any emissary other than Camacho quite unacceptable: it was Victoria himself who had proposed sending a minister, and it was this that had persuaded him and Morier of his good intentions. 'If' he told Victoria, 'after making a proposal of the greatest importance to the interests of the country, it appeared that the government had neither the right to make it without the concurrence of the Senate, nor influence enough to secure that concurrence now that the proposal was made, it would be weakness, and more than weakness on our part to allow His Majesty's Government to be trifled with any longer .... If ... Camacho's mission were now to be given up because the Senate conceived it to be an act of too great condescension on the part of Mexico towards Great Britain' the result would be fatal: there would be no treaty and His Majesty's Government might even decide to have no higher than consular relations with Mexico. The true position would have to be explained to the British Parliament and to the world. They 'would be told that, instead of the liberal views which were supposed to reign in Mexico, prejudice and suspicion were still all powerful, that the most important questions were decided not by their real merits but by a tissue of intrigues, and that even in a case where the vital interests of the country were at stake, nothing could be effected because the President and the legislative body were played off against one another by a junta of freemasons with a foreign Minister at their head'.[4]

Ward believed that he had succeeded, by using such language, in rousing Victoria from his irresolution; but he reinforced his attack with a letter to Dr José Manuel Ceballos, one of the senators he knew to be friendly, setting out the sequence of events leading up to Victoria's decision to send Camacho to England.[5] His tactics paid off. Camacho's appointment was approved by the senate by 23 votes to 4. Ward gave all the credit for this to Victoria who, he reported, had actually told some senators that he would no longer remain president 'if … the honour and plighted faith of the Government were to be again wantonly sacrificed'.[6] But he found it once again difficult to explain 'the anomaly of such energetic language being held at one time and such unaccountable apathy displayed at another. It is one of those contradictions peculiar to this country which one must take advantage of, but which it is impossible to account for.' At least, he felt, the delay in bringing the matter to a head had allowed time for his own propaganda to work, although he recognized the risk he had run 'of widening the breach, in the event of a second failure, in order to convince the Mexicans of the extreme importance of the point' and in threatening 'them with a positive rupture with Great Britain as the best means of preventing that rupture from taking place'. Ward, of course, had no authority to make such a threat, and once again had to seek retrospective approval from Canning for his actions: 'I am willing to confess, however, that nothing but the success with which [his strong words] has been attended could warrant the expedient to which I resorted, and it is to your indulgence that I must look for my justification.'

Poinsett may have failed to stop Victoria sending a minister to England, but in Ward's view he never missed an opportunity for making trouble for him. An example of this was described by Ward in a despatch to Canning dated 30 March.[7] The occasion was a St Patrick's Day dinner organized by the local Irish community. Ward had made sure, before agreeing to attend, that there was no intention of making it a political or religious event. Poinsett was also a guest and, in replying to a toast to the President of the United States, he referred to the many Irish who had taken refuge in the USA. His toast was: 'May those civil and religious privileges which the Irish enjoy to the full in [the USA] … be not long denied to them in their native country.' Ward decided not to react directly to this, but later in the dinner he took an opportunity to say publicly that he was glad the harmony of the evening had not been interrupted 'even by the very pointed allusion which had been made to the only subject upon which a difference could exist between the natives of Ireland and their British brethren'. And he went on to give a short lecture on what he thought to be the true position, particularly stressing that the Irish had never sought the interference or the sympathy of a foreign power. Poinsett made a reply to this, but Ward decided then to leave.

Ward was later told that Poinsett had then made several more derogatory statements. Despite this, he determined to say no more. But Poinsett next day called on O'Gorman, who was laid up at home, to make a 'very warm vindication of his conduct'. He accused Ward of allowing his opinion of himself (Poinsett) to be 'biassed by tale bearers' and professed 'the most amicable sentiments towards Great Britain'. O'Gorman sent Ward a written record of this interview. Ward felt he now had to respond and he decided to do so in the form of a letter to O'Gorman, to be shown to Poinsett if necessary. He explained that he had only gone to the dinner on receiving the assurance that it would not be political or religious and had assumed that Poinsett would have known about this. He asked O'Gorman to explain this to Poinsett and to assure him that any differences between them were political and not personal. He was aware that Poinsett had always personally shown great friendliness towards any Englishman with whom he had dealings. 'Were I fortunate enough to meet Mr Poinsett in any part of the world where I could be convinced that the interests of the two countries were indeed the same, there is no man whose intimacy I should more court.' Ward presumably felt he had to forestall any report that might reach Canning's ears through American channels and he asked him to accept that he was nonetheless justified by all that had passed and been reported by him since last September in continuing to have no confidence in Poinsett, which suggests that those last sentiments did not run deeper than diplomatic politeness.

Meanwhile, however, it was still not plain sailing for Ward in his efforts to get Camacho to England. He wrote to Admiral Sir Lawrence Halstead at Jamaica on 28 April asking him to make a ship available. Halstead did not receive this until 19 June and the best he could then do was to allocate HMS *Hussar*, a roomy 38/46 gun frigate of over 1000 tons, which he was expecting to be available in about three weeks. She eventually reached Vera Cruz on Monday 14 August and then had to spend some time loading nearly $1 million in specie before she could sail for Britain. During this long interval of waiting, further efforts were made to sabotage Camacho's mission, notably by Michelena who tried to convince Victoria, basing himself on his own experiences, that Camacho would not be received in England in a way appropriate to the dignity of Mexico. Ward assured both Victoria and Camacho that the circumstances, now that His Majesty's Government had given proper recognition to Mexico as an independent and sovereign state, would be very different.[8] Camacho himself had doubts about the wisdom of accepting this mission, although not for that reason or from any reluctance to make the journey. He was worried about what might happen in his absence over the negotiations for a treaty with the United States. He did not trust Esteva to stand up to Poinsett, and he told Victoria that he would not go to England unless he, Victoria, promised that 'not a single article of the American treaty' would be discussed until he returned.[9] Because of the delay over his departure, however, the negotiations with Poinsett were in fact completed and the treaty signed on 10 July (but not ratified), before Camacho left for England with formal instructions which empowered him to agree to anything 'deemed advisable' and emphasized that his mission was a continuation of the negotiations, not a new initiative. He was to sign the treaty in London and then return with it so that the other plenipotentiaries involved in the earlier rounds of negotiation could sign too. In reporting this to Canning, Ward indirectly hinted at his hope that he would thus be allowed to put his own signature to such an historic document, saying 'I will not pretend to deny the anxiety with which I shall look forward to the adoption or rejection [by Canning] of the plan proposed by the President in as far as it affects myself.'[10] But he laid particular stress on the importance of allowing Esteva to be one of the Mexican signatories because of the great store he set by this, and because his help would be needed in the future, particularly to secure ratification.

Ward was also anxious lest the Mexicans should find the cost of the journey excessive, and lest Camacho himself would suffer embarrassment, or worse, by finding himself a passenger in a ship calling at Havana. When consulted by Victoria about the sum which should be offered to the captain of *Hussar*, he suggested that as Camacho would be accompanied 'by only four people and very few servants', $5000 (£1000) would be appropriate. He wanted to avoid the unpleasant impression created when Captain Murray had charged such an excessive amount to take Michelena to England. And when telling Captain Harris of this he said: 'If, from the great expense of providing stock at Vera Cruz this sum should prove insufficient, the fault is mine and I only beg that I may be acquainted with it in order that it may be corrected. I am sure, however, that I have only done justice to your feelings as a British officer in stating, as I have done, that a sum sufficient to cover your expenses is all that you could desire or would accept.' At the same time he explained the importance of not touching at Havana on the way to England.[11] Harris was entirely amenable. In his reply he offered his 'unreserved and cordial acknowledgements of the handsome compliment you have so liberally bestowed upon my character. I confess that I am more than proud, and far better pleased, than if your suggestion had been thrice the amount, and I pray of you to dismiss any apprehensions as to the sum named not being ample .... I hope to be enabled to entertain the Minister with all the comforts that his distinguished rank entitles him to receive without any loss. Indeed, my only fears are that you have been too liberal.' Moreover, Harris assured Ward that although he was under orders to make communication with Havana on his passage, he would not anchor and would remain off as short a time as possible; and if he saw any sign that the Spanish authorities there might try to make mischief he would disregard his orders and sail direct to England.[12] This was indeed a refreshing change in the naval attitude.

In the event it did not go quite like that, although fortunately Camacho does not seem to have been put out by what did happen. (Ward described him in a letter to Vaughan as 'one of the most thoroughly good and honourable men whom it has been my lot to fall in with here'.)[13] He and his party (of three secretaries and four servants) were received on board *Hussar* on Saturday 26 August, with the full courtesy of a 15-gun salute. She set sail at 1.40 p.m. the next day; but instead of sailing direct for England, Harris chose to call at Tampico to load more specie. And, contrary to his earlier assurances, they actually moored in Havana harbour on 14 September for two days. However, the Spanish authorities made no trouble. On the contrary, the governor sent a member of his staff to call on Camacho, so the latter may even have felt that he had won a political bonus. *Hussar* anchored at Spithead at 2.40 p.m. on Friday 13 October.[14] There were no special arrangements for receiving Camacho, who asked one of the officers to take a note for Canning to London announcing his arrival and requesting customs clearance for the baggage. Whether he wished to make a point, or whether (as is the more likely) he genuinely thought this for the best, he explained that he had sent the note in this way 'in order to prevent any delay which might arise from [one of his own staff] not possessing the acquaintance with the country required for conveying my communication to Your Excellency's hands' with proper expedition.[15] No doubt he was well enough looked after at Southampton, and possibly Rocafuerte came down to escort him to London, which he reached on Thursday the 19th. There he settled into 24 Park Crescent which Rocafuerte had rented for him.

There was some confusion over his first call at the Foreign Office. Canning was absent in Paris, so Rocafuerte sent a note to Planta asking for an appointment to present Camacho to him. Planta was unwell at home, but he arranged for a reply to be sent inviting them to call on him at the office on Saturday the 21st at 2.0 p.m. By 2.30 his visitors had not arrived, and Planta then discovered that his instructions had not been carried out, so no reply had been sent to Rocafuerte's note. He immediately despatched a charming letter of apology (in French) to them, saying *he* would call upon *them* next day, Sunday, at the same time, or, if this was not convenient, receive them at the Foreign Office on Monday.[16] Rocafuerte replied that Camacho was 'vraiment reconnaissant à votre attention et politesse' and they would call at the Foreign Office on Monday.[17] Further balm was administered by Canning himself who, having received Camacho's note in Paris, had taken the trouble to reply with an apology for not being able to receive him at once.[18] When he was able to receive him, on his return from Paris, he did so in such a manner as to cause Camacho great pleasure. Ward was able to write to Canning on 15 January 1827 to tell him that Camacho had been taking 'every opportunity since his arrival of informing me of the deep sense which he entertains of the manner in which he has been received by you, and I can assure you that the conduct which you have been pleased to adopt towards this gentleman has created a strong and universal impression of gratitude throughout the country'.[19] Canning was no doubt himself well pleased with the letter which Victoria had sent him, written in his own hand, about Camacho's appointment, which included: 'Your Excellency's name which is heard with such pleasure and respect in America will acquire fresh claims to the affection and esteem of the Mexicans in addition to those which you have already so well merited' when the treaty is agreed.[20] And Canning told Ward in Mexico that 'no exertion will be wanting on my part to bring [Camacho's] Mission as speedily as possible to a favourable conclusion'.[21] By now, having had the benefit of discussions with Morier and many more despatches from Ward, he may have decided that it would be in Britain's interests to reach a harmonious understanding with Mexico as soon as possible. And he lost no time in doing so.

The first formal meeting between Canning and Camacho to begin discussion of the treaty was on 29 November 1826 when Canning was accompanied by Morier and the President of the Board of Trade, William Huskisson. He told Camacho to regard all three of them as the British plenipotentiaries, but explained that only Morier and Huskisson would sign the treaty.[22] He opened by expressing his sorrow at the Mexican attitude on the religious question, asking whether it would not be possible at least to include in the treaty a definite date by which the Mexican constitution would be changed in this respect. Camacho regretted that this was out of the question, but assured Canning that everything possible was being done to bring about what he wanted; and he agreed to a further amendment to the text agreed with Victoria to remove all doubt about the intention to modify the treaty in this respect as soon as it became possible. Canning then accepted that this was as much as he could get at this stage. He also accepted the need for a transition period during which the principle of full reciprocity over shipping would not apply. In return Camacho agreed to this being limited to ten years. It was also agreed, however, that Britain too would have the right to discriminate in British ports in favour of her own ships, but that neither party would apply greater discrimination against the other than against ships of the most favoured nation. After ten years the principle of full reciprocity would be applied if by then 'the interests of British navigation should be found to be prejudiced by the present exceptions'. With this excellent start it is surprising that it should then have taken a further four weeks to reach full agreement on a complete text, which was signed on 26 December (see Appendix II).[23] No doubt lawyers and others had to agree every comma.

It was Rocafuerte, not Camacho, who left on the 27th (in HMS *Caliope*) to take one of the signed copies to Mexico. Camacho remained in London for another seven months. He had brought with him credentials addressed to the king, signed by Victoria and Pedraza, which appointed him Envoy Extraordinary and Minister Plenipotentiary from 'the moment that the treaty … shall have been concluded and signed … to reside in that capacity with the Government of Your

Majesty for such a period as shall be necessary';[24] but he was not granted this status. He requested an audience with the king on the strength of these credentials, on which Canning noted: 'This will require a cautious answer.' There is no record now of what answer was given, but equally there is no evidence that Camacho took offence. He was active during his time in London in concluding agreements on behalf of Mexico with the Dutch and Prussia, and trying to do the same with France. But he had some problems with the Foreign Office. He gave up renting 24 Park Crescent and the owner, a Mr John Bainbridge, tried to dun him for damages to it to the extent of £184-12-9d. Camacho declined to pay and Bainbridge appealed to the Foreign Office for help. Camacho's secretary, Gutiérrez de Estrada, assured the Foreign Office on 17 March 1827 that it was only the amount claimed that was in dispute. This was being handled by agents appointed by Camacho and he was sure the matter would be settled.[25] Camacho then went off to Paris, but three weeks later the Foreign Office had to intervene again, this time with a remarkably stiff note to Murphy, who had been left in charge, saying 'the agents employed by M Camacho continue to raise frivolous objections and to put forward offers which you will forgive me for saying cannot be considered in any other light than derogatory to the dignity of their principal'. An offer of £25 had been made. The note continued: 'I trust, therefore, that you will see occasion as well out of respect to Mr Estrada's assurances as from regard for the honour of your Government, to direct M Camacho's agents to proceed forthwith to a fair and equitable adjustment of Mr Bainbridge's claim.'[26] Nevertheless the business dragged on. When Camacho returned from Paris, Estrada was at first refused an interview with John Backhouse, who had by now replaced Planta. One was eventually granted in June and it was then known that Camacho was about to return to Mexico, having suffered a relapse in his health. This led to agreement to put the matter to arbitration, but there is no record of what sum was eventually paid, or when.[27]

Camacho, however, did not leave in June. Whether his health problems were genuine, or simply diplomatic (perhaps he was getting tired of waiting around and having no proper home)[28] is not clear. He had asked for a naval vessel to take him back to Mexico,[29] but none was available before 15 July, and this turned out to be too small for his party. HM Sloop *Slaney* was then made available, to be ready at Woolwich by 21 July, and this was accepted.[30] This delay at least had one advantage. Ratification of the treaty had gone surprisingly smoothly after Rocafuerte had reached Mexico City with it on 22 February. The Council of Ministers had immediately sent it to a committee of the Chamber of Deputies, which had reported favourably on 3 March. Ward had taken action to forestall trouble at that stage. In December 1825 he had prepared a translation of the instructions from Canning brought out by Morier with a view to giving it circulation as a means of persuading members of Congress of the reasonableness of the British position. In view of the decision to transfer the negotiations to London, he had not used this at the time but he now passed it around because he felt that it gave the 'best and simplest explanation of the motives which induced His Majesty's Government not to ratify' the earlier text.[31] In addition, to obviate the possibility that Congress might give attention first to the treaty with the United States, which had been submitted to the Chamber of Deputies on 2 November 1826 but had not yet been debated, Ward suggested that one article of each treaty should be discussed alternately, a device which would have ensured that the British text of only 15 articles would breast the tape before the American of 35. The British treaty, however, was in fact approved unanimously by the deputies on 15 March, after only two days' discussion, and ratified unanimously by the Senate on the 31st. Rocafuerte reached London with the Mexican ratification just in time for the exchange of instruments to be carried out between Camacho, himself and Lord Dudley (who had by then replaced Canning as Foreign Secretary) on 19 July.

So far as British-Mexican relations were concerned, all was now set fair; but for Ward personally things had been going badly wrong.

16

WARD OFFENDS CANNING AND IS RECALLED – FEBRUARY 1826 TO MAY 1827

Morier had been sent back to Mexico at the end of 1825 as a special commissioner for the purpose of renegotiating the treaty. The Full Powers were drawn in his name and Ward's jointly, so that neither had the authority to agree anything on his own. In that function Morier was of course the senior; but he had no jurisdiction over the running of the permanent diplomatic mission by Ward, who remained Chargé d'affaires and was able, once the treaty negotiations had run into the sands at the end of January 1826, to resume that function fully. And he devoted himself to it during 1826 with conscientious energy, even though his health continued to give him trouble. Although he found Poinsett still a tiresome political opponent, and, after Morier's departure in March, he had to devote some time to fending off efforts to sabotage the Camacho mission to England, he managed to shower the Foreign Office with reports on every aspect of Mexico's politics, policies (particularly in relation to Texas) and economy. By the end of the year he had written 151 despatches and 13 additional official letters (as well as issuing 520 passports). His greatest enthusiasm, however, was for wide-ranging travel away from the capital so that he could really get to know the country and its people, particularly the state of mining and agriculture; and the book he published in 1828, on his return to England, provides ample proof of his capacity for absorbing and then conveying a mass of detail on these two activities. He wasted no time after the breakdown of the treaty negotiations, making two such trips, of a week each, in February. And so keen was he that he made another in May even though the birth of his second child was by then imminent and his liver was again playing up. (He wrote to Planta just before setting out that he could 'only keep going by dint of calomel and laudanum.'[1]) Others, of longer duration, followed in July, August and September.

Emily was clearly giving him tremendous support, not even objecting to his leaving her alone so near her term. Writing to Vaughan on his return from the May trip he said 'a wife is indeed a luxury in these out of the way countries'. But by then he was nevertheless again feeling the need of a break from Mexico. In the same letter he expressed his longing for home leave 'for Spain and Mexico together have ruined my constitution … my liver is in a most deplorable state which at 29 does not afford a man a very enlivening prospect. A winter in England wd possibly give me a new lease.'[2] He found dealing with Mexican bureaucracy a tiresome and time consuming chore. 'The detailed business of the Mission' he wrote to Planta 'is infinitely greater than I expected, and will continue to be so until these people become a little more familiarized with the customs of the civilized world. You must have seen how much trouble it requires to carry the commonest point, and yet I do not send you home by any means all my Notes .... I can assure you that I have never yet been able to obtain from this Gt redress – a satisfactory arrangement on any subject – or even an answer – without renewing my applications until they cd no longer decently defer coming to a decision.'[3] He could be tough with the Mexicans, however. For example, much concerned at an attempt by the authorities to confiscate a British merchant's business papers as a prelude to preferring charges which he thought to be trumped up, Ward took them under his own care at his house and defied the Mexicans to infringe his diplomatic immunity. Writing to Vaughan he said: 'In England they would send me my passports for doing this. Here I am pretty sure they will not, particularly as reason and justice are both on my side; and come what may, I feel sure that C will bear me out. In a new country, new measures must sometimes be resorted to, and I served too long an apprenticeship in Old Spain not duly to appreciate the difference between preferring a claim for *redress*, and disputing a point with possession in your favour.'[4] From one development, however, he drew comfort – a positive advance in religious tolerance.

It must have been just after Morier left that the authorities gave a remarkable open demonstration of a more relaxed attitude towards non-Catholics. Although the Wards had found it difficult to get at all intimate with Mexicans, they had by now made some real friends, among whom were in particular the Count and Countess of Regla. They asked these to be sponsors at the baptism of their first child (born in April 1825) and the Reglas responded with enthusiasm, on the one condition that they be allowed to arrange everything. Not only did they provide the baby with a beautiful locally made and embroidered robe, they organized a magnificent church ceremony 'with hundreds of wax-lights, and music, and crowds of attendants'. The Minister for Ecclesiastical Affairs, Pablo de la Llave, performed the ceremony and provided them with 'a certificate of baptism, printed on silk and inclosed in a gold frame'. To the Wards' own chosen name of Frances the sponsors insisted on adding 'Guadalupe (in honour both of the Virgin of that name, and of the President) and Felipa de Jesús, in commemoration of the only Mexican Saint acknowledged by the Church of Rome';[5] and they gave a dinner for 20 people and presents of diamonds.[6]

The Reglas, however, became the centre of a small scandal shortly after this – thanks partly to the machinations of Poinsett. In describing this to Canning, Ward referred to the countess (a considerable beauty by all accounts) as 'one of the cleverest women here'. He said that Poinsett had unsuccessfully tried to cultivate her 'partly I suppose because she is really a very superior person and partly because she was known to exercise very great influence over the President who frequently passed the evenings at her house'. Her rejection of Poinsett's overtures had led, however, to Victoria's having to drop this intimacy; for Poinsett 'began to declaim against her as a most dangerous woman, devoted to English interests and exercising baneful influence over the mind of the President'. He also intervened when she wanted to send two of her sons to England with Morier so that they could be educated there, persuading the count to withdraw his agreement by convincing him 'that the United States would be a more convenient and in all respects fitter place'. This caused a family quarrel and led to their separation. Victoria had wanted to mediate, but 'the most scandalous reports were immediately circulated, and General Victoria has been forced to drop all connexion with the Countess.'[7]

Another demonstration of religious tolerance came in August, when Victoria lent his help to Ward over the marriage he was asked to perform for two Protestant British subjects.[8] Victoria promised that if the ceremony were performed quietly in Ward's own house he would use all his influence 'to induce the ecclesiastical authorities to acknowledge its validity and to register the certificate of it at the office of the Provisor, which would be sufficient to reconcile the Mexicans to the idea of the ceremony being performed without the intervention of a clergyman' and thus enable the couple to live together as man and wife without social stigma.[9] So encouraged was Ward by these developments that he suggested to Canning the appointment of a chaplain to the staff of the mission. He felt sure that if he performed his duties discreetly, even if this should extend to divine worship at the residence for members of the local British community, there would be no trouble from the authorities. Ward had mentioned the possibility to Victoria, who was 'as well disposed as I could desire'. However, he did not want Victoria put in an impossible constitutional position by making a formal request, and he insisted that if a chaplain were appointed he should visit Mexico 'in the first instance as a traveller or at most charged with despatches' and should for some time assume no other character in public, remaining entirely under Ward's orders.[10] Thus Victoria continued, once the threat of having the religious question raised publicly in the context of the treaty had been removed, to demonstrate his sincerity in wishing to see more toleration in practice, and possibly this had some influence on Canning when it came to discussing religion with Camacho.[11]

Ward was impatient with bureaucracy of any kind, whether Mexican or British, and at this time he found the Foreign Office becoming particularly tiresome, the more so because their niggling, as he saw it, risked interfering with what gave him his greatest pleasure – his trips up country which he found 'a most agreeable relaxation after the confinement of the capital'.[12] For example, he was required to send home copies of all state papers; but he had to translate them into English. 'Since poor Waldegrave's death' he wrote to Planta, 'I am forced to do all the translations myself, for neither Ball nor Wilson [the mission doctor] can accomplish one fit to send.'[13] And he was still complaining about the lack of a direct confidential service for his despatches to London. This meant additional expense in paying special messengers to carry them on American ships to the USA for onward transmission by British ships, always assuming he could find someone reliable 'willing to undertake this service which at some seasons is by no means without danger and upon which one messenger has perished already during the last twelvemonth'.[14] And he did not always find the Foreign Office sympathetic over the expenses he incurred on his trips away from the capital, even though they had actually requested him to render a full report on the state of the mines. (Present day diplomats will no doubt recognize this phenomenon.) He did his best to assure Planta that he charged 'only mule hire and two pounds a day for my expenses, which does not half defray them .... My last journey alone cost me two horses of my own for each of which I had paid two hundred dollars [about £40].'[15] But by this time he was getting into deep trouble over his finances.

Ever since the end of the previous year Ward had been coming under increasing criticism from the Foreign Office because of what was conceived there to be his extravagances in the use of public funds and his casual approach to the rendering of his accounts. His troubles had begun when Planta had to write to him about his accounts to the end of May 1825 in which he had included his belated claim for the expenses of his journey out to Mexico with Emily at the end of 1824. The size of his travel claim horrified Planta. The total was £1588.19.8d, considerably higher than that for Morier's journey out a few months earlier. While a higher claim was to be expected from a married man, Planta considered that Ward had been too lavish with presents 'to the ship's company, to coxswains, to guards of honour and to the town and regimental music', none of which was he prepared to allow: while those 'to escorts appear unneedfully high'. Indeed, the whole principle of making such presents was questioned as 'generally speaking wholly inexpedient and ... likely to entail upon His Majesty's Government a future expense in many respects highly improper and inconvenient'. Moreover, Ward in addition had sent to the Foreign Office for payment a number of bills he had run up in England 'for presents in jewelry and cutlery'. These Planta returned for fuller explanation while agreeing, with reluctance, to meet the rest of his claim less £220. But Ward was reprimanded for extravagance, and told 'that what His Majesty's Government expects from you is rather a strict execution of your instructions than a display and representation which does not belong to the character which you hold and are to maintain in Mexico.'[16] The sin, in other words, was ostentation above his rank as much as the size of the actual claim. And at Planta's suggestion the official particularly charged with handling the Mexico mission accounts, Mr James Bandinel, wrote[17] to warn Ward of the bad impression he was in danger of creating at home:

> For your own sake do pray instantly bridle in. You are not expected here to make a show representation; you are not required to make presents in return for enthusiasm which is begotten by public acts of your country. The quieter you keep and live as an individual, as Mr Ward, the better you will please *here*. And as Chargé d'affaires they wish to hear of you not by dinners or parties, or representation or presents, but simply by attending to the body of your instructions.[18]

This mention of 'enthusiasm' arose from what Ward himself had written in the covering explanation of his accounts. He had a better understanding than those at home of the kind of sensitive courtesies with which Mexicans (and many other peoples) expect social intercourse to be decorated (and in which the British tend to be unskilled). He had explained that most of the expenses of his journey from the coast to the capital had been met by the generous hospitality of the Mexicans, who had received his party with great enthusiasm because its arrival was proof of Britain's friendship. He had explained 'the impossibility of not making the only return which the Mexicans could be induced to accept of. I had foreseen the enthusiasm and provided myself with some trifling presents which I knew would be highly acceptable here.' (These included sabres for the military, cases of razors and scissors, as well as inexpensive watches and jewellery.)[19] This was sensible: the omission of such courtesies could have caused offence. But he did not receive Bandinel's letter until October, while Planta's did not reach him until mid-December, with the other official mail which Morier brought out.

When he did receive these warnings, Ward realized that perhaps he had misinterpeted what Canning had said to him before leaving. His only guidance, so he claimed, had been what he had understood to be Canning's desire that he should 'give great dinners, balls etc' (see chapter 10). However, he does not seem to have sent home with Morier the estimate of his likely expenses as Chargé d'affaires which Canning had also asked for. But at that time he did not realize that he was going to be up against Poinsett, who was openly using indirect bribery to gain his ends. Ward, being convinced that British political and commercial interests could suffer if Poinsett were successful, had had to find ways of combatting this. With no specific instructions covering such a situation, and no clear guidance as to any limits on the expenditure he could charge to public funds as a mere Chargé d'affaires, he had decided he must try to win influence by expensive entertaining. It has been the cry down the years from diplomats abroad that the Treasury never understands the importance of not appearing mean and poverty stricken if Britain is to keep the respect of the host country and, indeed, that of the representatives of other countries. It is legitimate to question whether in the long run Britain's political or commercial prestige can be 'bought' by lavish diplomatic entertaining; but it is often true that, in the short term, vital influence among the 'ruling few' may need 'expense account' treatment from time to time if Britain's foreign policy objectives are to be secured. In the turbulence of Mexican politics at the time, Ward's expenditure may have played a vital part in the short term in securing support for the treaty against the machinations of Poinsett. Certainly Ward himself was convinced of this. Writing to the Foreign Office in August 1825 he had referred to entertainment expenses as 'the only means which can be made use of, in a country where no society exists among the natives, in order to acquire information and add to the number of friends of England', and to the need, 'in a country where Great Britain has an influence to establish and a formidable opposition Party to contend with', for Britain's diplomatic representative to be provided with 'appointments sufficient to enable him to support the dignity of the country which he represents'.[20] This was when he had sent in a supplementary account for over £2000, including the cost of celebrating the king's birthday.

In December Ward had also received later letters from Planta. One warned him that he must strictly observe expenditure regulations set out in instructions, and specifically that expenditure on 'the usual dinners etc given by His Majesty's diplomatic servants on anniversaries or on any occasion on which the sanction of the secretary of state has not previously been obtained' would not be reimbursed.[21] In another Planta queried the costs of Emily's confinement and of 'the cleaning and repairing of rooms after Mr Morier's departure [which] seems principally to consist in alterations effected in the house such as making alcoves etc .... The charge for the billiard table is an unusual one and ought not to have been in the accounts without sufficient reason.'[22] This was not entirely fair. Ward made clear that Morier had ordered the billiard table and had approved of the cleaning and repairs, some of which had been necessary for the king's birthday celebrations, which would have been held before Morier's departure but for the need to postpone it because of Emily's confinement.[23] Moreover, Planta had asked Morier (then in London) for his comments on the account, and Morier had confirmed these points. (But it is at least comforting to note that Planta did not object to the sad little item of £19 in respect of nursing and medicines for Ward's English footman and his subsequent burial.)

Ward had been very upset to learn in this way that he was considered to have been disregarding instructions to economize. In his view he had received none. He had therefore added a postscript to his personal letter of 17 December to Canning (see chapter 14), requesting his

> indulgent attention to one point which it is of the greatest importance to me to put in a proper light. It relates to my expenses here, which I perceive are thought excessive .... I beg that it may be most clearly understood that I have not to reproach myself with the additional error of having deviated from any instructions. I have *none* .... Circumstances which I have never attempted to conceal from you have forced me to take a line which I now most sincerely regret as I foresee that you will be dissatisfied with it; but now that I am aware of your intentions, & of the limits within which I am to confine myself, you may depend upon my never exceeding them in any way, or under any plea whatsoever. My connections here are formed and I hope that, this being the case, I shall be enabled to keep them up whatever be my income.

Possibly Planta never saw this letter, which Canning kept with his private papers, which could explain Ward's outburst in May 1826 after receiving further critical letters from him:

> Heaven is my witness that I would sooner have starved here on anything that you had chosen to allow me than have given cause for these reproofs, which as far as the best intentions went I am far from deserving .... My conduct under what Mr Canning termed most trying circumstances was honored with his approbation; and yet the means are blamed by which I did, and alone could, ensure success .... My only desire is to give satisfaction, and if at the end of my two years, which will I fancy expire before ratification of the treaty enables Mr Canning to appoint a Minister here, I can resign the business into his hands

> in as favourable a state as things are in at the moment, I shall have nothing further to wish for.[24]

At this time Ward was probably under domestic pressure following the birth of the second child, as well as once again suffering from his liver complaint, which could account for the irritability showing through this letter. But worse was to come. Shortly after this, out of the blue, he was suddenly told by the local merchant on whom he had been drawing his bills of exchange that the Foreign Office had refused to acknowledge some of them. This, of course, was a dire disgrace and likely to affect his standing locally, as well as making it difficult for him to obtain any more cash. Just what had happened in London is unclear. Planta had written to warn him that it might become necessary to have his bills accepted on his *private* account, but Ward had not by then received that letter.[25] Was there some misunderstanding by Bandinel? Or was Ward's private account out of funds and the local agent had not had the position properly explained to him? Whatever the truth, Ward *thought* the Foreign Office had dishonoured some of his bills without warning. Fortunately Mr Ruperti, the merchant concerned, behaved honourably and kept the matter private between them. But Ward was naturally very angry and wrote an intemperate letter to Planta:

> I cannot and will not refrain from telling you that I think I have been hardly treated .... By dishonouring my Bills you leave me no resource. You must feel that even if some items in my accounts are not allowed, still by far the greater part of the sum charged must ultimately be paid – you cannot in reason or justice refuse to do so! Why then disgrace me publicly by putting me, as you have done, into Mr Ruperti's power? .... What your instructions may be with regard to me I cannot conjecture: I have however made up my mind for the worst, and prepared to begin a life anew. If I am recalled in disgrace you will never see me in England again. I am conscious that I have not deserved it, and tho' you may ruin me, you shall not, and cannot, deprive me of this consolation. I have acted to the best of my judgment as the interests of my country required; nor could I have accomplished what little I have effected towards carrying Mr Canning's views into execution without having recourse to those means which I thought it necessary to adopt.[26]

After this outburst, Ward became calmer for a while, perhaps in consequence of getting over the latest trouble with his liver and having at last seen Camacho off to England. But back in London Planta was getting more and more exasperated by what seemed to him irresponsible and insubordinate behaviour. He had not received those outbursts when he remonstrated over the accounts to the end of December 1825, in which Ward had claimed reimbursement of nearly £2100, including $1350 for rent, $3392 on 'housekeeping' for three months, $375 for his English servants' wages, nearly $493 for 'stabling' and over $1041 on repairs to the house and furniture.[27] Planta had to point out that the corresponding mission in Colombia had claimed only about a quarter of this for the same period, and he conveyed Canning's 'displeasure that you have paid so little attention to the admonitions so frequently conveyed to you on the subject of the expenses' and 'his intention in consequence to take immediate measures for a change' in the mission.[28] Canning himself then wrote to confirm that when the treaty was concluded a 'regular' mission would be appointed, adding, however, that he would not 'lose any time in complying with the desire you have expressed to be relieved from your present situation' by sending out the future Secretary of Legation as Chargé d'affaires to replace him as soon as possible:

> An interval between your departure and the arrival of the King's Minister will be very useful for the purpose of reducing the enormous expense which your establishment has cost within the bounds at which alone it can be considered necessary or expedient for this country to maintain a Mission in Mexico. [One of the things Ward was being instructed to do at this time was find a more modest residence.] I have had occasion so repeatedly to address you on the subject of your expenditure that I have only in this despatch to instruct you that you will forthwith make every practicable reduction in your establishment and that you will not consider the approaching termination of your residence in Mexico as an occasion for any special extravagance or display.[29]

Ward received all this at the beginning of September while he was on tour up country. This time his reaction was extreme. On his return to the capital three days later he wrote formally to both Planta and Canning. To Planta he said:

> You have never done me the justice to reflect that a distance of seven thousand miles separates me from England, but appear on the contrary to have thought that because a letter with instructions respecting my accounts had been just despatched from the Foreign office, I ought to have acted upon its contents two months before it reached Mexico .... Without perhaps intending it you have done me an irreparable injury by not paying that attention to the dates of your correspondence with me which at such a distance is absolutely indispensable in order to avoid the most glaring injustice .... To your sense of justice I appeal to make me what amends may still be in your power by laying this letter before Mr Canning and stating to him your conviction that if I have upon *one* point mistaken his wishes [ie the expenditure to the end of December], you have been wrong in stating that I have ever wilfully disregarded him .... Did I feel myself guilty I should be humble enough ... but I cannot ... submit to be stigmatised as a mere thoughtless spendthrift.[30]

In his formal despatch to Canning, Ward emphasized that he could not have defeated Poinsett's views 'without making the house of His Majesty's Mission the rendezvous for the friends of England, as his was for the partisans of the United States' and that he

> had been forced to incur expenses which I knew had never been contemplated by His Majesty's Government .... Had I waited for your orders to act, instead of doing instantly what I conscientiously and to the best of my judgment believed that you would wish Mr Morier or any other British agent to do in my place, it was my firm conviction that not only a feeling, but a Party against England would have taken root here, which would have rendered the accomplishment of your views almost impossible whatever might have been the character of the persons entrusted with their execution.

He feared that his reputation would be ruined if he were recalled before the arrival of a full minister and emphasized that he had never solicited his recall earlier than that: he had only asked that he be allowed to return as soon as possible thereafter because of his health, 'an indulgence which is I believe generally accorded to any of His Majesty's servants who have passed three years in the New World'.[31]

Not content with this, Ward also wrote a personal letter to Canning, drawing his attention particularly to his formal despatch 'as my prospects in life depend almost entirely upon the impression' which it would produce. He said that although it had been written 'under feelings of considerable agitation', Canning would find proofs in every line of the 'respect which is due to your exalted situation' and of his own 'grateful recollection' of Canning's favours to him. But he

> could not … submit in silence to accusations such as those which have been brought against me, nor defend myself otherwise than in a tone which the consciousness of my innocence entitles me to assume .... My error has been too implicit a reliance upon that protection which I hoped you wd not deny me; a reliance which, where reference to England might have been fatal, induced me to take upon myself the responsibility of whatever measures were necessary in order to ensure success .... If … I am to be disgraced and dishonoured because … [of such action] … my fate will certainly be a warning to all not to expose themselves to pecuniary responsibility whatever may be the consequences to the cause which they may wish to advocate.[32]

On the same day that he wrote this personal letter to Canning, Ward wrote to Vaughan 'If, after having attained my object and risked everything in order to do so, I am to be sacrificed because, in the present pecuniary crisis,[33] expenses may be ill received by the House which a year ago would have been thought nothing of, it cannot be expected that I should submit in silence to such injustice'.[34] Ward would have realized that it would be some considerable time before any replacement would reach Mexico, and he seems to have simply decided then to make the best of the months that would be left to him. There is no sign of any dimunition in his conscientious attention to his work. And this unexpected news did not stop him fulfilling his promise to Emily that he would take her and the children on his next journey into the provinces. This was a remarkable decision. The second child had been born on 31 May[35] and was therefore barely four months old when he got back from his September trip. Perhaps it was fortunate that the elder child, Frances, became very ill then as a result of sunstroke and they were not able to set off until the beginning of November. But to undertake such a journey voluntarily with an 18-month-old child and a 5-month-old baby was adventurous indeed.

They shut up the house and took all their servants with them. The two children and two Mexican maids travelled in a large coach drawn by eight mules. Emily was supposed to travel with them, but she chose to make most of the journey on horseback, covering some 1400 miles in this way, rather than endure the shaking on the atrocious roads. The party included the French Consul-General as well as Dr Wilson, a young Mr Carrington and the mission messenger. All the men, 16 in all, were armed, and the caravan, as Ward said in his book, would have caused a sensation in Hyde Park – 'wild horses and mules, with the servants driving them at a gallop with the lassos whirling round their heads … the coach, in size like a Noah's Ark … with festoons of Tasajo (dried strips of beef sold by the yard) and handkerchiefs full of onions and tortillas attached to different parts of it'.[36] Sometimes they camped in the open, in hard frosts, sometimes they crowded into primitive inns, sometimes they were put up in haciendas. Emily would have to sit in the dark and bitter cold looking after the children for a couple of hours before sunrise while everything was packed up for another day's journey, but would then take every opportunity to make charming sketches of the countryside and the people they met.[37] Through it all she was still nursing the youngest child and, as it later transpired, she became pregnant again before they got back to Mexico City. Most of the time their journey passed as smoothly as the primitive roads allowed. But there was one incident which did cause some concern. A wheel of the coach collapsed when they were miles from anywhere and they had to leave the two girls and the maids with it while the rest of them rode on some 20 miles to the nearest place where they could get a replacement. This was then sent back on a mule, but by three next morning there was still no sign of the coach. Emily was by now in some distress, so Ward set off back to where they had left it. He found that it had not been possible to fit the new wheel, so the old one had been taken some 15 miles to the nearest hacienda to see if it could be repaired there. Ward, determined to get the child back to her mother as soon as possible, fastened her to his back with a shawl and rode the 20 miles back to where Emily was, not getting there until about nine in the morning after, as he put it, 'a ride rather longer than it often falls to the lot of a little creature of five months to undertake'.[38]

The party eventually returned to the capital on 23 January 1827 after an absence of nearly three months and covering some 2000 miles. They were a sturdy lot those Wards. And during their absence from the capital Ward still kept in touch with official business by means of the messenger he had taken with him, who would be sent back with Wards's own periodic reports on the conditions he found, and would return with whatever had arrived from London. But it was not until his return to the capital that he received, and replied to, some even more uncomfortable communications from Planta and Canning than those he had received before setting out. There had been little sign in fact of the 'respect which is due to' Canning's 'exalted situation' in what he had written in September and it is not surprising that Canning's reaction on receiving those outpourings on 5 December was stiff. This was particularly unfortunate for Ward, because Canning's view of his behaviour had begun to soften. He seems to have realized that Ward was continuing to act very conscientiously in Mexico, and he may have been impressed by what Camacho had to tell him of the difficulties Ward had had to overcome, and the very high regard in which he was held by Victoria. He had only just told Ward's father of his intention to recall his son, and the reason, but had also promised that he would be allowed the dignity of being a signatory to the treaty and would not be recalled in disgrace.[39] At least he stuck to the second part of this promise; but he did not in the end allow Ward to sign the treaty. And when Ward received Canning's formal notice of recall[40] in February 1827 he remained unrepentant, going no further than to acknowledge that he had protested earlier

> in terms stronger than custom warranted, but which the feelings of the moment might almost excuse. Had those letters been written under feelings of less agitation, I need not assure you that they would have been differently worded. I trust, therefore, that you will allow the excitement of the moment to plead as an excuse for any expression in which I may have been wanting in that respect which I owe to you both as my superior and as the man to whom I am indebted for whatever good has yet fallen to my lot in the world.[41]

But this crossed with a further reprimand from Canning of the greatest severity:

> Because in my despatches of the 9th December 1825 and January 1826 I gave you credit for the political conduct of your Mission, you think fit to infer that I must also have approved of

the enormous expenditure, which I had before and have since directly and repeatedly reprehended ....

I must take care not to append to a person who reasons thus any opportunity by leniency or forbearance on my part of raising fresh doubts as to the reality or extent of my disapprobation ....

I must ... express in the plainest terms my utmost displeasure and indignation at the ... language in which you have thought it decent and proper to express yourself personally to the Under Secretary ....

It is utterly impossible that any person, having permitted himself to use such language, should be continued in the discharge of any diplomatic functions, or restored to it, while his offensive despatches remained on the records of the office unatoned for by a direct expression of apology and contrition ....

Equally unjustifiable is the pretence which you set up for having persevered in a rate of expenditure which put your Mission at Mexico on the footing of the highest Embassies in Europe .... Until I am informed that the purse of the government of the United States was subjected to the desecration of Mr Poinsett in a proportion far beyond that in which any of its other Ministers abroad have been allowed to draw upon it, I must be permitted to doubt the necessity of an expenditure of £11000 per annum to maintain a competition with the representative of North America in any part of the world ....

I am extremely sorry that the contents and still more the tone of your despatches should have compelled me to speak to you in a language so different from that which I have heretofore had the satisfaction of addressing to you. But ... I cannot allow either the profuse expenditure of your Mission, or your very objectionable attempts to justify it, to pass without an unequivocal expression and an official record of disapprobation.[42]

Before he had received this, Ward had written privately to Canning in a slightly more penitent style, although still protesting his innocence of any improper motives in his actions:

> I wish … to assure you that if in any part of my despatches of Septr last I either in word or thought appeared to be wanting in those feelings of gratitude to you which I must ever retain, nothing could have been further from my intention .... And in one respect I confess that I have deserved my fate: I ought not to have written at all while my feelings were in so excited a state as to prevent me from being sensible to the impropriety of the tone of several parts of my answers .... As it is, I can only express my deep regret at the little command which I had at the time over my feelings, and my sorrow for the warmth of expression into which it betrayed me. I acknowledge it to be such as nothing can justify in an official correspondence with a superior, and I shall submit, without repining, to the consequences whatever they may be .... But I confess that to see my conduct attributed to the worst motives (I know of none worse than that indifference which would have led me to expose myself to your displeasure from wanton extravagance) is what I neither expected nor have deserved.[43]

But after receiving Canning's severe reprimand he realized that he had to put a contrite apology on record. He begged

> to express, publicly, both to yourself and to Mr Planta … my contrition as a feeble atonement for that breach of official decorum into which the extreme agitation of the moment could alone have betrayed me … not in the hope that any admission of my fault can be regarded as sufficient to expiate it, but because I have long felt that the most unlimited expression of my sorrow for what has passed was due to Mr Planta for that breach of official duty of which I have been guilty towards him .... For not having given to the cause of my recall that publicity which would have compelled me to begin the world anew under additional disadvantages, I most humbly thank you. I do so likewise for those favours which you conferred upon me at a time when, unknown and unconnected, I had no earthly claim upon your patronage. To it I am indebted for whatever good has fallen to my lot in life. For the Evil which may await me I confess that I have no one to accuse but myself.[44]

This was a sad ending to what had in fact been a tour of duty in which Ward had shown great ability; and later he was able to develop a career of distinction. But in any branch of the public service it has always been possible for young excellence to trip over the sensitivities of those in a position to make or break a promising career. He had perhaps acted at times with an apparent arrogance unjustified by his youth and early promotion, and no doubt Planta (whose influence surely must have affected Canning's actions) thought he needed teaching a lesson. If Ward felt bitterness at his treatment, who could blame him? But he at least had the comfort of knowing that he was held in high regard in Mexico. From the leading British merchants he received a formal address

> expressing the high sense they entertain of the zeal and talents you have displayed in His Majesty's service … [and] … their gratitude for the energy and activity you have ever evinced in the protection and furtherance of British interests, for the readiness with which you have received and attended to their many applications and for the urbanity and politeness they have experienced.[45]

And Victoria wrote personally, in his own hand, to Canning, referring to

> the esteem which the conduct of [Ward] has gained during the whole time that he sojourned in the Republic … by the conciliating and delicate manner with which he has known how to cultivate the relations subsisting between both governments and to perfect them to the degree which they now happily have attained.[46]

The Wards travelled back to England with Rocafuerte, who was taking the Mexican instrument of ratification of the treaty, and they sailed from Vera Cruz on 8 May 1827[47] in HMS *Primrose* (Captain Octavius V. Vernon RN), arriving at Spithead on 16 July, having spent a week in New York on the way.[48] Emily gave birth to a son, Charles Dudley Robert (who later became a judge in New Zealand), ten days before they reached Spithead, from where she was taken ashore to the Isle of Wight. Ward described the journey thus in his book:

> The Primrose was much too small for the accommodation of so large a party as ours; and as, after a thousand ingenious contrivances, there was only room for one female servant, a Mexican woman who was constantly unwell, the children, the eldest of whom was just two years old, could not be properly attended to, and were a frequent source of discomfort and trouble. They were nursed in turn, I believe, by all the ship's company and formed a particular alliance not only with the officers, who were very kind to them, but with the boatswain and many of the men, who used to carry them about the ship and introduce them to places which young ladies are not much in the habit of frequenting. To add to our embarrassments, Mrs Ward was confined on board, ten days before we reached Portsmouth, when the maid's attention was of course devoted to her. The little girls were transferred to my cabin below at night, and during the day were kept either upon deck or in the only part of the ship which Captain Vernon could call his own, half the poop-cabin where he slept and we all dined, separated from Mrs Ward by nothing but a light partition, with an opening below to allow the tiller to traverse.[49]

The British navy had once again showed its adaptability and regard for the welfare of its civilian passengers.

EPILOGUE

The British and Mexican exchange of ratifications of the Treaty of Friendship, Commerce and Navigation in July 1827, coinciding with the final return of Ward to England, closed the first chapter in the story of relations between the two countries. It had opened in 1822 with the departure from Mexico for England of Mackie and Wavell – separately. After five years of courtship the marriage contract had been sealed. There are some who argue that it was an unequal contract from which Britain gained more than Mexico. No one can deny that Britain was looking for commercial benefits from her treaties with the former Spanish colonies in America; but equally no one can deny that those colonies then needed the kind of support and help which only Britain of the European powers was able and willing to offer at that time. And any fair minded person must surely acknowledge that at least Britain made no attempt to secure exclusive privileges: the 'bride' was free to have the same relationship with others.

It was as well, however, that the marriage brokers did not realize what turbulence would follow. Within months of Ward's leaving Mexico, insurrection against constitutionally elected leadership again erupted, with Vice-President Bravo's (unsuccessful) attempt to seize power from Victoria. Santa Anna, that young man who had had to watch while O'Gorman carried off the girl he loved, and Guerrero supported Victoria and ensured that he could see out his allotted time as president. But they were less concerned with constitutionality when Victoria was succeeded in 1828 by Gómez Pedraza. They rebelled against him and Guerrero took over, only to be evicted in his turn and later executed. Santa Anna next rebelled against Guerrero's successor, Anastasio Bustamente, and in 1833 he won an overwhelming victory in the presidential elections of that year. Between then and August 1855 the presidency changed hands no fewer than 36 times, Santa Anna holding the post eleven times. In 1836 came the famous battle of the Álamo, when Santa Anna unsuccessfully tried to prevent Texas declaring for independence from Mexico. In 1838 there was a French invasion in an attempt to secure payment for damages suffered by French subjects in the various insurrections. From 1846 Mexico was at war for two years with the United States, following their annexation of Texas, and suffered American occupation of the capital. There was further civil war between 1858 and 1861, followed by another French incursion (in which they were briefly joined by Spain and Britain), in an attempt to force payment of debts. The French stayed and imposed the unfortunate Maximilian on the Mexicans as emperor until 1867, when he was overthrown and executed by Benito Juárez who then broke off diplomatic relations with Britain because she had recognized Maximilian. Juárez died in 1872, eight months after Porfirio Díaz began a revolt against him. Díaz was defeated in the subsequent election but was successful in 1876 in his armed revolt against the winner, Sebastian Lerdo de Tejada, and became President. After relinquishing the presidency four years later, in accordance with the constitution, he was succeeded by Manuel González for the next four years before being elected again in 1884 – the year in which diplomatic relations with Britain were restored, thanks partly to the efforts of another Lionel (Lionel Carden) and partly to Porfirio's anxiety to have a counterweight to the United States.[1] A new treaty was negotiated and signed in 1887.

So, 60 years after the ratification of the treaty over which Ward had laboured so valiantly, the course of British-Mexican relations came round full circle. And with this second election of Porfirio Díaz Mexico began her first substantial period of peace since the original revolt against Spain in 1810. Although not without its rough moments, it lasted 26 years, until civil war broke out again in 1910. Peace returned in 1920 when Álvaro Obregón was elected President, and this marked the final end of internal armed conflict, except for the violent suppression of the church-inspired revolt at the end of the decade – an ironical sequel to the efforts of Ward and Victoria to persuade the Catholic Church to be tolerant to Protestants.[2] From then forward Mexico has been able to devote her energies to efforts to build up her economy free from the scourge of insurrection, revolt and civil war. There was a further short break in relations with Britain in 1925, however, and a longer one in 1938 (connected with, but not directly caused by, the nationalization of oil companies). This was healed in 1941 and since then this thrice divorced couple have been able to maintain a harmonious friendship based on mutual respect and understanding.

At least none of the chief participants in the events leading up to the ratification of the treaty in 1827 lived to see the break in relations 40 years later. Victoria was the first to go, dying in 1843, in relative poverty. After laying down his office as Mexico's first constitutional President in 1829 he retired to look after his farms in the state of Vera Cruz, successfully persuading the Church to lend him money to develop them (over which there were legal wrangles for 18 years after his death from which the Church failed to recover all it was owed).[3] He was a senator for three years from 1833, during which time he was called upon to take charge of various military operations against insurrection. In 1836 he was put in military command of the state of Vera Cruz and when Spain finally recognized Mexican independence in that year he officially received the first Spanish ambassador, Angel Calderón de la Barca, and his Scottish wife Frances on their arrival at Vera Cruz. At the particular request of the commander of the French forces which invaded Mexico in 1838 it was Victoria who, after their withdrawal had been negotiated, raised the Mexican flag again over Ulloa in 1839 and escorted the French troops to their re-embarkation. (The British minister, Richard (later Sir Richard) Pakenham, played a significant part in negotiating this agreement.) But Victoria was developing epilepsy and, after unexpectedly marrying in 1841, he became more and more affected by it. He died dispirited by the evidence of the collapse of all his dreams of a strong and peaceful Mexico – but not the only great leader of independent Spanish America to see such dreams fade.

Ward rightly saw in Victoria the key to the successful prosecution of Canning's policy towards Mexico. He admired and liked him, even though he considered him flawed in some ways; and Victoria in his turn had great respect for Ward, with whom he obviously felt at ease. He trusted Ward completely – with justification. And Ward would probably have picked no serious quarrel with the opinion that Victoria

> was a man of remarkable purity of character, honest, unassuming, kind-hearted, and a true lover of freedom. By many his talents have been ignored, and his virtues set down as faults, the forethought and deliberation which marked his career being attributed to indolence and apathy. Because he would not uphold the schemes of those who wished to make him their tool, his errors have been ascribed to malice and his prudence to lack of decision, though in truth he was incapable of selfish ambition, and for the public welfare was ever ready to lay aside his private opinions.[4]

Ward, as we have seen, also thought him at times apathetic; and he thought he was honest. But he was not blinded to what he saw as faults. In October 1826 he described him to Canning thus:

> He is not a man of superior understanding, altho' he has many most excellent qualities; but when an idea, whether good or bad, once takes root with him, it is next to impossible ever to shake its hold upon his mind. His Party prejudices, his feelings towards individuals, are just as strong as that national hatred of Spain which induced him, at an earlier period of his life, to undergo unheard of hardships rather than submit to her yoke.
>
> With the recollection of what he has done and suffered for Mexico, the idea that he is the hero of the revolution, the man of the people *par excellence*, is deeply implanted in his breast. Not to admit this fact appears to him the height of injustice, to dispute it little less than treason ....
>
> Nor is this all. General Victoria has repeatedly stated to me his conviction that were his re-election possible ... the suffrage of the nation would be unanimous in his favour. He harps continually upon this idea, and as he is both too candid and too vain to conceal his sentiments upon the subject from those whom he supposes to be his friends, I much fear that advantage has been taken of this circumstance to induce him to believe that that which he considers almost as his right might not be so wholly unattainable as at first it appears.[5]

This was a shrewd analysis by Ward of a man for whom he had much respect. It is doubtful if he ever felt for him the degree of friendship that Victoria felt in the opposite direction, but he never gave Victoria cause to think otherwise of him. And it gave him no pleasure to have to submit this analysis. He ended the despatch by writing 'I am grieved, Sir, to be forced to give this opinion.'

If Ward was right – and he probably was – Victoria was not all that different from others who come to the top in political turbulence; he believed *he* knew how to ensure stability and that no one else could do it. Who knows what the outcome would have been had he been allowed to try? But he was a stickler for constitutionality and he made no attempt, as did others who followed him, to hold onto power unconstitutionally. (The Mexican constitution then, and now, forbids the re-election of an outgoing president.) Nor did he profit materially from his presidency. In December 1826 Ward reported that the Senate was debating, with some warmth, the validity of Michelena's expenditure in London, particularly the sum of $60,000 allegedly paid for a brig o' war which had never appeared in Mexico.[6] An attempt was made to implicate Victoria in peculation. Ward said that no one believed this and that Victoria would in fact 'quit the Presidency nearly as poor as when he entered it', despite the opportunities for enrichment and compensating himself for the loss of nearly all the family property during the independence struggle.[7] What he achieved during his presidency and before it, however, was significant for Mexico and for British-Mexican relations. In his valedictory despatch from Mexico, after his farewell audience with the President, Ward said of Victoria 'I have never applied to him for assistance without finding him most ready to exercise his influence both as President and as an individual in behalf of British interests, and whatever points have been carried here it is to his exertions that they are due.'[8]

Ward was the one who came nearest to having to see the break in relations in 1867, and it was only unexpected disease, cholera, that brought his life to a premature end in 1860 just after his arrival in Madras as governor, by then Sir Henry Ward GCMG. Nevertheless, he too must have been sorely disappointed at the way things turned out, not only for Mexico, but for himself personally. After his return to England in July 1827 he completed some reports for the Foreign Office while working on the book he published next year; but in January 1828 he had to appeal for a decision about his position. He wrote that he had been given to understand that he would be allowed to retain until 5 January 'that portion of my Mexican appointments' usually allowed 'on change of situation'. It was a low key letter, but he said that 'the consequence for me of having done in Mexico what it was my conviction that British interests required of me to do has been almost total ruin'. He explained that from January 1826 he had drawn bills amounting to nearly £2000 more than his allowances. In addition the Foreign Office had disallowed expenditure of nearly £1000 on such things as rent. He had by now paid off all his bills and part of what the Foreign Office had disallowed, but only by sacrificing nearly half of all the property he owned. He could pay off the rest if only he could have the allowances he thought were due to him from May 1827, which he had not received.[9] He was successful to the extent of getting £500 for the period from then to January 1828, half his annual salary as Secretary of Legation, and he then seems to have severed all connection with the Foreign Office. But he bobbed up again as MP for St Albans in 1832, a seat he retained until 1837, then holding Sheffield until 1849. During this time he demonstrated considerable hostility to the Irish Catholic Church (had he all along so disliked O'Gorman?) and founded and edited the *Weekly Chronicle*. He became Secretary to the Admiralty in 1846 and Lord High Commissioner of the Ionian Islands in May 1849. From there he went in April 1855 to be governor of Ceylon until he was made governor of Madras in June 1860. He and Emily had seven more children after the son born on board HMS *Primrose*, including another son who became a surgeon-general in the army. Emily survived him until 1882, when she died at the grace-and-favour home she had been granted at Hampton Court, being buried at St James's, Hampton Hill.

There was an odd little irony in Ward's appointment to Madras, where he was replacing Charles Trevelyan, who had been removed from office on the excuse that he had publicly disagreed with official policy over taxation. But, like Ward before him in Mexico, Trevelyan had also been accused of extravagance, and George Canning's son, then Governor-General of India, had written that his 'insubordination could not be excused. He must be recalled.' Trevelyan too was rewarded with the approbation of the community in which he had been living, receiving many addresses such as the one that said 'Our belief is that your departure is a public calamity.'[10] One wonders whether Ward knew of this and had time to reflect not only on the curious parallel but on the characters of Canning father and son.

George Canning himself lived but a few months after his sacking of Ward. In April 1827 he became Prime Minister; but he died at Chiswick House, after a short illness, on 8 August. Of his distinction as a statesman there can be no question, and it can even be argued that, even though in many respects he was carrying out after 1822 policies begun by his predecessor as Foreign Secretary, Britain's successes in Spanish America in the 1820s might not have been what they were if it had been Castlereagh rather than Canning who had remained in charge. (This is as good an occasion as any to correct the popular misconception that Canning's famous statement in the House of Commons 'I called the New World into existence to redress the balance of the Old' was made in connection with recognition of the independence of the Spanish-American colonies: it was actually made two years later, on 12 December 1826, when he was sending troops into Portugal to prevent Spain from attacking her. He wished to show that his policies in 1824/25 had resulted in Spain, without her American possessions, being no longer a danger.) But was Canning simply by nature someone who was liable to treat people like Hervey and Ward the way he did? Robert Bell, 20 years after his death, thought his 'temper was irritable and anxious, but wholly free from pettiness or malice. He held no ill-will, he concealed no rancour. The real fault was less what he felt than in the heat and arrogance of his manner and expressions. He was the most open, but the most unsparing adversary. He treated his opponents with haughtiness, amounting sometimes almost to scorn.'[11] He had a genuine interest in the development of a really professional diplomatic service. It is a pity his irritable temper, even if it was free from malice, and even if he concealed no rancour, led him to deprive that service of such an able young man as Ward.

Canning perhaps had more justification for being hard on Hervey. While Ward had been guilty of no more than extravagance and possibly what was taken to be insubordination, Hervey had actually caused Canning public embarrassment by his premature support of a government in conflict with Spain when Britain was still officially neutral in that dispute. But were there really grounds for abruptly ending a career which had seemed to be going so well? For Canning never fulfilled his promise to Michelena that Hervey would be promoted. He granted him a pension of £1200 a year from 5 April 1825[12] but no reply was sent to Hervey's acknowledgement of this in which he expressed the hope that he would nevertheless be given further employment.[13] And Canning never even thanked Hervey for his gifts of Mexican silver figures on his return to England: he merely annotated the letter accompanying them that his 'confinement' prevented him from answering as he could not 'yet use my own hand to thank him for his present'.[14] Hervey did get a note on Canning's behalf; but it does seem churlish not to have sent something more personal. After this, Hervey disappears from view.[15]

Morier was well treated. He seems to have continued to draw a salary up to 4 January 1827, but he had turned down the offer of being appointed minister in Mexico once the treaty had been ratified because the climate there did not suit him. On 5 January he presented a memorandum in which he asked for a temporary allowance until he was re-employed. In a covering letter to Planta, however, he made clear that he was looking for a pension, not further employment. He recalled his eight years of service in Persia, two of which were as minister *ad interim*, and the pension he then drew, from 1816 to 1824, of £800 a year. He very pointedly recalled that Sir Gore Ouseley (who had been his ambassador in Persia), after four years as ambassador in Russia and being allowed to accept Russian decorations, got a pension of £2000 a year: as he (Morier) had not been allowed to accept Persian decorations he thought this should be taken into account in fixing his pension.[16] Rather surprisingly, this presumption on Morier's part did not lead to a rebuff, but to the award of a pension from 5 January 1827 of £1100 a year instead of the old £800.[17] He should have had no cause to complain at this generous treatment, and indeed did not do so publicly; but he did write to his brother David that he did not see why Hervey, whose pension was £1200, should have got more. He continued to write books and evidently made a decent income out of them. What happened to Harriet is not clear. Some of the surviving family believe that they separated and that she renounced her right to his estate, which amounted to some £14,000 when he died in Brighton in 1849. But there are letters (held by the library of Balliol College, Oxford) showing that they were still together as late as July 1848 (although she was then very unwell and James was most concerned). Possibly she died shortly before he did, which would explain why his son Greville was the beneficiary of the estate.

Ward was far too gentlemanly to crow over the downfall of anyone with whom he had had differences. Nevertheless he may well have felt some quiet satisfaction if he ever heard of Poinsett's fate: he was recalled from his post in Mexico in 1829 after the Mexicans then in power made clear that his meddling in internal Mexican politics had gone too far. Moreover, the treaty he had so laboriously negotiated, and which he had expected to be ratified before the one the Mexicans concluded with Britain, did not get ratified, because of continuing arguments over the location of the frontier between Texas and the United States, until 1832. Poinsett himself continued to be active in politics at home, being Secretary of War from 1837 to 1841; and he showed his true worth by his strong opposition to the war with Mexico. Perhaps Ward had been right to assure him that away from political confrontation he would find him an admirable friend. He had a deep interest in science and nature, particularly botany, and was one of the founders of the National Institute for the Promotion of Science and the Useful Arts, the forerunner of the Smithsonian Institute. He died in 1851.

Alamán died in 1853 and is remembered mainly for his writings, including in particular his great history of Mexico in the first half of the nineteenth century, his contributions to the economic development of the country and improvements to the education system. After being out of government following his resignation as Foreign Minister in 1825 he returned to that post in January 1830 until May 1831, when he again resigned. During that time he tried, unsuccessfully, to get Britain to mediate again between Mexico and Spain (he found the British government sympathetic but unhelpful). In September 1835 he was appointed plenipotentiary to try to negotiate an agreement with the French and was then asked to go to Paris as ambassador but declined for family reasons. He was made a member of the Council of Government instead, and played a part in the negotiations for the French withdrawal in 1839. His attempt to resign from the Council that year was refused and he was made Vice-President until the end of 1840. In 1849 he was elected Municipal President for Mexico City and was once again Foreign Minister in April 1853, under Santa Anna who, being indisposed, made him acting president. But he became ill himself in May and died on 2 June, greatly distressed at the way his country was living in such political turmoil. He would have been distressed too at the break in British-Mexican relations in 1867; and he probably would not have agreed with the reason for it.

Wavell continued for some years to be in the service of the Mexican government, although he and his wife (he married Anne, daughter of Sir William Paxton, in 1828) left the country for a while during the disturbances after the end of Victoria's presidency. He was back again in 1831, when it is recorded that he was then given leave of absence for two years. During this time he was trying to make a success of his grant of land in Texas, and in 1833 his Mexican military service was terminated. From 1834 almost until his death in 1860 (at 43 Ladbroke Square, Notting Hill in London) he carried on a lengthy correspondence with the Foreign Office and others over his claims for arrears of pay from the Mexican government and his lands in Texas, and for a while he and his wife lived in France where their eldest son, Arthur Henry, was born. (The father of the field-marshal was the fourth son, Archibald Graham.) He was also active during the last ten years of his life in promoting the use of gun-rafts for bombarding enemy coastal fortifications. But to the end it was his interest in Texas that occupied him most. As late as March 1853 when writing to his agent there he said: 'Should we be tempted to transfer our establishment to Texas we shall bring out quite a colony for friends have already declared that whenever we go they will accompany us; indeed I think we could fill a vessel with our large family & friends. A friend says he will lend us one of his vessels.[18] And he was constantly enquiring whether land could not be found for his sons to settle. It cannot be said that he played more than a marginal role in the development of British-Mexican relations. Yet, despite becoming embittered over his treatment by the Mexicans, he had a genuine interest in their welfare and in fact his original object in trying to introduce British settlers to Texas had been to provide a buffer between the Americans and Mexico. In 1826 he had been the bearer of a letter from Ward to Vaughan, then in Washington, in which Ward said that he 'has been of very great use to me here and can give you a very good idea of the state of affairs here at the present moment [when the question of the border between Texas and the USA was preoccupying the Mexicans]. His only fault is being almost *too* zealous upon the subject, & from this the only differences which we have ever had have arisen.'[19]

It may seem, after this sad catalogue of the fates of some of the *dramatis personae* in this tale of the first five years of British-Mexican relations, that none of them had any lasting effect on the march of history, and that it has hardly been worth spilling so much ink over them. On a superficial level, indeed, one might be justified in commenting that 'plus ça change plus c'est la même chose'. To read, for example, Sir David Kelly's description of his tour of duty in Mexico, is to find echoes of Ward's experiences.[20] Kelly, who like Ward was only Chargé d'affaires, found that the business of pursuing British interests in 1926/27 was only possible through personal friendship with those in positions of power; and that the way to cultivate those to the stage when he could call on them in their homes to seek their help was through dinner parties – for men only in his case for the 'members of the Government much preferred dining out without their wives'. It has never become any easier to get those at home to loosen the purse strings to make the kind of gestures that are so important in cultivating that kind of relationship, or to get them to understand that others do not always see issues in the same light as the British. It may be easier in recent times to sympathize with Kelly's view that international problems are 'ultimately a religious question'; but Ward's difficulty in getting Canning to understand the delicacy of the religious question in Mexico in the 1820s was no more, perhaps, than a reflection of the difficulty, as Kelly put it, which the Englishman finds in grasping 'that the vast majority of the human race are far from sharing his exalted standards in administration, of justice in the Courts, and general respect for laws and regulations'.

It would be wrong to suggest that British-Mexican relations in the 1990s are affected as much as they were in Ward's day by the kind of close encounters with 'the ruling few' that this tale has tried to illustrate: there is now a sophisticated network of international business and banking which has far more influence over the development of relations between the 'new' world and the 'old' than anything experienced by Ward – or even by Kelly. Nevertheless, there will never come the day when important issues are not frequently decided by 'personal likes or dislikes, personal health, vanity, prejudice', to quote Kelly again; and this tale has perhaps shown how skilful Ward was in recognizing this (even if he did not always recognize how his own health could affect *his* outlook). It can be argued that what was achieved in terms of British-Mexican relations in those few years in the 1820s had little, if any, impact on the later development of those relations: the study of cause and effect in history can be as fanciful as Kipling's tale of the butterfly which stamped. But Ward was the first European diplomat to make an impression in Mexico, and the importance of how he made it is not to be underrated. Henry Bamford Parkes may possibly have gone too far in 1938 in referring to Ward as carrying out 'the instructions of the Imperial bagman in the Foreign Office', and in suggesting that 'for the success of the British economic penetration … Ward was largely responsible'.[21] But it may be reasonable to suggest that without him there might not have been that success, that somehow it was some relic of his influence that was acting on Porfirio Díaz when he determined to bring back British commercial influence as a counterweight to that of the United States. Parkes suggested that Ward achieved this by 'combining a British honesty and personal charm with an equally British conviction that the interests of British imperialism were identical with those of Mexico and that in serving his country he was also serving justice and civilization'. There can be no doubt whatsoever about his honesty and personal charm. (And it is possible that his success in his personal dealings with Victoria and others owed something to the Spanish blood in his veins: his paternal great-grandmother was certainly Spanish, and his grandmother, although born in Genoa, may also have been.) Moreover, there is absolutely no sign that he ever committed that most heinous of sins in a diplomat, becoming so attached to the country in which he serves that he cannot see when and where the interests of that country and his own should and must diverge.[22] That he believed in British imperialism is also sure, and there was nothing wrong with that. British imperialism may not have been the universal blessing some have claimed for it; but at the end of the eighteenth and early in the nineteenth centuries the way it was applied in relation to the emerging nations in Spanish America was fundamentally beneficial, the existence of some reprehensible get-rich-quick operators notwithstanding. Central to this, of course, were Castlereagh and Canning, without whose far-sightedness things might have turned out very differently.

As explained in chapter 1, Canning based much of his foreign policy on the principle that 'England should hold the balance, not only between contending nations, but between conflicting principles: that in order to prevent things from going to extremities she should keep a distinct middle ground, staying the plague both ways.' Ward understood this; but he also understood, as Canning did not, that even such intelligent people as Alamán had to be persuaded of it. It was Ward above all who could understand how someone like Victoria, leave alone the people of Mexico in general, was bound to see the success of the revolt against Spain as something of paramount importance requiring immediate recognition and support. He may occasionally have surrendered in his own mind to the belief held by Canning that Mexico had inflated ideas of her own importance and needed teaching a lesson; but it was he who struck the chord in Victoria's heart which persuaded him of the need for patience, and of the certainty of true British friendship if he would have faith. The theory put forward by Parkes that Ward acquired influence over Victoria 'by paying court to his mistress, the Countess Regla' is surely wrong. It was Ward who persisted, at the risk of his own career, in heading Canning off from what might have been a fatal head-on collision over the issue of religious tolerance. Without Ward, Victoria might have taken a wrong turning. Without Victoria, Ward could not have succeeded in holding Britain's position in Mexico, and there might have been no treaty. Hervey and Morier (and even the 'little Doctor' Mackie) played their parts, but they were not crucial. The true architects of British-Mexican friendship on the political level were Victoria and Ward. It is therefore all the more regrettable that Canning should have treated Ward so shamefully. But, as Kelly wrote, important issues are so often decided by personal health. Canning was not well when Ward's outbursts, sent when he himself was unwell, reached him. Had this not been so, possibly his treatment of Ward would have been gentler. By the time Ward got back to England, Canning was Prime Minister, so it might have been difficult to appeal to him, as his father's friend, for reinstatement in his chosen career. But Canning died within a few weeks of Ward's return, so that possibility was in any case closed to him. Perhaps, however, he had become disillusioned with the career of diplomacy, which he referred to in his book as one which 'was hitherto thought rather an easy, luxurious sort of metier; but a diplomatist in America requires stamina as well as head, and must have a talent for undergoing a good deal of very rough work, as well as for managing a delicate negotiation'.[23] Ward lacked none of those qualities; nor did his wife Emily, and his comment applied just as much to a wife, as it does to this day.

It was certainly not the physical difficulties of being a diplomat in the New World in those days which caused Ward to change careers. But it seems a tragedy that one so obviously possessing those characteristics should have been lost to the diplomatic service of the day in the way he was. However, it is not the only time that an involuntary separation from that service has led to a career of distinction greater, perhaps, than would have been attained within it. In the end neither Ward himself nor the interests of Britain suffered; and while it may be too fanciful to trace a generic line from him to present day relations between Britain and Mexico, at least one can have satisfaction in knowing that one so talented was on hand at their birth.

Postscript

At a very late stage the author came across a letter which Morier had written to his brother (who was considering investing in Mexican stock) in March 1827. As this revealed his real opinion of Mexico and her leading politicians, an extract is reproduced on page 292, note 24.

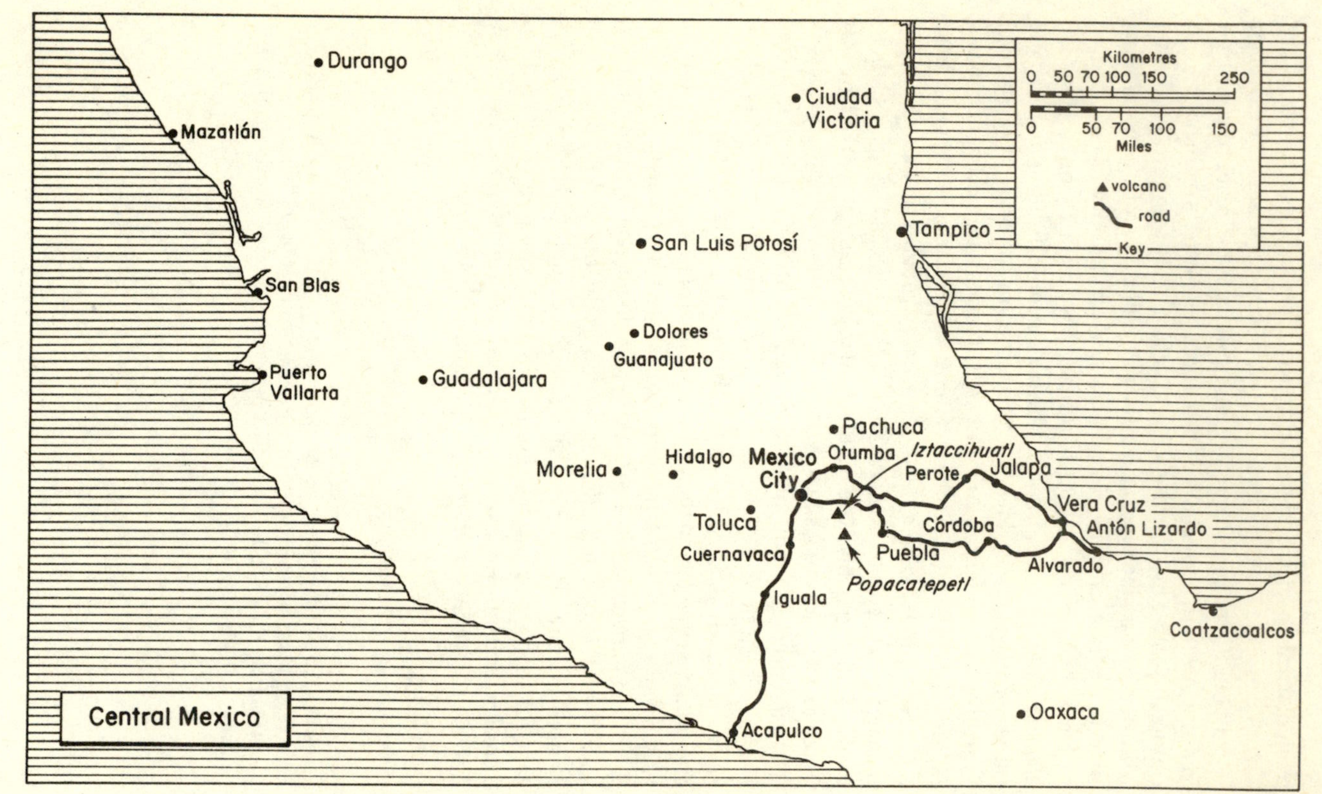

Central Mexico

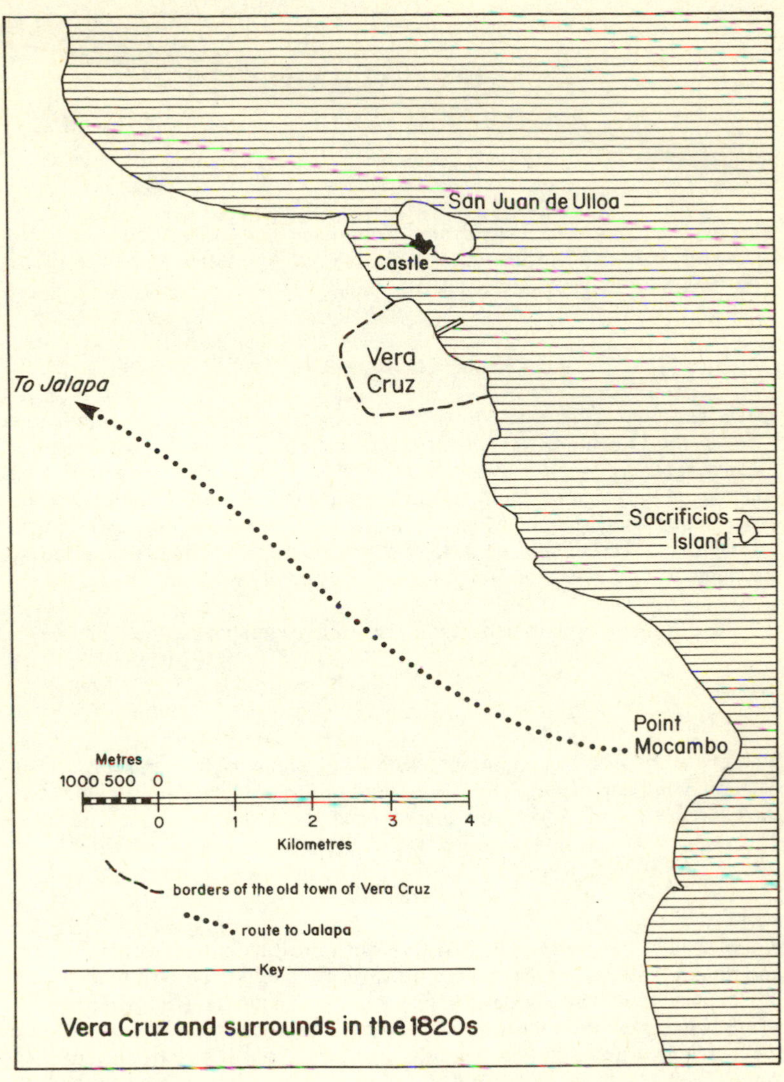

Vera Cruz and surrounds in the 1820s

APPENDIX I

Text of the Treaty of Friendship, Commerce and Navigation concluded between Britain and Mexico on 6 April 1825 but not ratified. (The text of the treaty finally ratified is at Appendix II).

In the Name of the Most Holy Trinity

Extensive commercial intercourse having been established for some time between the Dominions of His Britannic Majesty and the United States of Mexico, it seems good for the security, as well as the encouragement of such commercial intercourse and for the maintenance of good understanding between His said Britannic Majesty and the said States, that the relations now subsisting between them should be regularly acknowledged and confirmed by the signature of a Treaty of Amity, Commerce and Navigation.

For this purpose they have named their respective Plenipotentiaries ....

Article I

There shall be perpetual amity between the Dominions and subjects of His Majesty The King of the United Kingdom of Great Britain and Ireland, and the United States of Mexico and their citizens.

Article II

There shall be between all the Territories of His Britannic Majesty in Europe, and the Territories of Mexico, a reciprocal freedom of commerce. The inhabitants of the two countries respectively shall have liberty freely and securely to come, with their ships and cargoes, to all places, ports and rivers in the Territories aforesaid to which other foreigners are or may be permitted to come, to enter into the same, and to remain and reside in any part of the said Territories, respectively: also to hire and occupy houses and warehouses for the purposes of their commerce; and generally, the merchants and traders of each Nation, respectively, shall enjoy the most complete protection and security for their commerce, subject always to the laws and statutes of the two Countries respectively. By the rights of entering the places, ports, and rivers mentioned in this Article, the privilege of carrying on the coasting trade is not understood, in which national vessels only are permitted to engage.

Article III

His Majesty The King of the United Kingdom of Great Britain and Ireland engages further that the inhabitants of Mexico shall have the like liberty of commerce and navigation stipulated for in the preceding article in all His Dominions situated out of Europe, to the full extent in which the same is permitted at present or shall be permitted hereafter to any other nation.

Article IV

No higher or other duties shall be imposed on the importation into the Dominions of His Britannic Majesty of any article of the growth, produce or manufacture of Mexico, and no higher or other duties shall be imposed on the importation into the Territories of Mexico of any article of the growth, produce, or manufacture of His Britannic Majesty's Dominions than are or shall be payable on the like articles being the growth, produce or manufacture of any other foreign country; nor shall any other or higher duties or charges be imposed in the Territories or Dominions of either of the Contracting Parties on the exportation of any articles to the Territories of the other than such as are or may be payable on the exportation of the like articles to any other foreign country, nor shall any prohibition be imposed upon the exportation of any articles the growth, produce or manufacture of His Britannic Majesty's Dominions or of the said Territories of Mexico, to or from the said Dominions of His Britannic Majesty, or to or from the said Territories of Mexico, which shall not equally extend to all other Nations. Whatever concession or special privilege be granted either by His Britannic Majesty or by the States of Mexico to any other nation shall be extended respectively to the two Contracting Parties gratuitously if the concession in favor of that other nation shall have been gratuitous, and under the same conditions if the concession be conditional: excepting always the countries and provinces of America which were formerly Spanish possessions, and to which, in consideration of the ties of fraternity by which they are united to Mexico, peculiar privileges may be granted which cannot be extended to the subjects of His Britannic Majesty.

Article V

The provisions made by the preceding article with respect to the exportation and importation of goods are to be considered as extending, under the same conditions, and with the same exceptions, to all duties and charges on account of tonnage, light and harbour dues, pilotage, salvage in case of damage, shipwreck or re-capture of vessels, and all other charges which now are or hereafter may be established in the Dominions of His Britannic Majesty or the Territories of Mexico.

Article VI

If the importation into the Territories of Mexico of any article the growth, produce or manufacture of His Britannic Majesty's Dominions be made in a British vessel, no higher duties shall be paid than are paid or may hereafter be paid on the same article if imported in the vessels of the most favored nation: and in like manner, if the importation into the Dominions of His Britannic Majesty of any article the growth, produce or manufacture of Mexico be made in a Mexican vessel, no higher duties shall be paid than are paid or may hereafter be paid on the same article if imported in the vessels of the most favored nation. Articles of the growth, produce or manufacture of Mexico exported from the Territories of that State in British vessels shall pay no higher duties, and shall be entitled to the same drawbacks and bounties as articles of the same kind exported in the vessels of the most favored nation; and in like manner, articles of the growth, produce and manufacture of Great Britain exported from the Dominions of His Britannic Majesty in Mexican vessels shall pay no higher duties and shall be entitled to the same drawbacks and bounties as articles of the same kind if exported in the vessels of the most favored nation: the whole of these stipulations being subject to the conditions specified in the fourth Article. Should the trade of Mexico hereafter possess a sufficient number of ships for its commercial wants, the two Contracting Parties may establish perfect reciprocity with regard to all duties, bounties and drawbacks on the importation and exportation in their respective Dominions and Territories of articles the produce, growth or manufacture of such respective Dominions and Territories in vessels belonging to either of the two contracting parties.

Article VII

In order to avoid any misunderstanding with respect to the Regulations which may respectively constitute a British or Mexican vessel, it is hereby agreed that all vessels built in the Dominions of His Britannic Majesty and owned, navigated and registered according to the laws of Great Britain, shall be considered as British vessels: and that all vessels built in the Territories of Mexico, or nationalised there according to the law, owned by a Mexican citizen or citizens and whose Master or Captain is a Mexican either by birth or by naturalization and three parts of whose crew have been admitted into the Mexican service with the knowledge of the Government, shall be considered as a Mexican vessel. These regulations with respect to what is to constitute a Mexican vessel are to be in force for ten years, beginning with the day on which the ratifications of the present Treaty are exchanged, at the expiration of which time the Contracting Parties agree to take this Article again into consideration, and to assign, if they should think proper so to do, by mutual agreement, a new term for the duration of the said regulations.

Article VIII

Mexican citizens embarked on board a British man of war, or such Mexican property or effects as may be received on board, shall be covered and protected by His Britannic Majesty's flag; Mexican citizens, effects or property embarked on board a British merchant vessel shall be esteemed as much under the protection of the British flag as the persons, property or effects of the most favored nation. British property on board a Mexican man of war or merchant vessel shall enjoy reciprocally the same protection. The Mexican flag both in time of peace and in the event of a war between Great Britain and any other Power shall enjoy the same rights and privileges which His Majesty the King of the United Kingdom of Great Britain and Ireland either has granted or hereafter may grant to any other nation. The vessels belonging to either of the Contracting Parties can never be subject to embargo in the Dominions or Territories of the other under plea of military service or any other pretext whatsoever without a sufficient indemnification.

Article IX

All merchants, Commanders of ships, and others, the subjects of His Britannic Majesty, shall have full liberty in all the Territories of Mexico to manage their own affairs themselves, or to commit them to the management of whomsoever they please, as broker, factor, agent, or interpreter, nor shall they be obliged to employ any other persons for those purposes, than those employed by Mexicans, nor to pay them any other salary or remuneration, than such as is paid in like cases by Mexican citizens, and absolute freedom shall be allowed, in all cases, to the buyer and seller to bargain and fix the price of any goods, wares or merchandise imported into or exported from Mexico, as they shall see good, observing the laws and established customs of the country. The same privileges shall be enjoyed in the Dominions of His Britannic Majesty by the citizens of Mexico under the same conditions.

Article X

In whatever relates to the succession to personal estates, by Will or descent, and the disposal of personal property of every sort and denomination by sale, donation, exchange or testament, or in any other manner whatsoever, as also the administration of justice, the subjects and citizens of the two Contracting Parties shall enjoy in their respective Dominions and Territories the same privileges, liberties and rights as the most favored nation, and shall not be charged in any of these respects with any higher imposts or duties than those which are paid, or may be paid, by the native subjects or citizens of the Power in whose Dominions or Territories they may be resident.

Article XI

In all that relates to the police of the ports, the lading and unlading of ships, the safety of merchandize, goods and effects, the subjects of His Britannic Majesty and the citizens of Mexico, respectively, shall be subject to the local laws and regulations of the Dominions and Territories in which they may reside. They shall be exempted from all compulsory military service, whether by sea or land. No forced loans shall be levied upon them as foreigners, nor shall they be subject to any other charges, requisitions or exactions than such as are paid by the native subjects or citizens of the respective Dominions or Territories in which they may reside.

Article XII

It shall be free for each of the two Contracting Parties to appoint Consuls for the protection of trade, to reside in the Dominions and Territories of the other Party; but before any Consul shall act as such, he shall, in the usual form, be approved and admitted by the Government to which he is sent, and either of the Contracting Parties may except from the residence of Consuls such particular places as either of them may judge fit to be excepted. The Mexican Diplomatic Agents and Consuls shall enjoy in the Dominions of His Britannic Majesty all the privileges, exceptions and immunities which are granted to Agents of the same rank belonging to the most favoured nation, and in like manner the Diplomatic Agents and Consuls of His Britannic Majesty in the Mexican Territories shall enjoy according to the strictest reciprocity the same privileges, exceptions and immunities which may be granted to the Mexican Agents and Consuls in the Dominions of His Britannic Majesty.

Article XIII

For the better security of commerce between the subjects of His Britannic Majesty and the citizens of the Mexican States, it is agreed that if, at any time, any interruption of friendly intercourse, or any rupture should unfortunately take place between the two Contracting Parties, the merchants residing upon the coasts shall be allowed six months, and those of the interior a whole year, to wind up their accounts, and dispose of their property, and that a Safe Conduct shall be given them to embark at the port which they shall themselves select. All those who are established in the respective Dominions and Territories of the two Contracting Parties in the exercise of any trade or special employment shall have the privilege of remaining and continuing such trade and employment therein, without any manner of interruption, in full enjoyment of their liberty and property as long as they behave peaceably and commit no offence against the laws; and their goods and effects of whatever description they may be shall not be liable to seizure or sequestration, or to any other charges or demands than those which may be made upon the like effects or property belonging to the native subjects or citizens of the respective

Dominions or Territories in which such subjects or citizens may reside. In the same case, debts between individuals, public funds, and shares of Companies shall never be confiscated, sequestered or detained.

Article XIV

The Subjects of His Britannic Majesty residing in the Mexican Territories shall enjoy in their houses, persons and properties the protection of the Government; and continuing in possession of what they now enjoy, they shall not be disturbed, molested or annoyed in any manner on account of their religion, provided they respect that of the nation in which they reside, as well as the constitution, laws and customs of the country. They shall continue to enjoy to the full the privilege already granted to them of burying in the places already assigned for that purpose such subjects of His Britannic Majesty as may die within the Mexican Territories, nor shall the funerals and sepulchres of the dead be disturbed in any way, or upon any account. The citizens of Mexico shall enjoy in all the Dominions of His Britannic Majesty the same protection, and shall be allowed the free exercise of their religion in public or private, either within their own houses, or in the chapels and places of worship set apart for that purpose.

Article XV

The stipulations agreed to by the sixth Article of the Treaty of Versailles of the 3rd September 1783 shall remain in full force and vigour between His Britannic Majesty and the United States of Mexico with respect to that portion of the Mexican territory which they embrace, as shall also those of the Convention signed in London on the 14th July 1786 for explaining, enlarging and rendering effective the stipulations of the above mentioned article.

Article XVI

The Government of Mexico engages to co-operate with His Britannic Majesty for the total abolition of the Slave trade, and to prohibit all persons inhabiting within the Territories of Mexico, in the most effectual manner, from taking any share in such trade.

Article XVII

As many new and important points must naturally arise out of the intimate relations which are about to be established between the Dominions of His Britannic Majesty and the States of Mexico, which points may require a special arrangement, it is hereby agreed that these points shall be taken into consideration at the end of six years, to commence from the day on which the ratifications of the present Treaty are exchanged, and it is hereby further declared that such Articles as may then be agreed upon shall be regarded as forming a part of the present Treaty and shall have the same force as those now contained in it.

Article XVIII

The present Treaty shall be ratified, and the ratifications shall be exchanged at London within the space of four months or sooner if possible.

In Witness whereof the respective Plenipotentiaries have signed the same, and have affixed thereto their respective Seals.

Done at Mexico, the Sixth Day of April, in the Year of Our Lord Eighteen Hundred & Twenty Five.

Additional Article

Spain being the only European Power which in virtue of the last clause of the fourth Article of the Treaty signed this day, beginning with the words 'Whatever concessions' and continuing to the end of the Article, could pretend to privileges from the United States of Mexico which Great Britain could not obtain, it is hereby agreed that such commercial privileges as it may hereafter be the interest of Mexico to grant to Spain shall be in no wise exclusive or prohibitory, and shall be limited in point of time. The present additional Article shall have the same force and effect as if it were inserted, word for word, in the Treaty signed this day, and shall be ratified, and the ratifications exchanged at the same time.

In witness whereof the respective
Plenipotentiaries have signed it and have affixed therunto their respective seals. 6th April 1825 Mexico

Appendix II

Text of the Treaty of Friendship, Commerce and Navigation concluded between Britain and Mexico on 26 December 1826.

In the Name of the Most Holy Trinity

Extensive commercial intercourse having been established for some time between the Dominions of His Britannic Majesty and the United States of Mexico, it seems good for the security, as well as the encouragement of such commercial intercourse and for the maintenance of good understanding between His said Britannic Majesty and the said States, that the relations now subsisting between them should be regularly acknowledged and confirmed by the signature of a Treaty of Amity, Commerce and Navigation.

For this purpose they have named their respective Plenipotentiaries, that is to say, His Excellency the President of the United States of Mexico, His Excellency Señor Sebastian Camacho his First Minister of State and for the Department of Foreign Affairs, and His Majesty the King of the United Kingdom of Great Britain and Ireland, the Right Honorable William Huskisson, a member of His said Majesty's Most Honorable Privy Council, a Member of Parliament, President of the Committee of Privy Council for affairs of Trade and Foreign Plantations, and Treasurer of His Majesty's Navy, and James Morier Esquire, who, after having communicated to each other their Full Powers, found to be in due and proper form, have agreed upon and concluded the following articles.

Article I

There shall be perpetual amity between the Dominions and subjects of His Majesty The King of the United Kingdom of Great Britain and Ireland, and the United States of Mexico and their citizens.

Article II

There shall be between all the Territories of His Britannic Majesty in Europe, and the Territories of Mexico, a reciprocal freedom of commerce. The inhabitants of the two countries respectively shall have liberty freely and securely to come, with their ships and cargoes, to all places, ports and rivers in the Territories aforesaid, saving only such particular ports to which other foreigners shall not be permitted to come, to enter into the same, and to remain and reside in any part of the said Territories, respectively: also to hire and occupy houses and warehouses for the purposes of their commerce; and generally, the merchants and traders of each Nation, respectively, shall enjoy the most complete protection and security for their commerce. In like manner, the respective ships of war, and Post Office packets of the two countries shall have liberty freely and securely to come to all harbours, rivers and places, saving only such particular ports (if any) to which other foreign ships of war and packets shall not be permitted to come, to enter into the same, to anchor, and to remain there and refit, subject always to the laws and statutes of the two Countries respectively. By the rights of entering the places, ports, and rivers mentioned in this article, the privilege of carrying on the coasting trade is not understood, in which national vessels only are permitted to engage.

Article III

His Majesty The King of the United Kingdom of Great Britain and Ireland engages further, that the inhabitants of Mexico shall have the like liberty of commerce and navigation stipulated for in the preceding article, in all His Dominions situated out of Europe, to the full extent in which the same is permitted at present, or shall be permitted hereafter to any other nation.

Article IV

No higher or other duties shall be imposed on the importation into the Dominions of His Britannic Majesty of any article of the growth, produce or manufacture of Mexico, and no higher or other duties shall be imposed on the importation into the Territories of Mexico of any article of the growth, produce, or manufacture of His Britannic Majesty's Dominions than are or shall be payable on the like articles being the growth, produce or manufacture of any other foreign country; nor shall any other or higher duties or charges be imposed in the Territories or Dominions of either of the Contracting Parties on the exportation of any articles to the Territories of the other than such as are or may be payable on the exportation of the like articles to any other foreign country, nor shall any prohibition be imposed upon the exportation of any articles the growth, produce or manufacture of His Britannic Majesty's Dominions or of the said Territories of Mexico, to or from the said Dominions of His Britannic Majesty, or to or from the said Territories of Mexico, which shall not equally extend to all other Nations.

Article V

No higher or other duties or charges, on account of tonnage, light, or harbour dues, pilotage, salvage in case of damage or shipwreck, or any other local charges shall be imposed in any of the ports of Mexico on British vessels, than those payable in the same ports by foreign vessels, nor in the ports of His

Britannic Majesty's Territories on Mexican vessels, than shall be payable in the same ports on British vessels.

Article VI

The same duties shall be paid on the importation in to the Territories of Mexico of any article the growth, produce or manufacture of His Britannic Majesty's Dominions, whether such importation shall be in Mexican or in British vessels; and the same duties shall be paid on the importation into the Dominions of His Britannic Majesty of any articles the growth, produce or manufacture of Mexico, whether such importation shall be in British or in Mexican vessels. The same duties shall be paid, and the same bounties and drawbacks allowed on the exportation to Mexico of any articles of the growth, produce, or manufacture of His Britannic Majesty's Dominions, whether such exportation shall be in Mexican or in British vessels; and the same duties shall be paid, and the same bounties and drawbacks allowed, on the exportation of any articles the growth, produce or manufacture of Mexico to His Britannic Majesty's Dominions, whether such Exportation shall be in British or in Mexican vessels.

Article VII

In order to avoid any misunderstanding with respect to the Regulations which may respectively constitute a British or Mexican vessel, it is hereby agreed that all vessels built in the Dominions of His Britannic Majesty, or vessels which shall have been captured from an enemy by His Britannic Majesty's ships of war, or by subjects of His said Majesty furnished with Letters of Marque by the Lords Commissioners of the Admiralty, and regularly condemned in one of His said Majesty's Prize Courts as a lawful Prize, or which shall have been condemned in any competent Court for the breach of the laws made for the prevention of the Slave Trade, and owned, navigated and registered, according to the laws of Great Britain, shall be considered as British vessels: and that all vessels built in the Territories of Mexico, or captured from the enemy by the ships of Mexico, and condemned under similar circumstances, and which shall be owned by any citizen or citizens thereof and whereof the Master and three fourths of the mariners are citizens of Mexico, excepting where the laws provide for any extreme cases, shall be considered as Mexican vessels. And it is further agreed that every vessel qualified to trade as above described, under the provisions of this Treaty, shall be furnished with a Register, Passport, or Sea-Letter, under the signature of the proper person authorised to grant the same according to the laws of the respective countries (the form of which shall be communicated) certifying the name, occupation, and residence of the owner or owners in the Dominions of His Britannic Majesty, or in the Territories of Mexico, as the case may be, and that he or they is, or are, the sole owner or owners in the proportion to be specified, together with the name, burthen and description of the vessel, as to build and measurement, and the several particulars constituting the national character of the vessel, as the case may be.

Article VIII

All merchants, Commanders of ships, and others, the subjects of His Britannic Majesty, shall have full liberty in all the Territories of Mexico to manage their own affairs themselves, or to commit them to the management of whomsoever they please, as broker, factor, agent, or interpreter, nor shall they be obliged to employ any other persons for those purposes, than those employed by Mexicans, nor to pay them any other salary or remuneration, than such as is paid in like cases by Mexican citizens, and absolute freedom shall be allowed, in all cases, to the buyer and seller to bargain and fix the price of any goods, wares or merchandize imported into or exported from Mexico, as they shall see good, observing the laws and established customs of the country. The same privileges shall be enjoyed in the Dominions of His Britannic Majesty by the citizens of Mexico under the same conditions. The citizens and subjects of the Contracting Parties in the Territories of each other shall receive and enjoy full and perfect protection for their persons and property; and shall have free and open access to the Courts of Justice in the said countries respectively for the prosecution and defence of their just rights; and they shall be at liberty to employ in all cases, the advocates, attornies, or agents of whatever description whom they may think proper; and they shall enjoy in this respect the same rights and privileges therein as native citizens.

Article IX

In whatever relates to the succession to personal estates, by Will or otherwise, and the disposal of personal property of every sort and denomination by sale, donation, exchange or testament, or in any other manner whatsoever, as also the administration of justice, the subjects and citizens of the two Contracting Parties shall enjoy in their respective Dominions and Territories the same privileges, liberties and rights as native subjects, and shall not be charged in any of these respects with any higher imposts or duties than those which are paid, or may be paid, by the native subjects or citizens of the Power in whose Dominions or Territories they may be resident.

Article X

In all that relates to the police of the ports, the lading and unlading of ships, the safety of merchandize, goods and effects, the subjects of His Britannic Majesty and the citizens of Mexico, respectively, shall be subject to the local laws and regulations of the Dominions and Territories in which they may reside. They shall be exempted from all compulsory military service, whether by sea or land. No forced loans shall be levied upon them, nor shall their property be subject to any other charges, requisitions or taxes, than such as are paid by the native subjects or citizens of the Contracting Parties in their respective Dominions.

Article XI

It shall be free for each of the two Contracting Parties to appoint Consuls for the protection of trade, to reside in the Dominions and Territories of the other Party; but before any Consul shall act as such, he shall, in the usual form, be approved and admitted by the Government to which he is sent, and either of the Contracting Parties may except from the residence of Consuls such particular places as either of them may judge fit to be excepted. The Mexican Diplomatic Agents and Consuls shall enjoy in the Dominions of His Britannic Majesty whatever privileges, exceptions and immunities are or shall be granted to Agents of the same rank belonging to the most favoured nation, and in like manner the Diplomatic Agents and Consuls of His Britannic Majesty in the Mexican Territories shall enjoy according to the strictest reciprocity whatever privileges, exceptions and immunities are or may be granted to the Mexican Agents and Consuls in the Dominions of His Britannic Majesty.

Article XII

For the better security of commerce between the subjects of His Britannic Majesty and the citizens of the Mexican States, it is agreed that if, at any time, any interruption of friendly intercourse, or any rupture should unfortunately take place between the two Contracting Parties, the merchants residing upon the coasts shall be allowed six months, and those of the interior a whole year, to wind up their accounts, and dispose of their property, and that a Safe Conduct shall be given them to embark at the port which they shall themselves select. All those who are established in the respective Dominions and Territories of the two Contracting Parties in the exercise of any trade or special employment shall have the privilege of remaining and continuing such trade and employment therein, without any manner of interruption, in full enjoyment of their liberty and property as long as they behave peaceably and commit no offence against the laws; and their goods and effects of whatever description they may be shall not be liable to seizure or sequestration, or to any other charges or demands than those which may be made upon the like effects or property belonging to the native subjects or citizens of the respective Dominions or Territories in which such subjects or citizens may reside. In the same case, debts between individuals, public funds, and shares of Companies shall never be confiscated, sequestered or detained.

Article XIII

The Subjects of His Britannic Majesty residing in the Mexican Territories shall enjoy in their houses, persons and properties the protection of the Government; and continuing in possession of what they now enjoy, they shall not be disturbed, molested or annoyed in any manner on account of their religion, provided they respect that of the nation in which they reside, as well as the constitution, laws and customs of the country. They shall continue to enjoy to the full the privilege already granted to them of burying in the places already assigned for that purpose such subjects of His Britannic Majesty as may die within the Mexican Territories, nor shall the funerals and sepulchres of the dead be disturbed in any way, or upon any account. The citizens of Mexico shall enjoy in all the Dominions of His Britannic Majesty the same protection, and shall be allowed the free exercise of their religion in public or private, either within their own houses, or in the chapels and places of worship set apart for that purpose.

Article XIV

The Subjects of His Britannic Majesty shall on no account or pretext whatsoever be disturbed or molested in the peaceable possession and exercise of whatever rights, privileges and immunities they have at any time enjoyed within the limits described and laid down in a Convention signed between His said Majesty and the King of Spain on the 14th of July 1786, whether such rights, privileges and immunities shall be derived from the stipulations of the said Convention, or from any other concession which may, at any time, have been made by the King of Spain or His predecessors, to British subjects and settlers residing and following their lawful occupations within the limits aforesaid; the two Contracting Parties reserving, however, for some more fitting opportunity the further arrangement on this Article.

Article XV

The Government of Mexico engages to co-operate with His Britannic Majesty for the total abolition of the Slave trade, and to prohibit all persons inhabiting within the Territories of Mexico, in the most effectual manner, from taking any share in such trade.

Article XVI

The two Contracting Parties reserve to themselves the right of treating and agreeing hereafter, from time to time, upon such other articles as may appear to them to contribute still further to the improvement of their mutual intercourse and the advancement of the general interests of their respective subjects and citizens; and such articles as may be so agreed upon shall, when duly ratified, be regarded as forming a part of the present Treaty, and shall have the same force as those now contained in it.

Article XVII

The present Treaty shall be ratified, and the ratifications shall be exchanged at London within the space of six months or sooner if possible.

In Witness whereof the respective Plenipotentiaries have signed the same, and have affixed thereto their respective Seals.

Done at London, the Twenty Sixth Day of December, in the Year of Our Lord One Thousand Eight Hundred & Twenty Six.

Additional Articles

Article I

Whereas, in the present state of Mexican shipping it would not be possible for Mexico to receive the full advantage of the reciprocity established by the Articles V, VI, VII of the Treaty signed this day, if that part of the VII Article which stipulates that in order to be considered as a Mexican ship, a ship shall actually have been built in Mexico, should be strictly and literally observed and immediately brought in to operation, it is agreed that for the space of ten years, to be reckoned from the date of the exchange of the ratifications of this Treaty, any ships, wheresoever built, being *bona fide* the property of, and wholly owned by one or more citizens of Mexico, and whereof the Master and three fourths of the mariners, at least, are also natural-born citizens of Mexico, or persons domiciliated in Mexico by act of the Government, as lawful subjects of Mexico, to be certified according to the laws of that country, shall be considered as Mexican ships, His Majesty the King of the United Kingdom of Great Britain and Ireland reserving to Himself the right at the end of the said term of ten years to claim the principle of reciprocal restriction stipulated for in the article VII above referred to if the interests of British navigation shall be found to be prejudiced by the present exception to that reciprocity in favour of Mexican shipping.

Article II

It is further agreed that, for the like term of ten years, the stipulations contained in Articles V and VI of the present Treaty shall be suspended; and in lieu thereof, it is hereby agreed that, until the expiration of the said term of ten years, British ships entering into the ports of Mexico from the United Kingdom of Great Britain and Ireland, or any other of His Britannic Majesty's Dominions, and all articles the growth, produce, or manufacture of the United Kingdom or of any of the said Dominions, imported in such ships, shall pay no other or higher duties than are or may hereafter be payable in the said ports by the ships and the like goods, the growth, produce or manufacture of the most favoured nation; and reciprocally, it is agreed that Mexican ships entering into the ports of the United Kingdom of Great Britain and Ireland, or any other of

His Britannic Majesty's Dominions, from any port of the States of Mexico, and all articles the growth, produce or manufacture of the said States, imported in such ships, shall pay no other or higher duties than are or may hereafter be payable in the said ports by the ships and the like goods the growth, produce, or manufacture of the most favoured nation; and that no higher duties shall be paid or bounties or drawbacks allowed on the exportation of any article the growth, produce, or manufacture of the Dominions of either country in the ships of the other, than upon the exportation of the like articles in the ships of any other foreign country. It being understood that, at the end of the said term of ten years, the stipulations of the said V and VI Articles shall, from thenceforward, be in full force between the two countries.

The present additional articles shall have the same force and validity as if they were inserted word for word in the Treaty signed this day.

They shall be ratified, and the ratifications shall be exchanged at the same time.

In Witness whereof, the respective Plenipotentiaries have signed the same, and have affixed thereto their respective Seals.

Done in London, the Twenty Sixth day of December, in the Year of Our Lord One Thousand Eight Hundred and Twenty Six.

Notes: The treaty (to be found at FO 93/59/2) was written in both English and Spanish, the Mexican Plenipotentiary signing the Spanish version and the British Plenipotentiaries the English. The convention of 14th July 1786 referred to in Article XIV (incidentally written in French and to be found at FO 93/99/3) was an agreement between Britain and Spain whereby the latter, while having its sovereignty over the Mosquito Coast (a region of Nicaragua and Honduras) confirmed, allowed British settlers to continue, within a defined geographical area, in the enjoyment of their business of logwood cutting. The purpose of Article XIV was to ensure that the sovereignty of what later became British Honduras was not conceded to Mexico, a matter covered by R.A. Humphreys in his *Diplomatic History of British Honduras, 1638–1901*, published by Oxford University Press in 1961.

NOTES AND SOURCES

Most of the references are to papers in the Public Record Office at Kew in the FO series. The first figure following FO is the group number, the second the piece number within this group and the third the folio number within this piece (but folios are not always numbered). Where the text of a document in the FO series has been included in C.K. Webster's *Britain and the Independence of Latin America* this is indicated by a reference such as (W I 431) – i.e., Webster Volume I, page 431.

The prefix ADM indicates Admiralty files at the PRO with the group number followed by the piece number. The reference E 192/5 is that of a box held in the Chancery Lane section of the PRO containing a collection (unsorted) of Arthur Goodall Wavell's correspondence.

In addition to the above, the following abbreviations are used:

MFA: files in the archives of the Mexican Foreign Ministry showing the ministry reference number. Where the text of these is also included in *La Diplomacia Mexicana* (Mexican Foreign Ministry 1910–13) the volume and page number concerned is also given, e.g. (DM II 97)
Vaughan: the collection of letters from Henry George Ward to Charles Richard Vaughan in the Codrington Library, All Souls College, Oxford
Swinburne: the 'Swinburne (Capheaton) MSS' in the Northumberland County Record Office, Newcastle upon Tyne. The number shown is that of the particular letter in file ZSW 536
Canning: personal papers of George Canning forming part of the Harewood Collection in the Leeds District Archives

Prologue

1 ADM 51/3402. Log of HMS *Ranger*.
2 FO 72/265/157. Mackie's memo presented by Mr Broughton on 11/10/1822.
3 Hall, born in 1788, was the son of George Hall (1756–95), a merchant of

Dundee and, later, London; but the nature of the trade in which he was involved is not known. George's maternal grandfather was Alexander Gordon, understood to have been a Scottish writer; but whether this was the well-known antiquarian and writer of that name is not known.

4 FO 72/255/219. Hall's letter to Sir Henry Wellesley from Puebla dated 30/8/1821 received in Madrid and forwarded to the Foreign Office on 28/3/1822.

5 FO 72/255/23. Hall's letter from Vera Cruz dated 21/10/1821 forwarded by Madrid and received in the Foreign Office 24/1/1822. (A copy was sent from Madrid on 18/5/1822 and received in the Foreign Office 2/6/1822, to be found at FO 72/256/66).

6 FO 50/2/82. Note on docket covering Admiralty letter dated 12/9/1823.

7 FO 72/265/237. Mackie to Canning dated 30/10/1822.

8 FO 50/1/1. Mackie to Canning dated 28/11/1822.

9 FO 50/2/31. Admiralty letter dated 21/5/1823.

10 FO 50/1/3. Canning's instructions to Mackie dated 21/12/1822 (W I 431).

11 The quotation is taken from William Bullock, *Six Months' Residence and Travels in Mexico* (John Murray 1825), p. 15. The Roman Catholic Church was all powerful in Spain and her colonies, and non-Catholics, or 'heretics', were not allowed any religious privileges. The island had been so named by the Spanish explorer Juan de Grijalva in 1518. In *La Historia de la Conquista de México* by Antonio de Solís y Ribadenya, published 1704, as translated by Thomas Townsend (1724), the story of the naming is given as follows:

> They called it the Island of Sacrifices, because going in to view a House of Lime and Stone, which overlooked the rest, they found several Idols of a horrible Figure [in Spanish 'figura' means 'face'] and a more horrible Worship paid to them; for near the Steps where they were plac'd, were the Carkasses of six or seven Men, newly sacrificed, cut to Pieces, and their Entrails laid open. This miserable Sight struck our People with Horror, and affected them with different Sentiments, their Hearts being filled with Compassion, at the same Time that they were enraged at the Abomination.

From the same source comes the reason for naming the islet on which the castle of San Juan de Ulloa stood:

> They called it the Island of St Juan, because they arrived there on the Day of the Baptist, and likewise in Respect to the Name of their General, mixing Devotion with Flattery; and because an Indian, who was pointing with his Hand towards the Main Land, giving them to understand how it was called, repeated several Times, with a bad Pronunciation, the Word Culua! Culua! This gave the Occasion to the Sirname, by which they distinguished it from St Juan de Puerto Rico, calling it St Juan de Ulua.

12 Bullock, *Six Months' Residence and Travels in Mexico* p. 15.
13 FO 50/1/10. Mackie to Canning dated 17/3/1823.

Chapter 1

1 FO 50/1/10. Mackie letter from Havana dated 17/3/1823.
2 C.K. Webster, *The Foreign Policy of Castlereagh 1812–1815* (G. Bell and Sons 1931) p. 70.
3 FO 72/127/77. Foreign Office despatch No. 13 to Madrid dated 1/4/1812 (W II 309).
4 Foreign Office memorandum dated 20/8/1817 reproduced in C.K. Webster, *Britain and the Independence of Latin America* (Oxford University Press 1938) Vol. II pp. 352–8.
5 Quoted in Robert Bell *The Life of the Rt Hon. George Canning* (Chapman & Hall 1846) p. 334.
6 This speech is at column 1 of Hansard, New Series, Volume VIII and the relevant part reads: 'Faithful to the principles … constituting the rule of his conduct, His Majesty declined being party to any proceedings at Verona which could be deemed an interference in the internal concerns of Spain … and continues to use his most anxious endeavours and good offices, to allay the irritation unhappily subsisting between the French and Spanish governments and to avert, if possible, the calamity of war between France and Spain.
7 Canning's statement is at columns 872–96 of the same Hansard volume. In this statement he reiterated that the government's policy was guided by 'respect for the faith of treaties – respect for the independence of nations – respect for that established line of policy known by the name of "the balance of power" in Europe – and last but not least, respect for the honour and interests of this country'. In dealing with the question of the independence of the Spanish colonies in America he said that so long as Spain had no enemy in Europe it had been 'at British discretion' whether to leave this subject alone or, as she had done, to try to convince Spain that she had effectively lost all control over them. Now, however, Britain must come out into the open and declare that she 'considered the separation of the colonies from Spain to have been effected to such a degree that it would not tolerate for an instant any cession which Spain might make of colonies over which she did not exercise a direct and positive influence'.
8 Quoted by Augustus Granville Stapleton in *George Canning and His Times* (1859) p. 394.

Chapter 2

1 FO 50/1/10. Mackie letter from Havana dated 17/3/1823.
2 FO 50/1/24. Mackie letter from Havana dated 4/5/1823.
3 Mackie had in fact asked Captain Thomas Stopford RN commanding HMS *Icarus* then at Havana, to convey him to Vera Cruz, but Stopford was

willing to take him only as far as Jamaica. When Commodore Sir Edward Owen at Kingston heard about this he supported Stopford in his refusal to carry Mackie to Vera Cruz, saying that he would have arranged a passage for him from Kingston had he accepted Stopford's offer to get him there. This was all reported to the Admiralty, but the Foreign Office did not receive the papers until 13 September and they were then simply acknowledged (FO 50/2/82–87).

4 Lillian Briseño Senosiain, Laura Solares Robles and Laura Suárez de la Torre, *Guadalupe Victoria*: *Primer Presidente de México* (Secretaria de Educación Pública, México, 1986).

5 Carlos Bosch Garcia, *Problemas Diplomáticos del México Independiente* (El Colegio de México 1947, Universidad Nacional Autónoma de México 1986).

6 MFA 5-9-8124. Mackie letter dated 23/7/1823 (DM II 100).

7 Ibid., Victoria to Supreme Executive dated 23/7/1823 (DM II 97).

8 Ibid., Victoria to Alamán dated 23/7/1823 (DM II 99).

9 Ibid., formal instructions to Victoria dated 27/7/1823 (DM II 102).

10 The difficulty of guessing what really happened between Victoria and Mackie over the latter's credentials is enhanced by Victoria's own later statement that he had indeed broken off negotiations with the Spanish commissioners because of Mackie's representations (see chapter 6). Moreover it is impossible now to be sure how the Foreign Office received the various records of the talks. It appears from FO 50/1 that Mackie did not enclose copies of the Spanish language versions with his own report. But the Spanish language version at FO 50/1/68 (which Victoria himself signed with a statement certifying that a true copy was held in the archives at Jalapa) bears a note referring to it as having been enclosed with Victoria's own letter to Canning sent with Mackie. It is possible that Mackie was deliberately trying to conceal his deception from the Foreign Office and was unaware of what Victoria was sending to Canning.

11 Both Victoria and Mackie had presumably by then seen newspaper reports of the proceedings in Parliament on 14 April (see notes 6 and 7 to chapter 1). Mackie's instructions from Canning, which had been shown to Victoria, contained nothing on this subject.

12 MFA 59-8124. Victoria letter dated 8/8/1823 (DM II 115).

13 Ibid., Mackie to Alamán dated 8/8/1823 (DM II 118).

14 This request is mentioned in the three volume *Murillo – Catálogo Crítico* by Diego Angulo Iniguez (Espasa-Calpe SA, Madrid 1981). He says that these pictures were believed to have been commissioned by a devout Mexican for the Carmelite convent at Puebla. Four of them have disappeared and the remainder later became the property of Baron de Gorga Borras, reportedly in payment of a debt. It is thought that a picture now in the Hearst collection in New York may be one of these.

15 MFA 5-9-8124. Alamán to Victoria dated 13/8/1823 (DM II 120).

16 FO 50/1/64. Victoria to Canning dated 21/8/1823 (W I 432).

17 FO 50/1/60. Alamán to Canning dated 16/8/1823 (DM II 123).

18 FO 50/1/34. Mackie's final report dated 20/11/1823 (W I 438).

19 The Foreign Office agreed in February 1824 to pay £88 for the cost of his

passage in HMS *Phaeton* (FO 50/8/15); but why the journey took nearly three months instead of the more normal six or seven weeks is a mystery. Unfortunately her log for that period is not available.

Chapter 3

1 There is speculation of this kind in the excellent, unpublished Ph.D thesis presented at the University of London in 1954 by W. Cody, *British Interest in the Independence of Mexico, 1808-1821*, which was brought to the author's attention at a very late stage in the preparation of this book.
2 MFA 5-9-8235. Michelena to Alamán dated London 26/6/1824 (DM III 18).
3 Mackie's letter to Victoria was dated 23 August 1823 from Vera Cruz and is reproduced at p. 131 of Volume II of *La Diplomacia Mexicana* published by the Mexican Ministry of Foreign Affairs in 1910–13.
4 Information on these activities of Mackie is contained in official contemporary Mexican papers reproduced at pp. 176–83 of the work cited above, and at pp. 116–21 of Volume IV of *México a Través de los Siglos* edited by Vicente Riva Palacio and published in Mexico in 1888.
5 *The Diary of Benjamin Robert Haydon* (Harvard University Press 1963) entry for 16 August 1827 in Volume III, pp. 211–12.
6 Hall tried to get a consular post in Mexico but failed. He died, aged 36, in Vera Cruz in September 1824, leaving some $35,000 (about £7000) in 'safe custody' at the castle. What happened to this is not known. (Letter to the Foreign Office at FO 50/18/247 from his sister, Elizabeth, wife of Alexander Cowan, the founder of the paper-making firm of that name established then at Melville Mill, near Edinburgh.)
7 It is by no means certain that Mackie did know Iturbide personally. In one of his memoranda to the Foreign Office in 1822 he referred to Iturbide as being unmarried although he in fact had a wife and several children.
8 MFA 1-12-1220.
9 The only documentary evidence of Wavell's position in the Chilean army is the order (in the Texas State Archives) made by Bernardo O'Higgins on 6 July 1820 appointing him Colonel of Infantry on the General Staff.
10 The information in the papers in the Texas State Archives about Wavell's movements at this time, based as it is on his own later writings when he was claiming monetary compensation from the Mexican government, is suspect. And there would appear to be no warrant for the colourful description, in the late R.H. Kiernan's book *Wavell* (1945) about the field-marshal, of Arthur riding into Mexico City among Iturbide's staff on 27 September 1821: he was evidently not in Mexico at that time.
11 MFA 40-11-1.
12 Thomas, Earl of Dundonald, GCB, *Narrative of Services in the Liberation of Chili, Peru and Brazil* (James Ridgway 1859) Volume I, pp. 176–7.
13 Lucas Alamán, *Historia de Méjico desde 1808* (1852) Volume V, p. 474.
14 MFA 1-1-44. Letter from Wavell dated London 21/5/1823.
15 Annual Report of the American Historical Association for 1919, Volume

II, Part I, pp. 536, 544–5, 553.

16 Ibid. pp. 528–9 quoting letter from Wavell to Iturbide dated 4/7/1822 and his formal agreement with Austin of the same date.

17 Ibid. p. 553 quoting letter from Wavell to Austin dated London 21/11/1822.

18 MFA 1-1-44. Letter from Wavell dated London 7/5/1823.

19 British Library ref. ADD 38296/40357 and referred to in an item in the *Courier* of London dated 11/10/1823 reporting Wavell's departure for Mexico and describing him as one of 'the individuals who have exerted themselves in making known the actual situation of the Spanish Americas': it also referred to the publication of the pamphlet 'many months since' as having 'produced a considerable effect on public opinion'.

20 American Historical Association op. cit. p. 555 quoting letter from Wavell to Austin dated London 2/12/1822.

21 Wavell also learned then that as soon as Iturbide fell from power the 'regency' which took over for a period decided to send an 'ambassador' to England to seek recognition. This proposal fell through because the man chosen, Dr Josef Yañez, declined to go on account of his large family (letter from Wavell to Planta dated 22/7/1823 at FO 50/2/59). But Yañez later played a part in Wavell's commercial ventures in Mexican mines.

22 MFA 1-1-44. Letter from Wavell dated London 11/8/1823.

23 FO 50/4/168. Ward to Captain Murray dated 7/4/1824.

24 FO 50/2/37. Undated memo.

25 FO 50/2/41. Letter to Planta dated 29/6/1823.

26 *Despatches, Correspondence and Memoranda of the Duke of Wellington* 2nd Series (John Murray 1867) Volume 2, p. 117.

27 Adams was married to Jane Elizabeth, 4th daughter and co-heiress of Colonel George Rawson MP for Armagh, and in accordance with the wish expressed in his widowed mother-in-law's will, he became Sir William Rawson in March 1825.

28 In December 1824 Sir William was enthusiastic about the results of a demonstration before Wellington in which the gun 'at 60 atmospheres pressure liquified the ball at 100 feet distance from a target' and pierced 'four one inch deal boards, at an inch space from each other, which it is believed a musquet [*sic*] would not do' (letter from Sir William Adams to Wavell dated 16/12/1824).

29 FO 50/2/35. Wavell to Planta dated 19/6/1823.

30 The newspaper *El Sol* of 27 January 1824 carried a report from the port of Alvarado dated 6 January that the *Sarah* had just arrived there after a stop at Sacrificios, and that Wavell had disembarked at Vera Cruz.

31 A reference to Don Quixote's mistress Dulcinea much used at that time in England as a euphemism.

32 E 192/5. Adams to Wavell dated 10/10/1823.

33 E 192/5. Letter to Wavell from his father dated 8/7/1825.

34 Ibid. dated 12/7/1825.

35 FO 50/2/68. Migoni to Canning dated 1/9/1823.

36 Evidence suggests that these instructions were in fact carried by Mackie himself for delivery to Migoni: they were certainly sent in the same ship,

HMS *Phaeton*, since Migoni refers to this in his first communication with the Foreign Office.

37 MFA 5-9-8124. Alamán to Migoni dated 13/8/1823 (DM II 155).

38 FO 50/2/114. Marginal note on letter from Migoni dated 17/11/1823.

39 FO 50/2/132. Migoni to Canning dated 12/12/1823.

40 Harold Temperley, *The Foreign Policy of Canning, 1822–1827* (G. Bell and Sons 1925) p. 103.

41 FO 50/3/69. Foreign Office despatch No. 4 dated 23/4/1824 (W I 450).

Chapter 4

1 FO 72/259/35. Madrid despatch No. 11 dated 7/10/1822.

2 Vaughan C 121/1. Letter dated 26/8/1822.

3 Swinburne 20-22. Letters from Sir James Willoughby Gordon dated 3/6, 5/6 and 23/6/1823.

4 FO 72/257/218. Madrid despatch No. 113 dated 18/9/1822.

5 FO 72/268/74. Foreign Office despatch to Madrid No. 13 dated 28/1/1823.

6 FO 72/268/186. Madrid despatch No. 62 dated 13/3/1823.

7 O'Gorman's payments for the maintenance of his illegitimate daughter ceased in 1826, after his marriage in Mexico, and in 1834 the Spanish government formally requested the British government to arrange for their resumption (FO 72/427: Note from Spanish Foreign Ministry dated 17/10/1834 enclosed with private letter dated 22/10/1834 from the ambassador to the permanent secretary at the Foreign Office).

8 Vaughan C 121/12. Letter dated 2/5/1824.

9 On 1 June 1825 O'Gorman, then aged 40, married Anna Josefa Noriega y Vicario, aged only 14. She was the daughter of Colonel Juan Noriega and María Luisa Martín Vicario Elías. By that time Juan Noriega had died and María Luisa was married to Colonel Santiago Moreno. The witnesses at the O'Gorman wedding were Alamán and Ward. The marriage took place despite the efforts of Santa Anna to prevent it. He had fallen in love with Anna Josefa and wrote a passionate letter to her mother, when he heard of the proposed marriage to O'Gorman, begging her not to throw away her daughter on this elderly 'Englishman'. But María Luisa had been a staunch 'Iturbidista' and was contemptuous of the 'upstart' Santa Anna. The marriage was the start of a distinguished family, even though O'Gorman behaved cavalierly towards his young wife, going off to live in England without her. He took his son, John, with him to be educated at Eton; but John disliked this and returned to Mexico. He was the grandfather of two very distinguished Mexicans, Juan O'Gorman, the architect, and Edmundo the historian/philosopher (from whom this background has been obtained).

10 FO 72/123/3. Letter from Park Place, Edinburgh dated 9/9/1811.

11 E 192/5. Letter from Thos Kinder Jun. to Frederick Holdsworth dated 10/4/1826.

12 E 192/5. Letter from Adams, 26 Albermarle Street dated 10/10/1823.

13 In the second edition of the book about Mexico which Ward published in

1828 he inserted the following note in the preface: 'I have learnt with much regret that I have been thought by some friends of Mr Mackenzie not to have done justice to the assistance which I derived from his report on the Veracruz trade .... I am the more sorry for this because there are few persons to whom I have been so much indebted as to Mr Mackenzie, whose acute and laborious researches embraced not only the period of his residence at Veracruz, but the general state of the trade of that port for twenty-five years before his arrival.' And Hervey's successor as commissioner went so far as to recommend him to Canning because he had 'evinced so much zeal, integrity and intelligence in seconding my endeavours to obtain information' (Morier's despatch No. 17 dated 28/2/1825 at FO 50/11/86).

14 Hervey was granted £2000 p.a. for expenses, more if necessary, and £1000 outfit allowance. Ward got £300 p.a. for expenses and £500 outfit allowance. O'Gorman got a salary of £2500 and expenses of £700 p.a. The consuls were to have salaries of £1000 and £500 for expenses. Thomson's salary was £500 plus expenses of £200 p.a. (FO 50/3/21, 23, 32 and 36 and 50/7/1).

15 Swinburne 25. Ward to Sir John Swinburne dated 18/10/1823.

16 Canning. Letter dated 8/1/1824.

17 FO 50/10/164. Morier despatch No. 7 dated 10/2/1825.

18 FO 50/9/33. Foreign Office unnumbered despatch dated 3/1/1825.

19 One of Sir John's ancestors had supported the Royalists in the Civil War and as a reward was created baronet by Charles II, building Capheaton Hall in 1668. Emily was the fourth child (third daughter) of six, born 9/5/1798. She was the aunt of Algernon Charles Swinburne, the poet, and an accomplished amateur artist, having been taught by William Mulready, the Irish Royal Academician (1786–1863), who painted a portrait of her.

20 Vaughan C 121/11. Letter dated Capheaton 4/10/1823.

21 Swinburne 24. Ward to Sir John Swinburne dated 18/10/1823.

22 HMS *Thetis* unfortunately came to grief on 6 December 1830 when, under command of Captain Samuel Burgess, she ran aground in bad visibility at Cap Frio in Brazil while on passage back to England with a load of specie amounting to $810,000. She was a total loss, although the captain and most of the ship's company managed to reach the shore. But an ingenious salvage operation was mounted which, for a total expenditure of just over £13,000, led to the recovery of $760,000 (then worth just over £164,000) and over £2000 worth of other stores. The full story of this remarkable success, and of the subsequent court proceedings over salvage rights, can be found at ADM 7/598 and 599.

23 Dudley Pope, *Life in Nelson's Navy* (George Allen and Unwin 1981) p. 181.

24 Captain Basil Hall RN, *Fragments of Voyages and Travels*, first series, (Edward Moxon 1846) chap. 32, p. 139.

25 ADM 51/3490. Log of HMS *Thetis*.

26 FO 50/8/141. Admiralty letter to Foreign Office dated 10/5/1824.

27 Swinburne 25. Ward to Sir John Swinburne dated 30/10/23.

28 Swinburne 26. Ward to Sir John Swinburne begun at Vera Cruz and finished at Jalapa 22/12/1823.

29 FO 50/2/140. Captain Roberts to the Admiralty dated Havana 10/11/1823.

30 H.G. Ward, *Mexico in 1827* (Henry Colburn 1828) Volume II, p. 173 et. seq.
31 Ibid., p. 176.
32 FO 50/4/1. Hervey despatch No. 1 dated 14/12/1823.
33 H.G. Ward, op. cit. p. 178
34 Writing to Vaughan in January 1822 from Madrid Ward had referred to 'a banishment more complete from the whole civilized world than this it is hardly possible to conceive' (Vaughan papers C 120/7).

Chapter 5

1 FO 50/4/14. Hervey despatch No. 4 dated 23/12/1823.
2 Vaughan C 121/12. Letter dated 2/5/1824.
3 FO 50/4/8. Hervey despatch No. 3 dated 22/12/1823.
4 This was the ship in which Wavell was reported as having returned to Mexico, but this incident must have taken place on her return to Vera Cruz from visiting Alvarado, well after Wavell had disembarked.
5 The full correspondence is at FO 50/4/25-43.
6 MFA 1-4-889. Tradesmen's accounts.
7 Vaughan C 121/12. Letter dated 2/5/1824.
8 This house was on the street then called Mirador de la Alameda (now Ángela Peralta) and had been bought by one Antonio Terán as part of a conversion to private use of a section of the Convent of Santa Isabel on the site now occupied by the Palacio de Bellas Artes.
9 Translated from the original document in the private Alamán papers held by the Noriega family in Mexico City.
10 *Águila Mexicana* 7/1/1824.
11 *El Sol* 2/1/1824.
12 *Águila Mexicana* 11/1/1824.
13 FO 50/7/380. Canning note dated 10/10/1823.
14 Canning. Letter from Hervey dated 16/12/1823.
15 Swinburne 26. Letter begun at Vera Cruz and finished at Jalapa 22/12/1823.
16 FO 50/3/1. Foreign Office despatch No. 1 dated 10/10/1823 (W I 433).
17 FO 50/3/25. Foreign Office despatch No. 5 dated 10/10/1823 (W I 436).
18 In the original draft of these instructions Hervey was to 'declare … the readiness of your Government to meet any overtures from … Mexico for the establishment of friendly relations' before suggesting that Mexico should send an agent to London. It was Wellington who persuaded Canning to alter this, on the grounds that to express readiness to meet any overtures 'pledges us to everything', and it would be better not to 'appear to court an opportunity of recognising them'. (Letter to Canning dated 31/7/1823 printed in *Despatches, Correspondence and Memoranda of the Duke of Wellington*, 2nd Series (John Murray 1867), Volume 2, pp. 108–110).
19 This treaty 'for the abolition of the slave trade by Spain' was signed on 23 September 1817. It provided that the trade would be abolished 'throughout the entire dominions of Spain on the thirtieth day of May 1820', but that five months would be allowed thereafter for the completion

of any voyages which had already begun. And Britain provided Spain with £400,000 to be used to compensate for losses incurred by Spaniards in consequence of the treaty (FO 93/99/11).

20 FO 50/4/89. Hervey despatch No. 8 dated 18/1/1824.

21 FO 50/4/101. Translation of Mexican Law passed 15/1/1824.

22 FO 50/4/46. Hervey's formal report dated 18/1/1824 (W I 442).

23 Canning. Letter from Hervey dated 18/1/1824.

24 Ward boarded *Thetis* at Sacrificios for the return to England on 26 January 1824 but almost immediately went ashore again, presumably to see Victoria. Gales blew up on the 27th and 28th and 30th, and he did not finally get aboard until 2 February. They sailed next day.

Chapter 6

1 C.L. Meryon, *Memoirs of the Lady Hester Stanhope* (Henry Colburn 1845) Volume II, p. 105.

2 FO 50/4/4. Hervey despatch No. 2 dated 15/12/1823.

3 Vaughan C 120/5. Letter dated 23/4/1821.

4 From a letter from Mexico dated 31/1/1824 reported in *The Times* 8/4/1824.

5 FO 50/4/107. Hervey despatch No. 10 dated 20/1/1824.

6 FO 50/4/123. Hervey private letter to Canning dated 20/2/1824 (W I 445).

7 FO 50/4/133. Hervey despatch No. 13 dated 26/3/1824.

8 Rocafuerte was actually an Ecuadorean; but his native land was at that time part of 'Gran Colombia'. In these early days of Spanish-American independence from Spain there was considerable interchange between the regions of those active in politics. People like Rocafuerte had dreams of a great 'liberal' confederation of Spanish America and regarded themselves as Spanish Americans rather than Ecuadoreans, Colombians or whatever. Rocafuerte, for practical reasons, was given Mexican citizenship (but returned to his native Ecuador in 1833 when his pan-Spanish American dream began to fade). His controversial influence on Mexican diplomacy and politics is considered in some depth in *The Emergence of Spanish America* by Jaime E. Rodriguez O (University of California Press 1975). Murphy was a 'liberal' Spanish merchant who had lived for many years in Mexico and had been one of those representing that colony in the Cortes. He had already been used as a Mexican agent in France, and shortly after reaching London with Michelena he was sent back there to open up communications with the French government. He called upon the British ambassador to tell him of his instructions from Michelena and to assure him 'that he should not take any steps [under those instructions] without previous communication' with him. The ambassador, when reporting this to Canning, added 'that my personal knowledge of the character of Mr Murphy does not induce me to place very implicit reliance on this assurance' (FO 27/312 Sir Charles Stuart despatch No. 360 dated 15/7/1824).

9 FO 50/4/183. Hervey despatch No. 20 dated 23/5/1824.
10 Text carried in *El Sol* of 17 April 1824 (also in DM III 15).
11 MFA 5-9-8235. Michelena's first report from London dated 26/6/1824 (DM III 18).
12 FO 50/8/261. Croker (Admiralty) to Planta dated 14/10/1824.
13 FO 50/3/52. Foreign Office despatch No. 2 dated 9/4/1824.
14 There were two sets of proceedings. In the Commons on 4 March 1824 Canning laid the Polignac Memorandum and copies of some of his exchanges of despatches with à Court in Madrid and Spanish responses to proposals for mediation. In the Lords on 15 March there was a debate on a motion by the Marquess of Lansdowne calling for immediate recognition of the former Spanish colonies in America, in the course of which the prime minister, Lord Liverpool, said: 'He would ask [any Colombian, Chilean, Mexican or Peruvian] whether they believed that the appointment of a minister plenipotentiary, or a mere declaration of recognition, could be as satisfactory to them as the unqualified, undisguised avowal of Great Britain that she would never consent to the interference of any third power, and France [i.e. in the Polignac Memorandum] recording an abjuration of such an avowal. When it was a question of the good will and friendly disposition of Great Britain towards the South Americans, he would represent that such an avowal was worth the appointment of a thousand ambassadors.' (Columns 708–19 and 970–1009 of Hansard, New Series, Volume X).
15 FO 50/3/46. Planta letter dated 6/2/1824.
16 Hervey had actually been sent a copy of the Polignac Memorandum in strict confidence just before he sailed for Mexico (FO 204/1/127 letter from Planta dated 13/10/1823); but he never mentioned this in any of his subsequent correspondence with London. Either he never received it, or he was extraordinarily discreet.
17 The dating of this despatch is odd. The draft shows the date of 9 March, with March crossed out and April substituted. This is unlikely to have been a clerical error because the draft mentions that nothing had been received from Hervey at that time. Hervey's despatch reporting his arrival in Mexico City was received in the Foreign Office on 20 March, so the original drafting (which was not altered apart from the date) was obviously before this.
18 FO 50/3/75. Foreign Office despatch dated 23/4/1824.
19 FO 50/5/103. O'Gorman note to Alamán dated 1/7/1824.
20 FO 50/5/107. Alamán reply to O'Gorman dated 6/7/1824.
21 FO 50/5/47. Hervey despatch No. 31 dated 7/7/1824.
22 FO 50/5/136. Hervey despatch No. 41 dated 9/9/1824.
23 FO 50/7/105. O'Gorman to Planta dated 1/11/1824.
24 The ground provided for the British cemetery was at Tlaxpana, then outside the city limits and not far from the British Residence. The first burial in it was of the Honorable Augustus Waldegrave (see chapter 13) in 1827. It continued in use until 1926, by which time it contained 1129 graves and was full. In 1923, in anticipation of this, the British colony purchased a plot of 21,432 square metres in Tacuba, further out, at a cost

of 26,000 pesos, to be the new cemetery. In 1970 the grounds of the Tlaxpana cemetery were returned to Mexican ownership and in 1973, because an overpass for a new road was to be built over part of it, the bodies were transferred to the Tacuba cemetery and the remaining part became a public park.

25 H.G. Ward op. cit. pp. 712–3.
26 FO 72/284/70. Foreign Office despatch No. 13 to Madrid dated 31/3/1824 (W II 421).
27 FO 50/3/55. Foreign Office despatch No. 3 dated 23/4/1824 (W I 446).
28 Canning. Letter to Hervey dated Bath 23/4/1824.
29 FO 50/5/24. Hervey despatch No. 28 dated 30/6/1824.
30 FO 97/270/24. Michelena's memorandum of meeting with Planta 22/9/1824.
31 It is interesting that Michelena also asked Planta on this occasion whether Britain might agree to France taking part in the mediation attempt, because if so Mexico could 'have recourse to some expedient in her power' (translated as such in the Foreign Office from 'mover algunos resortes que estaban en la mano'). What he meant by this is obscure, and Planta is not recorded as having reacted.
32 FO 50/5/55. Hervey despatch No. 34 dated 9/7/1824 (W I 453).
33 FO 72/284/32. Foreign Office despatch No. 7 to Madrid dated 31/1/1824.
34 FO 50/3/69. Foreign Office despatch No. 4 dated 23/4/1824 (W I 450).
35 FO 50/5/51. Hervey despatch No. 33 dated 8/7/1824 (W I 452).
36 FO 50/5/1. Hervey despatch No. 24 dated 3/6/1824.
37 FO 50/5/202. Halstead to commander of Ulloa dated 10/8/1824.
38 FO 50/4/190. Halstead to Hervey dated 3/2/1824.
39 FO 50/4/150. Hervey despatch No. 15 dated 30/3/1824.
40 FO 50/7/1. Canning instruction to each consul dated 10/10/1823.
41 FO 50/7/175. Mackenzie to Canning dated 18/1/1824.
42 FO 50/7/153. Planta to Mackenzie dated 8/4/1824.
43 FO 50/7/242. Mackenzie to Planta dated 30/8/1824.
44 FO 50/5/40. Hervey despatch No. 30 dated 7/7/1824.
45 FO 50/18/186. Planta to Admiralty dated 18/6/1825.
46 E 192/5. Lady Adams (Rawson) to Wavell dated 11/7/1825.
47 E 192/5. Lady Adams (Rawson) to Wavell dated 5/9/1825.
48 E 192/5. Wavell senior to his son dated 8/7/1825.
49 E 192/5. Wavell senior to his son dated 23/1/1826.
50 E 192/5. Planta to Mackenzie dated 23/3/1826.
51 E 192/5. Mackenzie to Sir William Adams (Rawson) dated 20/8/1825.
52 E 192/5. Mackenzie to Wavell senior dated 25/3/1826.
53 E 192/5. Wavell senior to his son dated 1/5/1826.
54 Something of the character of Sir William can be deduced from a letter written to Lord Colchester by a friend who had met him by chance in a coach between London and Deptford on 2 June 1826. Sir William was on his way to 'make overtures of some kind to the French Government' about the steam gun, the rights to which he had purchased from the inventor. As France at that time was a potential enemy, his self-interest is clear. As the

writer ironically remarked, Sir William presumably feared that France might 'be behindhand in the knowledge of this new art of destruction' (*The Diary and Correspondence of Charles Abbot, Lord Colchester* (John Murray 1861), Vol. III, p. 443).

55 E 192/5. Thos Kinder Jun. to Frederick Holdsworth dated 10/4/1826.

56 When Mackenzie left Mexico he did so with a warm recommendation from Hervey's successor because he had 'evinced so much zeal, integrity and intelligence' (FO 50/11/86 letter to Foreign Office dated 28/2/1825), so he was evidently able to charm even his professional superiors.

57 Hervey started his provincial tour on 15 September, and on 17 October he reported from Guadalajara that he had covered nearly 700 miles, finding everything peaceful and settled (FO 50/5/175).

Chapter 7

1 Canning. Letter to his wife dated 20/3/1824.

2 Wellington op. cit. p. 241.

3 Wellington op. cit. p. 246 letter dated 4/4/1824.

4 Ibid.

5 FO 50/3/55. Foreign office despatch No. 3 dated 23/4/1824 (W I 446).

6 FO 50/5/26. Hervey despatch No. 29 dated 3/7/1824.

7 FO 50/4/129. Hervey despatch No. 12 dated 21/2/1824.

8 FO 50/3/79. Foreign Office despatch No. 6 dated 20/7/1824 (W I 455).

9 FO 50/7/342. Canning to Staples dated 22/7/1824.

10 Canning. Hervey letter dated 10/9/1824.

11 FO 50/5/210. Hervey unnumbered despatch dated 31/10/1824.

12 It is interesting to compare this formal despatch with the private letter Hervey had written only two weeks earlier from Guadalajara, where he had received a copy of the English newspaper in which the news of his action over the loan had broken. In this he had written: 'I think ... I am entitled to the support and confidence of H M's Ministers until it can be shown that I have disobeyed my instructions, and the instant I feel that I have lost either the one or the other I shall not hesitate to retire from the Post which has been entrusted to me. I feel however confident that these apprehensions are groundless whilst you remain at the head of the Department of Foreign Affairs.' (Letter dated 15/10/1824 in the Canning papers.)

13 MFA 5-9-8235. Michelena's record of meeting with Canning 31/7/1824.

14 FO 50/16/1. Hervey unnumbered despatch dated 15/12/1824.

Chapter 8

1 Swinburne 26. Ward to Sir John begun 9/12/1823 finished 14/12/1823.

2 Swinburne 27. Ward senior to Sir John 7/3/1824.

3 Swinburne 28. Ward to Sir John 26/3/1824.

4 Swinburne 29. Emily and Henry to Sir John undated but obviously 12/4/1824.

5 Swinburne 30. Ward to Sir John 13/7/1824.
6 Swinburne 32. Ward to Sir John 1/8/1824.
7 Swinburne 33. Emily to Sir John undated but obviously 1/8/1824.
8 Swinburne 34. Ward to Sir John 6/8/1824.
9 Swinburne 31. Ward senior to Sir John undated but obviously 30/7/1824.
10 Swinburne 34. Ward to Sir John 6/8/1824.
11 Margaret Morris Cloake (trans. and ed.), *A Persian at the Court of King George 1809–10*, the diary kept by Abul Hasan (Barrie & Jenkins 1988).
12 Sir Denis Wright, *The Persians Amongst the English* (I.B. Tauris 1985) p. 84.
13 Morier did well, financially, out of this. He continued to draw his pension of £700 a year in respect of his former service while being paid the full salary as a commissioner to Mexico. This appears to have been an administrative error, for in March 1825 Planta wrote to him to say that it could not continue. But Canning had given instructions, 'taking into consideration the circumstances in which you are placed', that he should be allowed to include the amount of £700 'in your Bills on account of the Mexican Commission, and to charge the same as an item in your accounts' (Planta letter dated 10/3/1825 at FO 50/9/46).
14 Although Morier did not claim to speak Spanish, he certainly had some knowledge of it. In a letter to his wife describing his arrival in Mexico he referred to a welcoming speech 'which I but partially understood'. It is probable that he gained some knowledge of Spanish from his business contacts in Smyrna with the Sephardic Jews there, whose language it was.
15 Swinburne 30. Ward to Sir John 13/7/1824.
16 Ibid.
17 ADM 52/3944. Log of HMS *Diamond*.

Chapter 9

1 FO 50/6/1. Foreign Office despatch No. 1 dated 20/7/1824.
2 FO 50/6/9. Foreign Office despatch No. 4 dated 30/7/1824 (W I 457).
3 ADM 52/3944. Log of HMS *Diamond*.
4 FO 50/6/17. Morier despatch No. 1 dated 1/11/1824.
5 FO 50/6/94. Morier despatch No. 10 dated 19/11/1824.
6 FO 50/6/108. Morier despatch No. 13 dated 27/12/1824.
7 FO 50/5/119. Hervey despatch No. 38 dated 28/7/1824.
8 FO 97/270/9.
9 National Library of Scotland MS 2268 folios 24–7.
10 FO 50/6/115. Morier despatch No. 14 dated 27/12/1824.
11 FO 50/10/181. Morier despatch No. 10 dated 10/2/1825.
12 Morier also learned that the consular clerk, Smith, had 'moved to a hut' about a mile and a half away but was still attending to his duties of arranging the forwarding of mail. Morier asked Planta to agree that as a reward for this devotion to duty he should be made consul and receive a salary of £300 a year. This was agreed personally by Canning (FO 50/6/135).
13 FO 50/6/125. Captain Forrest to Morier dated 22/11/1824.

14 FO 50/6/131. Morier to Forrest dated 27/11/1824.
15 FO 50/18/162. Hervey to Napier dated 6/1/1825.
16 FO 50/18/160. Hervey to Napier dated 6/1/1825.
17 FO 50/18/155. Croker (Admiralty) to Planta dated 2/2/1825.
18 FO 50/10/123. Napier letter dated 6/1/1825.
19 FO 50/10/126. Secretary for War and Marine note dated 15/1/1825.
20 FO 50/10/110. Morier despatch No. 4 dated 18/1/1825.
21 FO 50/10/140. Morier/O'Gorman note to Alamán dated 17/1/1825.
22 FO 50/6/147. Morier/O'Gorman note to Guzmán dated 27/12/1824.
23 FO 50/6/150. Guzmán note dated 29/12/1825.
24 FO 50/11/66. Morier despatch No. 15 dated 28/2/1825.
25 FO 50/6/164. Guzmán note dated 26/12/1824.
26 FO 50/6/169. Morier note dated 28/12/1824.
27 FO 50/6/172. Guzmán note dated 29/12/1824.
28 FO 50/10/181. Morier despatch No. 10 dated 10/2/1825.
29 MFA 5-9-8235. Michelena despatch dated 26/6/1824 (DM III 18).
30 MFA 5-9-8235. Michelena despatch dated 3/7/1824 (DM III 27).
31 MFA 5-9-8235. Michelena despatch dated 12/7/1824 (DM III 38).
32 This mention of the King of the Sandwich Islands was made rather savagely only ten days after his death in London on 14 July and the consequent great attention paid publicly to this sad event, which in turn had followed the death of his queen only six days earlier. The monarch had been on an official visit to England 'with his Prime Minister and his Admiral' during which lavish attentions had been bestowed upon him. He had been escorted everywhere by a Foreign Office official to whom King George had given £2500 for paying the expenses; and it was apparently only illness that had prevented the queen accompanying the party on a visit to the British Museum (diary entry for 8 June 1824 by Lord Colchester op. cit. p. 320).
33 MFA 5-9-8235. Michelena despatch dated 25/7/1824 (DM III 46).
34 MFA 5-9-8235. Michelena despatch dated 31/8/1824 (DM III 72).
35 The very great difficulties which Michelena faced in his mission to London are in themselves of considerable interest, but have deliberately been omitted from this work. They are well covered by Jaime E. Rodríguez O in his op. cit. particularly chapters V and VI.
36 MFA 5-9-8235. Michelena despatches dated 13/10 and 30/11/1824 (DM III 93 and 124).
37 There is a mystery about these letters from Victoria. At FO 50/1/64 there is a letter in Spanish from Victoria to Canning dated 21/8/1823 which appears to have been written and signed personally by Victoria. This is now filed with a translation obviously made in the Foreign Office, and immediately after Mackie's own report of his proceedings. But when Ward returned to Mexico (see chapter 10) he carried a letter to Victoria in which Canning acknowledged having received a 'message' sent to him with Ward, but specifically denying ever having had a letter by hand of Mackie. Indeed, he told Victoria that he 'had so much reason to be dissatisfied' with Mackie's actions (which of course Victoria by now knew – see chapter 6) that he had 'ceased to have any intercourse with him'. Ward had suggested

that possibly the letter should have been delivered by Migoni, and Canning added to Victoria that he had never seen that person although he had 'heard that of his proceedings here which did not make me desirous of cultivating his acquaintance'. (This may have been a reference to an apparent deceit by Migoni in telling people in Mexico that he had had 'repeated' meetings with Huskisson, the President of the Board of Trade (who had in fact never met him) in an attempt to persuade the agents of British firms in Mexico that the British government approved of all he was doing so that they would take up Mexican bonds. There is a Foreign Office memorandum about this dated 10/5/1824 at FO 50/8/153; but Migoni himself hotly denied the deceit when called to see Huskisson and Planta on 16/5/1824, at least as stated by him in a report to the Mexican government reproduced in volume IV of *Mexico a Través de los Siglos* edited by Vicente Riva Palacio and published in Mexico in 1888. However, in this letter to Victoria, Canning suggested that all that was 'in the past', assuring him that he had never intended any slight and that 'it shall be no fault of mine if the good understanding which is about to be established … is not established at the same time and maintained with great cordiality between Your Excellency and me'. None of this, however, explains why Canning never received the letter allegedly brought by Michelena. The suspicion comes to mind that Canning had received it but had decided not to reply personally to Victoria until he was ready to propose a formal treaty and thus establish *de facto* relations. (FO 50/17/390 for Canning's letter of 1/1/1825 and –/296 for Victoria's very warm reply of 21/5/1825).

38 FO 50/11/116. Morier despatch No. 19 dated 3/3/1825.

39 FO 50/11/135. Morier despatch No. 22 dated 12/3/1825.

40 Canning had had to exercise all his political skill to get approval from cabinet and the king for this. He had come under considerable pressure from his parliamentary constituency in Liverpool (from where much of the trade with America was carried on) to extend recognition, as well as being convinced that it was necessary for the prosecution of British foreign policy. The somewhat reactionary Wellington had been lukewarm, if not downright opposed, writing, for instance, that 'we must take care not to give additional examples in these times of the encouragement of insurrection, and we must not be induced by clamour, by self-interested views, by stock-jobbing or by faction, to give the sanction of approbation to what are called the governments of those provinces' (Wellington op. cit. p. 247, letter to Canning dated 12/9/1824). The king, worried by the 'revolutionary spirit' abroad, suggested 'it would be wisdom to look to the ultimate consequences which the result of our intended recognition … may probably produce on the evil and discontented'. He asked whether 'the great abettors of this Spanish question … give their support [to recognition] in relation to the great mercantile advantages … or from their love of democracy in opposition to a monarchical aristocracy' (A.G. Stapleton, *George Canning and His Times* (John Parker 1859) pp. 416–7, memorandum to Lord Liverpool in December 1824). But Canning had been firm in putting his case to cabinet: 'Suppose the New States were to impose high and exclusive duties upon the ships and commerce of all the

Powers resorting to their ports which did not acknowledge them ...? Can the British government shut its eyes to what is the interest of Great Britain in this question? .... it cannot be doubted that if we provoke the New States of America to give a decided preference in their ports to the people of the United States over ourselves, the navigation of these extensive dominions will be lost to us .... The disposition of the New States is at present highly favourable to England .... Let us not, then, throw the present golden opportunity away, which once lost may never be recovered.' (Wellington op. cit. pp. 354–9, Canning's memorandum to cabinet dated 30/11/1824.) And when he had at last obtained the king's relucant agreement he wrote: 'The fight has been hard but it is won. The deed is done. The nail is driven. Spanish America is free.' (Wellington op. cit. p. 411, letter from Canning to Granville in Paris dated 17/12/1824.)

41 FO 50/11/142. Morier despatch No. 23 dated 17/3/1825.

Chapter 10

1 Swinburne 35. Letter dated 23/12/1824.
2 L.E.O. Charlton (ed.), *Recollections of a Northumbrian Lady 1815–1866: Memoirs of Barbara Charlton* 2nd Edn (The Spredden Press 1989) p. 126.
3 Swinburne 36. Ward senior to Sir John Swinburne dated 24/12/1824.
4 Swinburne 37. Ward to Sir John dated 29/12/1824.
5 Swinburne 39. Ward to Sir John undated, probably 3/1/1825.
6 FO 97/272/107. Ward to Planta dated 2/1/1825.
7 FO 50/9/40. Planta to Ward dated 5/1/1825.
8 Swinburne 40. Emily to her father dated 12–14/1/1825.
9 Swinburne 41. Ward to Sir John dated 17/2/1825.
10 H.G. Ward op. cit. pp. 257 and 260–1.
11 This incident is not recorded in the log of HMS *Egeria*, where reference is simply made to frequent soundings over the three days 6 to 8 March, although going only as shallow as four and a half fathoms against the two and three quarters mentioned by Ward in his book as having been found on the 6th. But one expects sailors to be more laconic than land lubbers. The log does, however, confirm rough weather at the start of the journey, and indeed records that although the civilians boarded on 14 January and anchor was weighed next day, the ship had to return to Plymouth on the 18th because of damage and to put ashore a sailor who had been badly injured in a fall from the rigging. They eventually got away only on the 20th, after which they still had several days of bad weather.
12 Canning. Ward to Canning dated 18/3/1825.
13 FO 50/12/1. Morier/Ward despatch No. 1 dated 10/4/1825.
14 FO 50/9/9. Foreign Office despatch No. 2 dated 3/1/1825 (W I 463).
15 FO 50/6/30. Morier despatch No. 3 dated 2/11/1824.
16 FO 50/5/101. Hervey despatch No. 36 dated 18/7/1824.
17 Canning. Ward to Canning dated 18/3/1825.
18 FO 50/12/189. Declaration dated 6/4/1825 enclosed with Morier/Ward despatch No. 2 dated 12/4/1825.

Chapter 11

1 The reports of the ratification process are at FO 50/12/207–306 and 318–381 in two despatches signed jointly by Morier and Ward, No. 6 dated 30/4/1825 and No. 8 dated 17–30/5/1825.
2 When it became known in England that Morier and Ward had taken this stand, *The Times*, however, was very approving. In its editorial on 6 July 1825 it referred to the 'dirty littleness' of the Mexican behaviour and the 'childish drivelling to talk of our having claims upon the gratitude of the American Republics. We acknowledged them, not because it was an act of kindness or indulgence, but being one of strict justice towards them.'
3 FO 50/12/293. Translation of editorial in *El Sol* of 25/4/1825.
4 Canning. Ward to Canning dated 10/3/1826.
5 FO 50/12/1. Morier/Ward unnumbered despatch dated 10/4/1825.
6 FO 50/12/177. Ward unnumbered despatch dated 10/4/1825.

Chapter 12

1 Planta may already have begun to take against Ward a year earlier when he received his request to be allowed to take out of customs, without paying duty, six cases of books he had brought back from Spain in 1823 in order that he could repack them more suitably for taking to Mexico if he were sent back there. Ward promised 'that not one book liable to duty shall remain in England' (FO 72/297/170, letter dated 16/7/1824). Planta rather stuffily replied that 'they may remain in custody at the Custom House, or they may be repacked there; but they cannot be delivered except on payment of duty'. Ward should have been warned by this of the need for care in dealing with Planta (who later became MP for Hastings in 1827 and Joint Secretary to the Treasury, and a privy councillor in 1834).
2 Baring Brothers archives DEP 193.74.2. Letter dated 23/4/1825 from Francis Baring to Humphrey Mildmay.
3 Swinburne 42. Ward to Sir John Swinburne dated 21/5/1825.
4 FO 50/12/311. Morier unnumbered despatch dated 8/5/1825.
5 FO 50/13/1. Ward despatch No. 1 dated 21/5/1825.
6 FO 50/13/28. Ward despatch No. 6 dated 2/6/1825.
7 FO 50/13/72. Ward despatch No. 12 dated 23/6/1825.
8 Michelena was in fact born in Mexico; but he had been active in Spain politically as a supporter of the 'liberal' movement.
9 FO 50/9/19. Foreign Office unnumbered despatch dated 3/1/1825 (W I 459).
10 FO 50/15/66. Ward despatch No. 52 dated 10/11/1825.
11 Alamán papers held in Texas State Archives, microfilm copy in Mexican Archivos Generales roll 36/117: Michelena letter dated 23/11/1824.
12 MFA 5-9-8235. See for example Michelena's despatches 46 and 47 dated August 1824.
13 E 192/5. Lady Adams to Wavell dated 30/5/1825.

14 E 192/5. Lady Adams to Wavell dated 9/2/1825.
15 MFA 4-25-7373. Michelena letter dated 30/10/1824.
16 FO 50/18/33. Michelena memorandum to Planta dated 4/3/1825 (W I 466).
17 FO 50/14/194. Ward despatch No. 37 dated 24/9/1825.
18 FO 50/15/1. Ward despatch No. 44 dated 8–17/10/1825.
19 FO 50/15/66. Ward despatch No. 52 dated 10/11/1825.
20 FO 50/28/219. Michelena to Planta dated 19/7/1826.
21 Even Jaime E. Rodríguez O, in his op. cit., can only suggest possible reasons. And it is of interest that Alamán, in his *Historia de Méjico desde 1808*, published in 1852, wrote of Michelena that in London 'although he did not always carry out his duties with skill, at least he acted with integrity' (Volume V p. 783).
22 FO 50/12/191. Morier/Ward despatch No. 3 dated 12/4/1825.
23 FO 50/13/106. Ward despatch No. 15 dated 6/7/1825.
24 FO 50/15/76. Ward despatch No. 53 dated 14/11/1825.
25 FO 50/13/176. Ward despatch No. 21 dated 14/7/1825.
26 FO 50/13/135. Ward despatch No. 20 dated 12/7/1825.
27 FO 50/14/1. Ward despatch No. 25 dated 12/8/1825.
28 FO 50/14/155. Ward despatch No. 34 dated 19/9/1825.
29 In the end Ward could do nothing for Baring because in November a decree was passed, with retrospective effect, that land could only be sold to foreigners if they had become naturalized Mexicans. Time was given for the buyer of any land who did not thus qualify to dispose of it (and presumably Baring's loss arose out of such a forced sale). Moreover, the condition that owners of land must be Catholics was got in through the back door because it was impossible to be naturalized unless one declared oneself to be an adherent to the Catholic faith. As Ward put it when reporting this, no proof of such adherence was required, but no 'conscientious and respectable man' would cheat (Ward despatch No. 59 dated 23/11/1825 at FO 50/15/133).
30 FO 50/14/76. Ward to Planta dated 24/8/1825 enclosing copy of note dated 18/8/1825 addressed to Alamán.
31 Swinburne 43. Emily to her father dated 17/8/1825.
32 In reporting this to Canning, Ward actually said he had assured Alamán that Britain was 'pledged' to intervene in such circumstances. When Canning later told him he had gone too far in using that word, he explained that he had mistranslated the Spanish phrase he had used – 'se veria compremetido' – and should have rendered it in English as 'compromised' (Ward despatch No. 70 dated 25/12/1825 at FO 50/15/219).
33 FO 50/14/19. Ward despatch No. 26 dated 16-17/8 1825.
34 FO 50/14/76. Ward to Planta dated 24/8/1825.
35 Ibid.
36 FO 27/330. Granville despatch 'Separate' to Canning 6/6/1825 (W II 182).
37 FO 27/328. Foreign Office despatch No. 50 to Paris dated 12/7/1825.
38 FO 27/331. Granville despatch No. 148 dated 18/7/1825 (W II 185).
39 FO 50/9/108. Foreign Office despatch No. 11 dated 9/9/1825 (W I 477).

40 It is doubtful if Canning really was satisfied that the French were not up to something. In June, writing to Viscount Granville at Paris about the earlier incident, he had confessed that he had 'doubts whether it was not (a prescribed I will not say, but) a permitted experiment to see how far a French force might be incidentally and imperceptibly slipped into the Havannah' (*Some Official Correspondence of George Canning*, Edward J. Stapleton (ed.) (Longmans, Green 1887) volume I p. 277 – letter to Viscount Granville dated 21/6/1825).

41 FO 50/9/162. Foreign Office despatch No. 14 dated 14/10/1825.

Chapter 13

1 FO 50/13/22. Ward despatch No. 5 dated 1/6/1825. (W I 470).

2 Carlos Bosch García, *El Mester Político de Poinsett* (Universidad Nacional Autónoma de México 1983) quoted at p. 79.

3 FO 50/13/118. Ward despatch No. 17 dated 9/7/1825 (W I 472).

4 Carlos Bosch García op. cit. quoted at p. 82.

5 The rivalry between the USA and Britain is here deliberately treated in a narrow way, related to a limited aspect of the personal relations between Ward and Poinsett. For a wider view, and coverage of Poinsett's background, see J. Fred Rippy, *Rivalry of the United States and Great Britain Over Latin America, 1808-1830* (Baltimore and London 1929).

6 The part played by freemasonry in Mexican internal politics at that time was very significant. The details, which are of Byzantine complexity, are covered in Professor Michael Costeloe's excellent book *Parties and Politics in Independent Mexico – A Study of the First Federal Republic 1824–1835* (published only in Spanish by the Fondo de Cultura Económica in Mexico in 1975); but they are not necessary to an understanding of Ward's difficulties.

7 FO 50/14/68. Note dated 9/8/1825 enclosed with Ward despatch No. 27 dated 22/8/1825.

8 FO 50/14/229. Ward despatch No. 42 dated 27/9/1825 (W I 485).

9 Ward need not have worried. Canning told him later that 'in all that relates to the watching and counteracting of the intrigues of the American Minister you appear to have exercised a judgment as sound as your zeal has been meritorious' (Canning despatch to Ward dated 7/1/1826 at FO 50/19/1).

10 Canning. Ward letter dated 30/9/1825.

11 FO 50/14/212. Ward to Canning dated 30/9/1825 (W I 489).

12 FO 50/15/1. Ward despatch No. 44 dated 8-17/10/1825.

13 Professor Costeloe's book also covers this in some depth.

14 It is of interest that Ward had been told by Victoria some weeks earlier that he wanted to get rid of Alamán (Ward despatch No. 40 dated 25/9/1825 at FO 50/14/208).

15 Carlos Bosch García op. cit. quoted at p. 123.

16 FO 50/15/19. Ward despatch No. 45 dated 17/10/1825.

17 FO 50/14/208. Ward despatch No. 40 dated 20/9/1825.

18 José C Valadés, *Alamán: Estadística y Historiador* (Universidad Nacional Autónoma de México 1977).
19 FO 50/14/208. Ward despatch No. 40 dated 20/9/1825.
20 FO 50/15/19. Ward despatch No. 45 dated 17/10/1825.
21 FO 50/15/61. Ward despatch No. 51 dated 31/10/1825.
22 FO 50/15/161. Ward despatch No. 61 dated 24/11/1825.
23 FO 50/15/141. Ward despatch No. 60 dated 23/11/1825.
24 Canning. Ward letter dated 25/11/1825.
25 Swinburne 44. Ward to Sir John dated 18-30/9/1825.
26 Vaughan C 122/5. Letter dated 10/9/1825.
27 Canning. Ward letter dated 25/11/1825.
28 Vaughan C 122/3. Letter dated 9/12/1825.
29 FO 50/12/205. Morier unnumbered despatch dated 24/4/1825.
30 FO 50/9/182. Planta letter dated 14/10/1825.
31 FO 50/15/51. Ward despatch No. 50 dated 30/10/1825.
32 Waldegrave's body was later moved to the new British cemetery, being the first interment there.
33 FO 50/13/36. Ward despatch No. 8 dated 3/6/1825.
34 FO 50/13/40. Ward despatch No. 9 dated 5/6/1825.
35 Rocafuerte too had been showing considerable anxiety about the treaty, seeking (unsuccessfully) several interviews with Canning in the summer and early autumn of 1825. What he sent home was probably the outcome of a meeting with Planta on 15 October. But Canning got irritated by Rocafuerte's persistence and over Mexican impatience, minuting a memorandum by Rocafuerte dated 18 October 'The Treaty – The Treaty – The Treaty ...' (FO 50/18/66). And in November Planta minuted another request from Rocafuerte to see Canning 'I can see this man for you when you are gone', and did so on the 16th (FO 50/18/66).
36 FO 50/15/183. Ward despatch No. 67 dated 13/12/1825.

Chapter 14

1 FO 50/15/183. Ward despatch No. 67 dated 13/12/1825.
2 There was a curious incident while they were making up the coast back to Vera Cruz. On 2 December a strange vessel 'apparently American' bore down on them and when within musket range fired a shot over them. *Vigilant* fired back and the other vessel then hoisted a white flag and bore away. *Vigilant* tried to give chase, but under jury rig was unable to do so successfully. There is simply a laconic entry in the log to this effect.
3 ADM 51/3531. Log of HM Cutter *Vigilant*.
4 FO 50/9/60. Foreign Office despatch No. 9 dated 9/9/1825 (W I 475)
5 FO 50/9/102. Foreign Office despatch No. 10 dated 9/9/1825 (W I 476).
6 FO 50/15/190. Ward despatch No. 68 dated 14/12/1825.
7 ADM 51/3350. Log of HMS *Pyramus*.
8 FO 50/9/150. Foreign Office despatch No. 13 dated 14/10/1825 (W I 495).
9 Canning expressed his feelings even more strongly in a letter to Viscount

Granville at Paris on 21 October 1825 in which he said he was delighted to be arranging to present the representatives of Buenos Aires and Colombia to the king as ministers plenipotentiary and thus able 'to show Mexico what she had lost by her selfish and silly policy in overreaching Morier and Ward [and Alamán's boasting]. I delighted in raising these people into States; but I shall not let them fancy themselves too fine fellows, as they would be apt to do if not snubbed when they deserve it' (Augustus Granville Stapleton, *George Canning and his Times* (John Parker & Son 1859) pp. 445-6).

10 FO 50/9/162. Foreign Office despatch No. 14 dated 14/10/1825 (W I 498).

11 FO 50/17/400. Canning to Victoria dated 13/10/1825 (W I 494).

12 FO 50/15/223. Ward despatch No. 71 dated 26/12/1825.

13 This is reproduced exactly as written in the draft of this letter in the Foreign Office file. It is to be hoped that when copied out for signature by Canning the syntax had been improved. But the signed copy is no longer available.

14 FO 50/17/404. Canning to Victoria dated 15/10/1825 (W I 500).

15 FO 50/15/246. Ward note to Ministry of Foreign Affairs dated 17/12/1825.

16 FO 50/15/242. Ward despatch No. 75 dated 29/12/1825.

17 FO 50/15/205. Ward despatch No. 69 dated 16/12/1825.

18 Canning. Ward letter dated 17/12/1825.

19 FO 50/15/217. Morier unnumbered despatch dated 19/12/1825.

20 FO 50/15/236. Ward despatch No. 74 dated 29/12/1825.

21 H.G. Ward op. cit. p. 274.

22 FO 50/20/10. Ward to Victoria dated 3/1/1826.

23 FO 50/20/3. Ward despatch No. 2 dated 6/1/1826.

24 FO 97/271/1. Morier/Ward despatch No. 1 dated 15/1/1826 (W I 502).

25 FO 50/19/9. Planta to Ward dated 15/2/1826.

26 FO 97/271/11. Morier/Ward despatch No. 2 dated 30/1/1826 reporting the negotiations.

27 FO 97/271/89. Ward memorandum of interview with Victoria on 25/1/1826.

28 It is interesting that Morier had a somewhat similar experience in Persia in 1814 when, as Minister *ad interim*, he received instructions brought out by a junior, Ellis, to get the Persians to agree to modifications to the treaty which had been signed with Sir Gore Ouseley in March 1812. He foresaw difficulties, which he pointed out to the Foreign Office, because he had to tell the Persians that they would no longer be receiving the subsidy they had been relying on for some time. Nevertheless he gave his assurance that 'no arguments shall induce us to depart from the line of conduct' in his instructions. In the end he persuaded the Persians to sign and ratify the treaty as Britain wanted it (with only a couple of minor variations, which were accepted in London) on the understanding that Ellis would take it back to London personally with a letter from the Shah appealing for a change of heart over the subsidy (his despatch No. 4 from Tehran dated 30/11/1814 at FO 60/9/118). Nevertheless, in a letter to his brother David he made clear that he had to some extent bowed to the views of Ellis

('had I not made many great sacrifices of my own inclinations to secure the public good' and 'thanks to my unremitting moderation'). But then also he was longing to get away from Persia (which he had no chance of doing unless he could get the treaty agreed with the Persians) so his motives then, and now in Mexico were similar. On neither occasion was his heart really in the business in hand.

29 Canning. Ward letter dated 30/1/1826.
30 Canning. Morier letter dated 30/1/1826.

Chapter 15

1 FO 97/271/108. Morier/Ward despatch No. 3 dated 17/3/1826.
2 Morier boarded HMS *Pyramus* on 28 March and they sailed on the 31st, going via New York, where they spent 12 days, and reaching Spithead on 6 June (ADM 51/3350 log of HMS *Pyramus*).
3 FO 50/20/167. Ward unnumbered despatch dated 18/3/1826.
4 FO 50/20/204. Ward despatch No. 22 dated 25/3/1826.
5 FO 50/20/220. Ward to Dr Cevallos dated 20/3/1826.
6 FO 50/20/282. Ward despatch No. 26 dated 7/4/1826.
7 FO 50/20/255. Ward despatch No. 24 dated 30/3/1826.
8 FO 50/22/48. Ward despatch No. 80 dated 6/7/1826.
9 FO 50/20/309. Ward despatch No. 29 dated 10/4/1826.
10 FO 50/22/53. Ward despatch No. 81 dated 7/7/1826.
11 FO 50/23/57. Ward to Captain Harris dated 20/8/1826.
12 FO 50/23/91. Captain Harris to Ward dated 24/8/1826.
13 Vaughan C 123/3. Letter dated 7/7/1826.
14 ADM 51/3228. Log of HMS *Hussar*.
15 FO 50/29/35. Camacho note to Canning dated 13/10/1826.
16 FO 50/29/25. Planta to Rocafuerte dated 21/10/1826.
17 FO 50/29/27. Rocafuerte to Planta dated 22/10/1826.
18 FO 50/29/41. Canning to Camacho dated Paris 20/10/1826.
19 FO 50/31A/45. Ward despatch No. 5 dated 15/1/1827.
20 FO 50/28/215. Victoria to Canning dated 9/4/1826.
21 FO 50/19/109. Foreign Office despatch No. 11 dated 16/11/1826.
22 FO 50/29/55. Memo of conference on 29/11/1826.
23 FO 50/19/121. Foreign Office despatch No. 14 dated 27/12/1826.
24 FO 50/29/45. Camacho's credentials.
25 FO 50/40/31. Estrada to Planta dated 17/3/1827.
26 FO 50/40/41. Planta letter dated 10/4/1827.
27 FO 50/40/86. Backhouse letter dated 14/6/1827.
28 After Camacho moved out of 24 Park Crescent, he stayed in the Grillons Hotel in Albermarle Street. On his return from Paris he moved into Hannay's Hotel in Leicester Square. At this time Murphy was living at 67 Regent's Quadrant (various letters at FO 50/40/23-53). When Michelena was in London he resided, at least for some of the time, at 2 Hanover Square (see for example FO 50/18/33), while Rocafuerte was at times at the Hanover Hotel, Hanover Square (e.g. FO 50/18/54) and at

18 Welbeck Street (e.g. FO 50/18/58).

29 FO 50/40/72. Camacho letter dated 21/6/1827.

30 Camacho eventually boarded *Slaney* (Commander James Campbell RN) at Spithead at 10.30 a.m. on Friday 17 August 1827, receiving a salute of 11 guns. The journey was uneventful and mostly in fine weather. They reached Funchal on 27 August and left two days later. They spent three days at Port Royal in Jamaica between 23 and 26 September, and finally anchored below Ulloa on 7 October, Camacho then going ashore to a salute of 13 guns (log of HM Sloop *Slaney* at ADM 51/3468).

31 FO 50/31B/98. Ward despatch No. 39 dated 2/3/1827.

Chapter 16

1 FO 50/21/3. Ward to Planta dated 1/5/1826.

2 Vaughan C 122/7. Letter dated 23/5/1826.

3 FO 50/22/253. Ward to Planta dated 18/8/1826.

4 Vaughan C 123/2. Letter dated 22/6/1826.

5 The christening robe is still in the possession of the present owners of Capheaton Hall, the Browne-Swinburnes, having been left to them by Nora Frances de Sausmarez, the child's granddaughter, together with a number of other possessions of Emily's. Unfortunately the 'certificate of baptism' has not survived, so it is not possible to check these names, quoted by Ward in his book, against the existing family records which show them as 'Guadalupe Felipa *Maria*'. Felipe de Jesús was born in Mexico of Spanish parents in the sixteenth century. On a voyage from Manilla to North America he was forced by a storm to land in Japan just as the great persecution there was about to begin. He was crucified as a Christian in 1597 and venerated as the first martyr of Japan, his 'day' being 5 February.

6 H.G. Ward op. cit. pp. 711-12.

7 FO 50/20/248. Ward unnumbered despatch dated 25/3/1826.

8 The couple where Charles Conrad Lavater, born in Liverpool on 24 September 1800, a 'respected merchant', and Fermina Susan Agassiz, born in Finsbury Square, London on 1 August 1810, the daughter of the Treasurer and Commissioner of the United Mexican Mining Company of which Alamán was a partner. He himself was a witness at the marriage, and possibly he too had exerted some influence with the authorities.

9 FO 50/22/176. Ward despatch No. 87 dated 3/8/1826.

10 FO 50/22/198. Ward despatch No. 88 dated 4/8/1826.

11 Ward was able to report another concession (although this time rather grudgingly given) at the end of October when two more British subjects wanted to get married. This time one was Protestant the other Catholic. Despite the efforts of the Minister for Justice and Ecclesiastical Affairs, Ramos Arispe, no Mexican priest could be persuaded to perform the ceremony because the groom was not a Catholic. However, a French priest came to the rescue, agreeing 'to take upon himself the whole responsibility of the match in the next world provided the Provisor would engage that he should not be called to account in this' (Ward despatch No. 150 dated

29/12/1826 at FO 50/25/208). This was agreed to and the marriage was duly registered by the Mexican authorities.

12 H.G. Ward op. cit. p. 317.
13 FO 50/22/253. Ward to Planta dated 18/8/1826.
14 Ibid.
15 FO 50/22/63. Ward to Planta dated 7/7/1826.
16 FO 50/19/70. Planta to Ward dated 27/8/1825.
17 FO 97/272/1. Bandinel to Ward dated 3/8/1825.
18 Bandinel may have been only carrying out instructions, but such an unfeeling attitude towards those in the field has ever been a tendency on the part of officials at home who have never themselves served overseas. Bandinel was a Clerk in the Foreign Office for 50 years (at that time he was aged 42). He was a member of a Jersey family of Italian extraction, brother of the Rev. Bulkeley Bandinel who became Keeper of the Bodleian Library in Oxford.
19 FO 97/272/110. Ward to Planta dated 9/5/1825.
20 FO 97/272/128. Ward unnumbered despatch dated 17/8/1825.
21 FO 50/19/76. Planta to Ward dated 14/10/1825.
22 FO 50/19/80. Planta to Ward dated 19/10/1825.
23 FO 97/272/153. Ward to Planta dated 1/2/1826.
24 FO 50/21/69. Ward to Planta dated 23/5/1826.
25 FO 50/19/29. Planta to Ward dated 8/6/1826.
26 FO 50/21/172. Ward to Planta dated 8/6/1826.
27 FO 97/272/142. Ward unnumbered despatch dated 5/1/1826.
28 FO 50/19/24. Planta to Ward dated 8/6/1826.
29 FO 50/19/54. Foreign Office despatch No. 7 dated 8/10/1826.
30 FO 50/23/96. Ward to Planta dated 10/9/1826.
31 FO 50/23/61. Ward despatch No. 102 dated 8/9/1826.
32 FO 50/23/190. Ward to Canning dated 15/9/1826.
33 This must have been a reference to the harsh criticisms of extravagance by the government in the armed and other public services voiced in a debate on 'The State of the Nation' in the Commons on 4 May 1826 (Hansard, New Series, Volume XV columns 841–97). No doubt the Foreign Office had been instructed after this to make economies. The criticisms made during the debate were remarkably similar to those that have been made in the same place in the late twentieth century, not to say at other times between.
34 Vaughan C 123/5. Letter dated 15/9/1826.
35 This second child was later christened Georgina Katherine Petronella; but the Wards felt too embarrassed by the generosity of the Reglas over the baptism of Frances to ask any of their friends in Mexico to be sponsors lest they would have thought it necessary to match what the Reglas had done.
36 H.G. Ward op. cit. p. 407.
37 Some of Emily's sketchbooks are still in the possession of a member of the Ward family. And many of her drawings were worked up into illustrations for her husband's book. Some were published separately by Henry Colburn in 1829 under the title *Six Views of the Most Important Towns and Mining Districts Upon the Table Land of Mexico*.
38 H.G. Ward op. cit. pp. 413–4.

39 In a letter to Canning (in the Canning private papers) dated 5/5/1827 Ward told him that he had only that day received from his father a letter dated 9/12/1826 saying that Canning had told him of his intention to let him sign the treaty and not to recall him in disgrace.
40 FO 50/19/119. Foreign Office despatch No. 13 dated 21/12/1826.
41 FO 50/31B/77. Ward despatch No. 35 dated 21/2/1827.
42 FO 97/272/25. Foreign Office despatch No. 1 dated 15/1/1827.
43 Canning. Ward letter dated 3/3/1827.
44 FO 50/32/41. Ward despatch No. 54 dated 12/4/1827.
45 FO 50/32/85. Address to Ward dated 9/4/1827.
46 FO 50/39/247. Victoria to Canning dated 3/4/1827 (the letter itself is now illegible: the translation made at the time in the Foreign Office has been used).
47 The Municipality of Mexico City sent with them 'packages' addressed to the king and Canning, and an 'author of some celebrity' sent a book to Canning. These gifts were apparently sent to Ward at Vera Cruz, but someone there simply put them with his heavy baggage which was sent separately and not opened until some time after their arrival. When Ward discovered them on 30 August he sent them on to the Foreign Office (by which time Canning had died) with an explanation (FO 50/40/308). What these gifts were and what happened to them is not recorded.
48 The purpose of the call at New York was to have a meeting with Vaughan and give him an oral briefing about the troubles Ward could already see brewing over Texas. Captain Vernon had evidently been unhappy at being required to make this diversion (FO 50/40/296) and reported to the Admiralty on his arrival in England. The Admiralty got an assurance from the Foreign Office that this diversion had been in the public interest (FO 50/40/300), so Ward must have given them a report himself.
49 H.G. Ward op. cit. pp. 704–5.

Epilogue

1 Ironically this resumption of British-Mexican relations was marked by a piece of extravagance of the kind that caused Ward's downfall. The new British minister, Sir Spenser St John, decided in March 1885 that the best way to start making up for the way the United States had gained influence at the expense of Britain during the period of rupture was to give a masked ball in honour of the wife of the new president (Alfred Tischendorf, *Great Britain and Mexico in the Era of Porfirio Díaz*, Duke University Press 1961, p. 20).
2 Ward's proposal that there should be a chaplain attached to the British diplomatic mission was never realized, even though the idea was taken up by the Bishop of London in 1829 when he drew Lord Aberdeen's attention 'to the present state of the English residents in South America with respect to the want of all provision for religious worship & instruction according to the doctrines & disciplines of the Protestant Church' from which people were defecting to the Catholic, despite the activities of Presbyterians in

some parts. He thought that chaplains should be appointed to Mexico, Colombia and Buenos Aires where he believed there would be no objection on the part of the authorities to the 'private celebration of Protestant worship'; and he suggested that the expense could be met from the profits accruing to the Revenue from the trade carried on in South America (letter dated 16/2/1829 in the Lambeth Palace Library under reference Ms 2165, ff 50–1). James Thompson, a Scottish Baptist preacher, was active in Mexico on behalf of the British and Foreign Mission Society from April 1827 until 1830; and Vicente Rocafuerte, who helped him, was tried for sedition, but acquitted, in 1831 for publishing an 'Essay on Religious Toleration'. But it was not until the constitution of 1857 that Protestantism was officially legalized, and it was 1872 before the Episcopal Church of the United States became properly established in Mexico (see Deborah J. Baldwin, *Protestantism and the Mexican Revolution*, University of Illinois Press 1990 and also Jaime E. Rodríguez O op. cit. chapters 10 and 11).

3 In those days, before the establishment of commercial banks, the Catholic Church was the major lender of money for industrial and agrarian development. (See the article by Professor Costeloe published in January 1969 in 'The Americas' (Academy of American Franciscan History), Vol XXV, No. 3, which discusses this loan to Victoria.)

4 Hubert Howe Bancroft, *A Popular History of the Mexican People* (Trübser London, 1888) p. 404.

5 FO 50/25/33. Ward unnumbered despatch dated 22 & 25/10/1826.

6 Jaime E. Rodríguez also deals with the tragically farcical attempt to buy a 'submarine'.

7 FO 50/25/178. Ward despatch No. 145 dated 15/12/1826.

8 FO 50/32/71. Ward despatch No. 59 dated 18/4/1827.

9 FO 50/51/44. Ward to Backhouse dated 9/1/1828.

10 Raleigh Trevelyan, *The Golden Oriole* (Oxford University Press 1988) pp. 389-96.

11 Robert Bell op. cit. p. 247.

12 FO 50/16/142. Planta to Hervey dated 4/5/1825.

13 FO 50/16/161. Hervey to Planta dated 4/6/1825.

14 Canning. Hervey letter dated 18/4/1825.

15 As a Foreign Office pensioner Hervey's whereabouts were of course always known, and the Foreign Office got in touch with him in July 1828 about papers which had been reported missing from the legation files in Mexico (FO 50/51/89). Hervey replied that he had in his possession the despatches from the Foreign Office mentioned, but he assumed that copies would have been retained in the files at Mexico. He made no offer to return what he held and presumably the matter was left like that.

16 FO 50/40/151. Morier to Planta dated 5/1/1827.

17 FO 50/40/212. Canning formal letter to Treasury dated 30/3/1827.

18 Letter dated 18 March 1853 from Wavell to The Hon. Asbel Smith (Texas State Archives)

19 Vaughan C 122/5. Letter dated 5/4/1826.

20 Sir David Kelly, *The Ruling Few* (Hollis and Carter 1952) chapter 7.

21 Henry Bamford Parkes, *A History of Mexico* (Methuen 1938).

22 A diplomat can avoid this sin even when convinced of the quality of the people among whom he serves. Ward wrote in his book (Volume II p. 710): 'From what I have seen of the Mexicans, I should say that they possess great natural shrewdness and ability: they are brave, hospitable, warm hearted where met with kindness, and only too magnificent in their ideas of what the intercourse of society requires. From a fear of not doing enough, they often do too little; but whatever they attempt is executed with a splendour which is at times almost embarrassing.' That analysis remains valid.

23 H.G. Ward op. cit. p. 259.

24 Morier to his brother, March 1827.
'For my part, if the Mexican Government be honest, prudent and able, I think the country has enough resources within itself to give confidence to those who hold Mexican stock and await interest thereon. But they are in general such a set of narrow minded [? illeg.] that until a few years of good straightforward government can be passed over their heads, I should be loath to risk any think [sic] of much magnitude among them or to endanger my fortunes and independence. The President is a weak, well meaning, uninformed (and obstinate withal) man: the Minister of Finance Esteva (formerly a chocolatero of Vera Cruz) a clever, knavish sort of animal, keeping the President under his clutch: the Minister for Ecclesiastical Affairs a downright rogue and clever: the Minister of War the best of the bunch but one who would exclude foreigners and have nothing to do with foreign politics. I do believe he would be happy to make a China of Mexico and/or keep her where she was under the Spanish rule. The Senate and deputies! such a lot of animals never were to be seen! Intractable, ignorant and every thing you choose to make a government go crooked. They want one master head to cut them all straight and frighten them occasionally.'

BACKGROUND READING

A very selective short list of works in English

Mexican History

Meyer, Michael C. & Sherman, William L. *The Course of Mexican History*. Oxford University Press, New York 1979.

Cheetham, Nicolas J.A. *A History of Mexico*. Hart-Davis 1970.

Cheetham, Nicolas J.A. *New Spain: The Birth of Modern Mexico* Victor Gollancz 1974 – up to independence.

Rodríguez O, Jaime E. (ed.) *The Independence of Mexico and the Creation of the New Nation*. University of California Press 1989 – a collection of essays.

Green, Stanley C. *The Mexican Republic: the First Decade 1823–1832*. University of Pittsburgh Press 1987.

Calvert, Peter A.R. *Mexico*. Ernest Benn 1973 – post-independence.

Cumberland, Charles C. *Mexico: the Struggle for Modernity*. Oxford University Press 1968 – a good general study of the social and economic background of Mexico both pre- and post-independence.

Background to Independence

The Cambridge History of Latin America, Volume III. Cambridge University Press 1985.

Domínguez, Jorge I. *Insurrection or Loyalty*. Harvard University Press 1980.

Hamnett, Brian R. *Roots of Insurgency*. Cambridge University Press 1986.

Lynch, John *The Spanish American Revolutions 1808–1826*. Weidenfeld & Nicolson 1973.

Nicholson, Irene *The Liberators*. Faber & Faber 1969.

British Policies

Webster, C.K. *Britain and the Independence of Latin America*. Oxford University Press 1938.

Webster, C.K. *The Foreign Policy of Castlereagh*. G Bell & Sons 1947.
Temperley, H.W.V. *The Foreign Policy of Canning*. G Bell & Sons 1925.

Canning

Bell, Robert *The Life of the Rt Hon. George Canning*. Chapman & Hall 1846.
Hinde, Wendy *George Canning*. Collins 1973.
Marshall, Dorothy *The Rise of George Canning*. Longman & Green 1938.
Rolo, P.J.V. *George Canning: Three Biographical Studies*. Macmillan 1965.
Petrie, Charles *George Canning*. Eyre & Spottiswoode 1930.
Temperley, H.W.V. *Life of Canning*. James Finch 1905.

History of Latin America in General

Camacho, George *Latin America*. Allen Lane 1973.

United States Policies

Vásquez, J.Z. & Meyer, L. *The United States and Mexico*. University of Chicago Press 1985.
Rippy, J. Fred *Rivalry of the United States and Great Britain over Latin America, 1808–1830*. Baltimore and London 1929.

Also to be recommended is the book by Jaime E. Rodríguez O *The Emergence of Spanish America: Vicente Rocafuerte and Spanish Americanism 1808–1832* (University of California Press 1975) which does not fall neatly into one of the above broad classifications. Although it covers aspects of the background to revolt in Spanish America, it is in fact concerned largely with the events in Mexico immediately preceding and following independence, and it deals in some detail with aspects of British-Mexican relations then from the Mexican point of view (but unfortunately the chapter on the treaty with Britain contains some inaccuracies).

INDEX